I had long dreamed of entering Central High. I could not have imagined what that privilege could cost me.

Me, at fifteen, the year I entered the battlefield of Little Rock
Central High.

Author collection

My mother, Lois Peyton Pattillo, gave me strength and kept me focused on my goal.
Author collection

Without my grandmother, India Anette Peyton, I would not have survived my year at Central.
Author collection

Almost every day I came home from Central, my brother, Conrad, would meet me on his bike and tell me: "Sis, remember, I like you," or "You're not bad for a big sis." He was always a support.
Author collection

On the day I watched Elizabeth Eckford being brave in the face
of the mob, I felt both helpless and vulnerable.

I will always be grateful to the men of the 101st Airborne, who did their personal best to protect us from attacks.

George Silk/*Life* magazine

The NAACP chief counsel, Justice Thurgood Marshall, visited with us on the steps of the Supreme Court. From left to right: me; Jefferson Thomas; Gloria Ray; Mrs. C. Bates, President of the NAACP in Little Rock; Thurgood Marshall; Carlotta Walls; Minnijean Brown; and Elizabeth Eckford.

UPI/Bettmann Newsphotos

Our family home, which had always been my sanctuary, became a prison during the year of integration.

Author collection

Thelma Mothershed sits on the arm of my chair as we do our Central High homework.

AP/Wide World Photos

We nine students involved in the integration of Central High
School became a closely knit family with one goal—to survive.
Front row: Thelma Mothershed, Elizabeth Eckford, and me.
Back row: Jefferson Thomas, Ernest Green, Minnijean Brown,
Carlotta Walls, Terrence Roberts, and Gloria Ray.

Praise for Melba Pattillo Beals's
WARRIORS DON'T CRY

"Beals . . . writes movingly . . . a highly readable tale of courage in the face of persecution that deserves to be read, especially by young people."
—Donna L. Cole, *Library Journal*

"Ms. Beals's story is vivid and moving. . . ."
—Keith Dixon, *The New York Times Book Review*

"Profoundly uplifting. . . . The sense of immediacy in Beals's well-crafted account makes the events seem like they happened yesterday."
—*Kirkus Reviews*

"A sad and compelling tale of a naive young girl who was, like the other eight black teenagers, unwittingly pushed to the front lines of one of the nation's hottest battlegrounds."
—Ozzie Roberts, *San Diego Union-Tribune*

"Beals recounts that traumatic year with drama and detail. . . . tell[s] not only of the ugly harassment she was subjected to, but also of the impressive dignity of a 15-year-old forced to grow up fast."
—*Publishers Weekly*

"Beals's distress and anguish from the experience simply leap from these pages. . . ."
—Donald V. Adderton, *Savannah News-Press*

WARRIORS DON'T CRY

A Searing Memoir of the Battle to Integrate Little Rock's Central High

MELBA PATTILLO BEALS

WASHINGTON SQUARE PRESS

New York   London   Toronto   Sydney

For information regarding special discounts for bulk purchases,
please contact Simon & Schuster Special Sales at 1-800-456-6798
or business@simonandschuster.com

W A Washington Square Press Publication of
POCKET BOOKS, a division of Simon & Schuster Inc.
1230 Avenue of the Americas, New York, NY 10020

Beals, Melba.
    Warriors don't cry : a searing memoir of the battle to integrate
Little Rock's Central High / Melba Pattillo Beals.
        p.   cm.
    ISBN-13: 978-0-671-86639-6
    ISBN-10:   0-671-86639-7
    1. School integration—Arkansas—Little Rock—History—20th
century.   2. Central High School (Little Rock, Ark.)—History.
3. Beals, Melba.   4. Afro-American students—Arkansas—Little Rock—
Biography.   I. Title.
LC214.23.L56B43   1994
370.19'342—dc20   93-44590
                                                                CIP

First Washington Square Press trade paperback printing February 1995

20 19 18

Acknowledgments

I am grateful to:

the late Supreme Court Justice Thurgood Marshall—our guiding light, our protector—a brave warrior whose tenacity and courage will be an inspirational banner to mankind for all eternity.

Federal Judge Robert Carter, like Justice Marshall an untiring architect of the *Brown* v. *Board of Education of Topeka, Kansas* decision, also a warrior who has forged a path with his own life.

L. C. Bates, Daisy Bates, Wiley Branton, Sr., and the ministers who stood beside our parents to cheer us on.

Federal Judge Ronald Davies—a man with the courage of his convictions.

The brave men of the 101st Airborne who guarded us.

the memory of the late Eugene Smith, and to all Little Rock police officers who risked their own lives to shield us from the mob.

Grace Lorch and Benjamin Fine, who gave comfort to Elizabeth in the face of a mob.

Mrs. Pickwick, my shorthand teacher at Central High, who exhibited a sense of fair play.

Elizabeth Huckaby, girls' vice-principal at Central High, who tried to give Personal Best.

the very few nameless Central High students who dared to smile or cast a pleasant glance or refused to torture us.

Link, who dared to be my friend.

George and Carol McCabe, the white surrogate parents who took

Acknowledgments

me into their home, gave me unconditional love, and walked with me over the bridge to adulthood.

Judy, Joan, Dory, and Rick McCabe, who welcomed me as their sister.

my spiritual family, always at my side when I needed them: Aliaster and Consi Smith; Maria and Jean Picard; Sanford and Catherine Rosen and family; Dr. Mimi Silbert; Babette Wurtz, and Dr. David Geisinger.

my dear sisters and brothers, Dorothy Divack, Leslie Divack, Jim Harris, Dana Durst Lawrence, Richard Lawrence, Martha Jane McNally, Patricia O'Neil, Saemi Ladue, and Claudette Jeminez.

my colleagues who encouraged me to the finish line: Jim Frey, Mollie Giles, Jay Schaefer, Sandra Dijkstra, and "Danno."

Julie Rubenstein and Molly Allen, kindred souls who understood and shared my vision of this book.

Dedication

I dedicate this book to the eight brave and gentle warriors
with whom I attended Central High School in 1957:

Elizabeth Eckford
Ernest Green
Gloria Ray Karlmark
Carlotta Walls LaNier
Minnijean Brown Trickey
Terrence Roberts
Jefferson Thomas
Thelma Mothershed Wair

and to our mothers, fathers, and family members who
supported us through this incredible experience

Special Thanks to:

my mother, Lois Marie Pattillo, M.A., Ph.D.
my grandmother, India Anette Peyton
my brother, Conrad Pattillo
my daughter, Kellie Beals
my nephews, Barry and Conrad Pattillo

Author's Note

Some people call me a heroine because I was one of nine black teenagers who integrated Central High School in Little Rock, Arkansas, in 1957. At the age of fifteen I faced angry mobs, violent enough to compel President Eisenhower to send combat-ready 101st Airborne soldiers to quell the violence. I endured a year of school days filled with events unlike any others in the history of this country.

Although this happened over thirty-five years ago, I remember being inside Central High School as though it were yesterday. Memories leap out in a heartbeat, summoned by the sound of a helicopter, the wrath in a shouting voice, or the expression on a scowling face.

From the beginning I kept a diary, and my mother, Dr. Lois Pattillo, a high school English teacher, kept copious notes and clipped a sea of newspaper articles. I began the first draft of this book when I was eighteen, but in the ensuing years, I could not face the ghosts that its pages called up. During intervals of renewed strength and commitment, I would find myself compelled to return to the manuscript, only to have the pain of reliving my past undo my good intentions. Now enough time has elapsed to allow healing to take place, enabling me to tell my story without bitterness.

Author's Note

In some instances I have changed people's names to protect their identities. But all the incidents recounted here are based on the diary I kept, on news clippings, and on the recollections of my family and myself. While some of the conversations have been re-created, the story is accurate and conveys my truth of what it was like to live in the midst of a civil rights firestorm.

Introduction:
Little Rock Warriors
Thirty Years Later

THE LITTLE ROCK NINE COME TOGETHER
FOR THE FIRST TIME SINCE '57
—Headline, *Arkansas Gazette*, Friday, October 23, 1987

The stone steps are slippery with morning drizzle as we begin the tedious climb up to the front door of Central High School. It is the first time in thirty years that we nine black alumni have entered this school together.

In 1957, as teenagers trying to reach the front door, we were trapped between a rampaging mob, threatening to kill us to keep us out, and armed soldiers of the Arkansas National Guard dispatched by the governor to block our entry.

On this day Arkansas Governor Billy Clinton, who in less than six years will be President of the United States, greets us warmly with a welcoming smile as he extends his hand. We are honored guests, celebrating both our reunion and thirty years of progress in Little Rock's race relations. Cameras flash, reporters shout questions, dignitaries lavish enthusiastic praise on us, and fans ask for our autographs.

And yet all this pomp and circumstance and the presence of my eight colleagues does not numb the pain I feel at entering Central High School, a building I remember only as a hellish torture chamber. I pause to look up at this massive school—two blocks square and seven stories high, a place that was meant to nourish us and prepare us for adulthood. But, because we dared to challenge the Southern tradition of segregation, this school became, instead, a furnace that consumed our youth and forged us into reluctant warriors.

On this occasion, we nine ascend the stairs amid a group of reporters and dignitaries gathered here for the National Association for the Advancement of Colored People convention. I have a slight tension headache and, like some of the others, I am yawning. Even though each one of us is forty-something, we were up very late last night enjoying one another's company and giggling just as we did when we were teenagers.

Long past the hour that should have been bedtime, we gathered in Ernie's suite to catch up on the years when we were separated from each other. Our senior member and now a Shearson Lehman Hutton vice president, Ernie treated us to all the room service we could handle. Still, the fun we enjoyed last night does not make it easier to appear nonchalant on this occasion. Some of us take another's arm to brace ourselves as we prepare to face the ghosts in this building. Even as we speak of how much we dread touring this school, some of us blink back tears to smile for the media, shake hands, and sign autographs.

"How does it feel to be in Little Rock again?" a reporter shouts.

"Weird," I reply.

We nine have come from our homes around the world. Gloria, a magazine publisher, is a citizen of the Netherlands. Minnijean, a Canadian citizen, is a writer and raises her six children on a farm. Shearson V.P. Ernie comes from New York; Thelma has come from her Illinois teaching duties; and Dr. Terry Roberts comes from his UCLA professor's post. Carlotta is a Denver realtor, and Jeff is a Defense Department accountant from California. Only Elizabeth stayed on in Little Rock, where she is a social worker. It is significant that almost all of us chose not to remain in Little Rock but sought lives elsewhere.

All of us bring children—some are adults now like my daughter, Kellie. Others are toddlers, or the same age as we were when we attended Central. We have observed each other's graying hair and balding spots and noted paunches brought on by the years. Time has, nonetheless, been kind to us.

Our relationships with one another and the joy of our camaraderie have not changed. For me our reunion has been a rediscovery of a part of myself that was lost—a part that I longed to be in touch with. I have missed these eight people who by virtue of fate's hand are most dear to me. Since our arrival in Little Rock, we have laughed and cried together and talked nonstop. We have both relished and dreaded this moment when we would again walk up these stairs.

Today, if I let the memories flood in and listen closely, on these same stone steps I can hear the click-clack of leather boots—boots worn by soldiers of the 101st Airborne, dispatched to escort us past the raging mob. I hear the raspy voices of their leaders commanding, "Forward march," as we first walked through these front doors on September 25, 1957.

"What was it like to attend Central?" asks one reporter.

"I got up every morning, polished my saddle shoes, and went off to war," I reply. "It was like being a soldier on a battlefield."

"It was a teenager's worst nightmare," someone else shouts. "What's worse than to be rejected by all your classmates and teachers."

"What's it like to be back here again?" another reporter asks.

"Frightening," one voice says. Most of us have rarely come back to Arkansas as adults. Even though my mother and brother continue to live here, I have only found the strength to visit five times in thirty years because of the uneasy feeling the city gives me. Three of those visits have been since Bill and Hillary Clinton took over the governor's mansion, because they set a tone that made me feel safer here.

"How does the city look to you now?"

I answer the question to myself. Very different from when I

lived here. Today, I could not find my way around its newly built freeways, its thriving industrial complexes, its racially mixed, upscale suburban sprawl. It is a town that now boasts a black woman mayor. My brother, Conrad, is the first and only black captain of the Arkansas State Troopers—the same troopers that held me at bay as a teenager when I tried to enter Central.

We reach the crest of the first bank of stairs, turn right at the landing, and begin mounting the next set of steps when we hear more shouting from the reporters: "Stop. Look this way, please. Can you wave?"

I am annoyed. You'd think I'd be more patient with their questions, since I am a former NBC television news reporter and have been a working journalist for twenty years. But it's different when you're the person being barraged by questions. I resent their relentless observation of the nine of us during such a personal time. Still, I try to smile graciously, because these reporters have traveled a great distance from their posts around the world to be here.

Where is Governor Faubus, I wonder. Where is the man who dispatched armed soldiers to keep nine children out of school, who bet his life and his career that he could halt integration?

"Faubus is quoted on the news wires today saying if he had it to do over again, he'd do the same thing. What do you think about that?" a reporter asks.

"If we had it to do again, we'd do the same," Terry quips.

"Why isn't Faubus here?" someone asks.

"Because he wasn't invited," a reporter replies. "At least that's what he says. He retired to some small town in Arkansas."

As we near the top of the second bank of stairs, I sense that something is missing. I look below and see that the fountain has disappeared. It once stood directly in front of the hundred-foot-wide neo-Gothic entryway, with stairs ascending to it on both sides. Hearing my expression of surprise, a man I do not know explains: Someone threw Jell-O into it, so they concreted it over. I pause as I recall what a treacherous place that fountain was in 1957 when students repeatedly tried to push us the sixty feet or so down into the water. Nobody thought to close it then.

All at once, I realize the questions have suddenly stopped. I am surrounded by an anxious silence—like the hush of an audience as the curtain is about to rise. The main entrance of the school is now clearly in sight. I feel a familiar twinge; a cold fist clamps about my stomach and twists it into a wrenching knot, and just at that instant, it is October of 1957, and I am a helpless, frightened fifteen-year-old, terrified of what awaits me behind those doors. What will they do to me today? Will I make it to my homeroom? Who will be the first to slap me, to kick me in the shin, or call me nigger?

Suddenly one of the huge front doors swings open. A black teenager impeccably dressed in morning coat and bow tie emerges. He is slight, perhaps five feet six inches tall, with closely cropped hair, wearing wire-rimmed spectacles. He bows slightly as we approach.

"Good morning. I am Derrick Noble, president of the student body. Welcome to Central High School."

1

IN 1957, WHILE MOST TEENAGE GIRLS WERE LISTENING TO BUDDY Holly's "Peggy Sue," watching Elvis gyrate, and collecting crinoline slips, I was escaping the hanging rope of a lynch mob, dodging lighted sticks of dynamite, and washing away burning acid sprayed into my eyes.

During my junior year in high school, I lived at the center of a violent civil rights conflict. In 1954, the Supreme Court had decreed an end to segregated schools. Arkansas Governor Orval Faubus and states' rights segregationists defied that ruling. President Eisenhower was compelled to confront Faubus—to use U.S. soldiers to force him to obey the law of the land. It was a historic confrontation that generated worldwide attention. At the center of the controversy were nine black children who wanted only to have the opportunity for a better education.

On our first day at Central High, Governor Faubus dispatched gun-toting Arkansas National Guard soldiers to prevent us from entering. Mother and I got separated from the others. The two of us narrowly escaped a rope-carrying lynch mob of men and women shouting that they they'd kill us rather than see me go to school with their children.

Three weeks later, having won a federal court order, we black

1

children maneuvered our way past an angry mob to enter the side door of Central High. But by eleven that morning, hundreds of people outside were running wild, crashing through police barriers to get us out of school. Some of the police sent to control the mob threw down their badges and joined the rampage. But a few other brave members of the Little Rock police force saved our lives by spiriting us past the mob to safety.

To uphold the law and protect lives, President Eisenhower sent soldiers of the 101st Airborne Division, the elite "Screaming Eagles"—Korean War heroes.

On my third trip to Central High, I rode with the 101st in an army station wagon guarded by jeeps with turret guns mounted on their hoods and helicopters roaring overhead. With the protection of our 101st bodyguards, we black students walked through the front door of the school and completed a full day of classes.

But I quickly learned from those who opposed integration that the soldiers' presence meant a declaration of war. Segregationists mounted a brutal campaign against us, both inside and out of school.

My eight friends and I paid for the integration of Central High with our innocence. During those years when we desperately needed approval from our peers, we were victims of the most harsh rejection imaginable. The physical and psychological punishment we endured profoundly affected all our lives. It transformed us into warriors who dared not cry even when we suffered intolerable pain.

I became an instant adult, forced to take stock of what I believed and what I was willing to sacrifice to back up my beliefs. The experience endowed me with an indestructible faith in God.

I am proud to report that the Little Rock experience also gave us courage, strength, and hope. We nine grew up to become productive citizens, with special insights about how important it is to respect the value of every human life.

I am often asked, in view of the state of race relations today, if our effort was in vain. Would I integrate Central if I had it to do over again? My answer is yes, unequivocally yes. I take pride in the fact that, although the fight for equality must continue, our 1957 effort catapulted the civil rights movement forward a giant step and shifted the fight to a more dignified battlefield. For the first time in history, a President took a very bold step to defend civil rights—our civil rights.

Back then, I naively believed that if we could end segregation in the schools, all barriers of inequality would fall. If you had asked me in 1957 what I expected, I would have told you that by this time our struggle for human rights would have been won. Not so. But I am consoled by the words my grandmother spoke: "Even when the battle is long and the path is steep, a true warrior does not give up. If each one of us does not step forward to claim our rights, we are doomed to an eternal wait *older* in hopes those who would usurp them will become benevolent. *people* The Bible says, WATCH, FIGHT, and PRAY." *are wiser.*

Although I am perplexed by the state of race relations in this country today, I am at the same time very hopeful because I have ample evidence that what Grandmother promised me is true. With time and love, God solves all our problems. When we returned to Central High School for our first reunion in 1987, many Little Rock residents, white and black, greeted the nine of us as heroines and heroes. Hometown white folk in the mall smiled and said hello and offered directions even when they did not recognize us from our newspaper photos.

During all the fancy ceremonies, some of Arkansas's highest officials and businessmen came from far and wide to welcome us. And perhaps the most astounding evidence that things have indeed changed for the better was the attitude of Governor Bill Clinton.

"Call me Bill," he said, extending his hand, looking me in the eye. "You'all come on up to the house and sit a while." He flashed that charming grin of his. A few minutes of conversation assured me that his warm invitation was genuine. He is, after all, a man my brother refers to as "good people," based on their *So* working relationship over the years. *her brother has worked with Bill Clinton*

3

So my eight friends and I found ourselves hanging out at the governor's mansion, the one Faubus built. Governor Clinton sauntered about serving soft drinks and peanuts. He and his wife, Hillary, were the kind of host and hostess who could make me feel at home even in the place where Faubus had hatched his devilish strategies to get the nine of us out of Central High School by any means possible.

"You'all ought to think about coming on back home now. Things are different," Governor Clinton said. He had been eleven years old when Faubus waged his segregationist battle against us. He displayed genuine respect for our contribution to the civil rights struggle. That visit was to become an evening I shall always treasure. As Chelsea played the piano and Bill and Hillary talked to me as though we'd known each other always, I found myself thinking, "Oh, Mr. Faubus, if only you and your friends could see us now."

My grandmother India always said God had pointed a finger at our family, asking for just a bit more discipline, more praying, and more hard work because He had blessed us with good health and good brains. My mother was one of the first few blacks to integrate the University of Arkansas, graduating in 1954. Three years later, when Grandma discovered I would be one of the first blacks to attend Central High School, she said the nightmare that had surrounded my birth was proof positive that destiny had assigned me a special task.

First off, I was born on Pearl Harbor Day, December 7, 1941. Mother says while she was giving birth to me, there was a big uproar, with the announcement that the Japanese had bombed Pearl Harbor. She remembers how astonished she was, and yet her focus was necessarily on the task at hand. There was trouble with my delivery because Mom was tiny and I was nine pounds. The doctor used forceps to deliver me and injured my scalp. A few days later, I fell ill with a massive infection. Mother took me to the white hospital, which reluctantly treated the families of black men who worked on the railroad. A doctor operated to save my life by inserting a drainage system beneath my scalp.

4

Twenty-four hours later I wasn't getting better. Whenever Mother sought help, neither nurses nor doctors would take her seriously enough to examine me. Instead, they said, "Just give it time."

Two days after my operation, my temperature soared to 106 and I started convulsing. Mother sent for the minister to give me the last rites, and relatives were gathering to say farewell.

That evening, while Grandmother sat in my hospital room, rocking me back and forth as she hummed her favorite hymn, "On the Battlefield for My Lord," Mother paced the floor weeping aloud in her despair. A black janitor who was sweeping the hallway asked why she was crying. She explained that I was dying because the infection in my head had grown worse.

The man extended his sympathy. As he turned to walk away, dragging his broom behind him, he mumbled that he guessed the Epsom salts hadn't worked after all. Mother ran after him asking what he meant. He explained that a couple of days before, he had been cleaning the operating room as they finished up with my surgery. He had heard the doctor tell the white nurse to irrigate my head with Epsom salts and warm water every two or three hours or I wouldn't make it.

Mother shouted the words "Epsom salts and water" as she raced down the hall, desperately searching for a nurse. The woman was indignant, saying, yes, come to think of it, the doctor had said something about Epsom salts. "But we don't coddle niggers," she growled.

Mother didn't talk back to the nurse. She knew Daddy's job was at stake. Instead, she sent for Epsom salts and began the treatment right away. Within two days, I was remarkably better. The minister went home, and the sisters from the church abandoned their death watch, declaring they had witnessed a miracle.

So fifteen years later, when I was selected to integrate Central High, Grandmother said, "Now you see, that's the reason God spared your life. You're supposed to carry this banner for our people."

5

2

BLACK FOLKS AREN'T BORN EXPECTING SEGREGATION, PREPARED from day one to follow its confining rules. Nobody presents you with a handbook when you're teething and says, "Here's how you must behave as a second-class citizen." Instead, the humiliating expectations and traditions of segregation creep over you, slowly stealing a teaspoonful of your self-esteem each day.

By the time I was three years old, I was already so afraid of white people that when my red-haired, white-skinned cousin, Brenda, came to babysit, I hid beneath Mother's bed. Like many nonwhite Southern families, ours included people with a variety of skin tones and physical features. Although Daddy's skin was brown like mine, some of his relatives looked white.

My mother was fair-skinned as well, but Brenda's skin color was made more stark by her flaming red hair. As a toddler, growing up in Little Rock, Arkansas, in 1945, I felt safe only in my sepia-toned world, a cocoon of familiar people and places. I knew there were white people living somewhere far away and we didn't do things together. My folks never explained that I should be frightened of those white people. My fear developed as I observed adults and listened to their conversations. With alarmed expressions, they often whispered, "The white folks

6

won't like us to do that," or "We don't wanna anger the white folks."

Whenever we walked uptown, among white people, Mother held my hand too tight. I could see the fear in her eyes, feel the stiffening of her body as white people walked past. If we happened to be in their path, she quickly shoved me aside, according them the privilege of first passage.

If white adults were accompanied by children, those kids scowled or stuck their tongues out at us. Even worse, they'd sometimes say, "Mama, look at that there nigger."

Those trips to town became my primer on relating to white people. While shopping in the five-and-dime one hot summer day, I urged my mother to ask the waitress behind the lunch counter to give me a glass of water. She clutched my arm and whispered that we had to use our own drinking fountain. I started to cry aloud. I looked over to see the shiny chrome fountain the white people used. I didn't want to go to our fountain marked "Colored." It was the old dusty one located in an isolated part of the store, where I was afraid to go even with Mother.

Mother says when she tried to usher me to our drinking fountain, I caused such a fuss that the store manager chided her and asked if we were some of those uppity niggers from the North come to stir up trouble.

By the time I was four years old, I was asking questions neither my mother nor grandmother cared to answer. "Why do the white people write 'Colored' on all the ugly drinking fountains, the dingy restrooms, and the back of the buses? When will we get our turn to be in charge?" Grandma India would only say, "In God's time. Be patient, child, and tell God all about it."

I remember sitting on the dining room floor, writing letters to God in my Indian Head tablet. I painstakingly formed the alphabet just as Grandma had taught me to do in order to distract me from my asthma cough. I could do the multiplication table through ten and read and write simple sentences by the age of four as a result of all those long nights working with her.

I also wrote to God about getting a park where I could swim and ride the merry-go-round. Whenever we went to Fair Park, the grownups warned me not to walk near the pool. We had to stay in a separate area. If I asked about riding the merry-go-round, Mother Lois and Grandmother India got very nervous. They would tell me there was no space for me as they dragged me away.

When the mailman failed to bring a reply from God, and things at the park didn't change, even after a year, my patience wore thin. With each passing day, I realized just how different things really were for me.

When I was five, I had my first true bout with testing the harsh realities of segregation. My family—Grandmother, Mother, Daddy, and Conrad, plus most of my aunts and uncles—had gathered at Fair Park for a Fourth of July picnic. As usual we were separated from the white people, set apart in a wooded section away from the pool and the merry-go-round. While the grownups busied themselves setting up the meal, I made my escape, sneaking away to ride the merry-go-round. I had had my eye on one horse in particular, Prancer, the one I had dreamed about during all those months as I saved up the five pennies I needed to ride him.

I reached up to give the concessionaire my money. "There's no space for you here," the man said. But I pointed to Prancer's empty saddle. That's when he shouted at me and banged hard on the counter, spilling my coins on the ground. "You don't belong here, picaninny." I didn't know what that word meant. But his growling voice hurt my ears and made my knees shake. Angry faces glared at me as though I'd done something terribly wrong. Scurrying past the people waiting in line, I was so terrified that I didn't even take the time to pick up my precious pennies. At five I learned that there was to be no space for me on that merry-go-round no matter how many saddles stood empty.

As a young child, my life was centered around the big, old, white wood-frame house at 1121 Cross Street that was my home.

I lived there with my mother, Lois, her mother—my grand-mother India—my father, Howell, and my brother, Conrad. Seven red cement stairs led up to the front door. A giant rubber plant stood just inside the front hallway next to tall mahogany bookcases that held the cherished volumes of Shakespeare, Chaucer, and Emily Dickinson, and of James Welden Johnson and Langston Hughes that Grandma and Mother loved so much. Some of the shelves held the textbooks Mother used for teaching seventh-grade English and for the night classes she took to get her master's degree.

Next came the living room with its tattered, overstuffed green velvet chair and matching couch. The half-moon-shaped radio with brass knobs sat on a round mahogany table. Wine-colored leather chairs stood on either side. Great-grandma Ripley's clock and a copper horse that had belonged to Great-grandpa rested on the mantel over the fireplace.

The kitchen had a huge old-fashioned stove, a red chrome-trimmed breakfast table and chairs, bright yellow walls, and a linoleum floor with visible marks of wear and tear. Grandma could usually be found scrubbing it sparkling clean or baking cornbread, simmering collard greens, or preparing her special gourmet salmon soufflé. She had learned to cook some of her fancy dishes when she worked as a maid in white ladies' kitchens on Park Hill. Much of that time, she earned only a dollar a day, which she used to support her three children after Grandpa died. Since they had very little money, my uncle and aunt worked to help Grandma put my mother through college.

My favorite place in our house was Grandma India's bedroom, filled with her "dibbies," the name she gave the personal things that "a body treasures and holds close to the heart." Her room always smelled of fresh flowers. Antique velvet scarves with satin fringe draped the back of her rocking chair and the back of the overstuffed maroon velvet chair in the corner by the window. There were photographs of her travels—to an Indian reservation where her husband, Grandpa Charles Peyton, had grown up with his people in Canada. There were also old tin-plate photos of her travels as a young woman to Italy with her father, Great-grandpa Ripley, when he accompanied his boss to Rome on business.

I couldn't decide which of her treasures I loved most—her eight-foot-tall antique armoire with its ornate Oriental carvings, her iridescent green music box that played "Stardust," or the special Dutch-girl quilts she created with colorful fabric profiles in each square.

I don't remember life without Grandmother India. Mother and Daddy had lived with her in North Little Rock even before I was born. When they purchased our Little Rock house, Grandma came with them. Unlike Mother, who was delicate and fair, Grandma was tall and copper-skinned. She had pronounced cheekbones and huge, deep-set almond-shaped eyes that peered at me from behind wire-rimmed spectacles. She had a regal posture and a fearless attitude. My happiest evenings were spent listening to her read aloud from the Bible, from Archie comic books, or from Shakespeare. I sometimes gave up my favorite radio programs like *The Edgar Bergen and Charlie McCarthy Show*, *Our Miss Brooks*, and *The Aldrich Family* to hear her read to me.

For as long as I can remember, I spent late afternoons with Grandma India in her garden, tending her four o'clock plants. I would stand beside her holding on to her skirt as she pulled the weeds or held the water hose. That's when we had our private talks. Once when I was six or so, I explained to her that I believed each human being was really only a spirit—made by God, and that our bodies were like clothes hanging in the closet. I said I thought that one day I would be able to exchange my body for a white body, and then I could be in charge.

"Some of your thinking is right, child. We are not these bodies, we are spirits, God's ideas. But you must strive to be the best of what God made you. You don't want to be white, what you really want is to be free, and freedom is a state of mind."

"Yes, ma'am, but . . ."

"I hope you haven't told anyone else about spirits and bodies." She squeezed my hand. "Well, have you?"

"No, ma'am."

"Good. It's time you started keeping a diary so's you can write down these thoughts and share them with me sometimes, but mostly keep them to yourself and tell God."

The next time she went to town she brought me a pink diary *Her grand-ma is very special to her* that I could lock with a little key. Most evenings before sleeping, I looked forward to going to my bedroom to write to God. I was actually giving God an exam because He hadn't kept His promise so far. I had asked Grandma could I still trust Him, and she had said, "Always, child, but remember, it's His schedule, not yours. His good will come when you least expect it."

My room was a place for my stuffed animals to live and a home for my huge brown Raggedy Ann doll, the one Grandma India made for me. It was a magical place where I daydreamed for hours as I listened to music or radio shows. There I could be whoever I wanted; I could be white—I could be free.

My brother, Conrad's, bedroom was filled with strange trucks, glass jars of crawly bugs, and a wooden train Daddy made for him. Conrad spent lots of time counting marbles, putting puzzles together, and playing Monopoly. His room always seemed to be cluttered with pieces and parts of things, and Daddy would often march into Conrad's room and demand that he put all his toys and trucks back into the red wooden box they had built together.

Daddy worked for the Missouri Pacific Railroad as a hostler's helper. He would arrive home, his huge muscular body obviously tired from the physical labor of his job. Mother constantly reminded him that if he'd finish just one more course, he could graduate from college and have a professional job that paid more. But he resisted, saying he preferred to work outside in the fresh air, where he was free. He loved hunting and fishing and getting away to the wilds where nobody could bother him. It made Mother very angry that he wouldn't follow her advice. I worried they might do what my friend Carolyn's parents did— get a divorce. At the time, I didn't know the meaning of that word, but I knew that when it happened, her daddy was gone forever.

11

The dining room with its big oval table was the place we gathered each night for dinner and evening games. Daddy sat in the brown leather chair, reading his newspaper and working his crossword puzzles. Grandma entertained us with reading or checkers and chess so we wouldn't bother Mother as she studied for her night-school exams. She was determined to complete her master's degree.

When she began graduate school, our people couldn't attend classes with whites at the University of Arkansas. After much grumbling and dickering, white folks had begun to allow small departments to integrate, class by class. She would tell us the story of the lone black man who was trying to integrate the law school. In the classroom, he was forced to sit confined by a white picket fence erected around his desk and chair. When he needed to come or go, he sometimes stumbled over that fence. White people around him sometimes stumbled over that fence, too. And still each day when he arrived, there it was, encircling him, keeping him separate but equal.

Mother began meeting with a few others from our community who were also determined to be admitted to the graduate school of education at the university. At the time, they were attending extension classes but in a separate space set aside for our people. Sometimes we got telephone calls from people warning us not to push any further to integrate the university. Nevertheless, Mother Lois continued her meetings and her classes.

I will always remember the night she casually looked up from her papers to tell us she would be one of the first of our people to attend the University of Arkansas. There was a nervous quiver in her voice. The glance she exchanged with Grandma made me realize they were both frightened of what lay ahead. "I can't turn back now," Mother said. "Forward is the only way our people can march."

Later that winter, she smiled as she talked across the dinner table about the integrated classes. Some nights she would come home exhausted, her face pale and drawn, her teary eyes reflecting the discomfort of her plight. When I asked what hap-

12

pened, she would only say white folks were stubborn about seeing our people as God's ideas.

Nevertheless, she survived. A few years later in 1954, she tugged me forward by my hand as Conrad and Grandma walked just behind us up the sidewalk to her graduation. It was a rare occasion, for I saw a few white folks look at Mother with a pleasant expression. This time she didn't seem as nervous around them, maybe because she was wearing the same black cap and gown they were as she held the diploma in her hand. "It's the first graduate degree I know of in this family," Grandma India said, stroking the document as though it were the same precious tablet given Moses in the Bible.

Within our community, we were considered middle-class folk. The middle-class label was mostly because of Mother's teaching job. It didn't mean we had lots of money or lived without struggling to pay our mortgage or the bills. Preachers, teachers, and doctors were usually the only professionals in our community, and hence they were accorded a special kind of respect because they had educational degrees. Certainly we were not considered radical integrationists or people who made waves. We were quiet churchgoing folks. Daddy's Uncle Benjamin Pattillo was a preacher who traveled from city to city conducting revivals. I remember spending many a night sitting and fanning myself in churches as he preached, while aunts and cousins joined in the choir.

We lived in the heart of my community, a short distance from the church and school I attended. As I grew older, I began going places on my own, like to ballet or piano lessons and to Girl Scout meetings. Still, my immediate neighborhood and its people continued to be the most important threads of the tapestry that was my life.

With the passage of time, I became increasingly aware of how all of the adults around me behaved the same. They were living with constant fear and apprehension. It felt as though we always had a white foot pressed against the back of our necks. I was feeling more and more vulnerable as I watched them continually struggle to solve the mystery of what white folks expected of them. They behaved as though it were an awful sin to overlook even one of those unspoken rules and step out of "their place," to cross some invisible line. And yet lots of discussions in my household were about how to cross that line, when to cross that line, and who could cross that invisible line without getting hurt.

On those rare occasions when a white person came into our house, children and adults alike would all stand at attention, staring, waiting for them to give orders. There was the milkman, blond and smiling, who leered at Mother Lois every time he delivered our milk. Usually he would insist that she bring him a drink of water, even when she pleaded she didn't have time. He'd set down his metal case with its glass bottles of undelivered milk and wink at her as he gulped his water.

She would clasp her shaking hands, nervously waiting for him to finish and go away. Finally, he would hand the bottle of milk to her; but when she tried to take it from him, he wouldn't let go and kept holding it tight, forcing her to plead for it. And that's when he would offer her free milk and ice cream if she "cooperated" with him.

Mother Lois's face would turn red and her mouth would tighten just the same way it did when the insurance man offered her free premiums if she'd be his special colored lady. As always when either of these men behaved inappropriately, she would urge me to go inside. But somehow I knew I had to disobey—I had to stay with her.

Even though they were all adults, the milkman seemed to have some strange power over her, just as the insurance man and other white people did. I watched as she struggled to stay calm while the milkman hassled her.

Sometimes my father stood silent in the next room peeking through a crack in the door and listening to those men insult Mother. He would clench his fist and clear his throat loud, but he wouldn't show his face or say anything. Afterward, he would either storm out, mumbling under his breath, or sit down in the chair at the dining room table and bury his face in his hands.

14

Sometimes he talked loud as though he were really going to do something awful, but only after the white men left our house. I could tell he really loved Mother and wanted to protect her, but there was an awful big fear keeping him silent.

I would sit beside him as he took his shotgun out, oiled and cleaned it. There was a sad, pained look in his eyes as he would turn to me and say, "You understand, don't you, that man's got no call to talk to your mama that way." He stood, then paced as he wrung his hands and whispered, "God, give me strength and patience to do Your will." He would stroke my cheek and smile as he continued to answer as though he could hear all the questions in my head. "Someday things will be different, someday our men will be respected and not be called 'boy' and treated like children." Then he would calm down and smile, describing his visits to states like North Dakota and Pennsylvania where our men were treated, as equals—where they looked white men in the eye fearlessly, where they could protect their women. These were places where we would all move—someday.

There were so many times when I felt shame, and all the hope drained from my soul as I watched the adults in my family kowtow to white people. Whenever we shopped at the grocery store, they behaved as though they were worried about something.

The grocer, tall, skinny Mr. Waylan, with his Adam's apple sticking out above his collar, his fish-belly blue-white skin and oversized fingernails, was the white man I saw most often. At least twice a week, I would accompany one or more of the adults in my family to his store. Looking through horn-rimmed glasses, with what Grandma India called "criminal eyes," Mr. Waylan sometimes greeted us cordially. There were even times when he inspired a nervous laugh from Mother and Daddy with his placating chatter.

His store was one of my favorite places because going there was sometimes like going to a neighborhood party. Mostly our people shopped there, although a few whites from a nearby neighborhood came there, too. There was sawdust on the floor, and the air was filled with the aroma of spices, fruits, onions, nuts, and potatoes. Maybe it was the festive colors and sounds that reminded me of a party.

Early one Friday evening, when the store was crowded, our entire family went in for a shopping spree. We had Mama's teaching check, Daddy's railroad check, and the money Grandma India had earned from her work as a maid. It was one of those times when we all felt joy and peace and lots of hope. I looked forward to the bill paying because the grocer sometimes rewarded Conrad and me with Sugar Daddy suckers after the grown-ups handed over the money.

Grandma was the first to look over Mr. Waylan's bill. Her forehead wrinkled; she mumbled and handed it to Daddy. He looked it over and talked to her with his eyes. By the time Mother examined the bill, all their faces were grim. They quickly moved Conrad and me with them to a corner of the store.

They were certain the bill overcharged them by twenty-two dollars. That was more than a day's pay, Daddy said. Still, they seemed frightened to speak up. After lots of whispered angry words, they decided to complain. Although Grandma approached the grocer in a calm, respectful way, he shouted back at her in an angry voice—loud enough for everyone within a block to hear. He said he gave us credit when we didn't have eating money, so he expected us to pay without complaining.

Seeing Daddy's jaw tighten and his eyes narrow, Grandma touched his hand to stay him. There was an ominous silence in the store. Everybody was staring at us. Other people in the store, some of them our friends, stood absolutely still, fear in their eyes.

At first, Mother, Grandma, and Daddy stood paralyzed. Then Mother took a deep breath, stepped forward, and said in a commanding voice, "Even when we're being overcharged?"

"You just watch your mouth or you'all will be eating beans next month." The grocer was shaking his fist at Mother Lois. There was fire in Daddy's eyes, but once again, Grandma looked at him and he backed down; the three of them cowered like children before a chastising parent. There was a long moment

of complete silence. All at once Grandma started to pull dollars
out of her purse and Daddy did the same. Together, they paid
the full amount.

Mama quickly shoved Conrad and me out the door. We'd
make do with what was in our cupboards for the next few days,
Daddy said. We wouldn't be going to that store anymore.

On the way home Grandma fussed and fumed, saying she
was fed up with buying day-old bread and slightly rotting meat
for one and a half times the price fresh food was sold to white
folks. I couldn't stop wondering why Mama, Grandma, and
Daddy couldn't talk back to that white man.

Daddy was a tall man, over six feet four, with broad shoulders
and big muscles in his arms. He could toss me in the air and
catch me or hoist me over the fence with ease. Until that moment, I had thought he could take on the world, if he had to
protect me. But watching him kowtow to the grocer made me
know it wasn't so. It frightened me and made me think a lot
about how, if I got into trouble with white people, the folks I
counted on most in my life for protection couldn't help me at
all. I was beginning to resign myself to the fact that white people
were definitely in charge, and there was nothing we could do
about it.

The next day, Grandma called all her friends and tried to get
them to agree to form a group to shop across town. All but one
person warned her not to cause trouble. After she had dialed
at least ten numbers, she sank down into her chair with a sad
face and placed the receiver in its cradle. She sat silent for a
long while. Then she picked up her Bible and read aloud the
verse that cleared away the tears in her eyes: "And Ethiopia
shall stretch forth her wings." With a smile on her face and fire
in her eyes she said, "Be patient, our people's turn will come.
You'll see. Your lifetime will be different from mine. I might not
live to see the changes, but you will. . . . Oh, yes, my child,
you will."

But as time passed without significant changes in my life, I
was becoming increasingly anxious waiting for Ethiopia to
stretch forth her wings. In my diary I wrote:

What if Grandma is wrong?—what if God can't fix things. What if the white people are always gonna be in charge. God, now, please give me some sign you are there and you are gonna do something to change my life. Please hurry!
—Melba Pattillo—age eight—a Sunday School student

I was as impatient for change as I was with the location of the rest rooms marked "Colored." As a child it seemed they were always located miles away from wherever I was when I felt the urge to go. When we shopped in the downtown stores, the rest rooms were usually located at the end of a dark hallway, or at the bottom of a dingy stairwell. It never failed that either I dampened my pants trying to get there in time or, worse yet, got a horrible ache in my side trying to hold my water until I got home.

An experience I endured on a December morning would forever affect any decision I made to go "potty" in a public place. We were Christmas shopping when I felt the twinge of emergency. I convinced Mother and Grandmother that I knew the way to the rest room by myself. I was moving as fast as I could when suddenly I knew I wasn't going to make it all the way down those stairs and across the warehouse walkway to the "Colored Ladies" toilet.

So I pushed open the door marked "White Ladies" and, taking a deep breath, I crossed the threshold. It was just as bright and pretty as I had imagined it to be. At first I could only hear voices nearby, but when I stepped through a second doorway, I saw several white ladies chatting and fussing with their makeup. Across the room, other white ladies sat on a couch reading the newspaper. Suddenly realizing I was there, two of them looked up at me in astonishment. Unless I was the maid, they said, I was in the wrong place. But it was clear I was too young to be the maid. While they shouted at me to "get out," my throbbing bladder consumed my attention as I frantically headed for the unoccupied stall.

They kept shouting, "Good Lord, do something." I was doing something by that time, seated comfortably on the toilet, listening to the hysteria building outside my locked stall. One woman even knelt down to peep beneath the door to make certain I didn't put my bottom on the toilet seat. She ordered me not to pee.

At first there was so much carrying-on outside my stall that I was afraid to come out. But I wanted to see all the special things about the white ladies' rest room, so I had no choice. A chorus of "Nigger" and other nasty words billowed around me as I washed my hands. One woman waved her finger in my face, warning me that her friend had gone after the police and they would teach me a thing or two. Hearing the word "police" terrified me. Daddy and Mother Lois were afraid of the police. The ladies were hurrying out through the door saying they were going to tell the manager that they would never shop in that store again.

Just then I heard a familiar voice: "Melba Joy Pattillo, just what are you doing in there." It was Grandma India calling out to me. She stepped inside the room. I was so happy to see her that I rushed to give her a hug. Her embrace made me feel safe, but the fear in her voice brought back my fear. My curiosity had gotten us into a real mess, she said. The police and a whole bunch of white folks were outside waiting for me. Grandma pushed me away and wiped my tears. And even as she straightened the bow on my braid, those voices were shouting at us through the door.

"I'm demanding you'all get out here right now. I'm with the Little Rock Police. Don't make us come in after you."

Grandma straightened her shoulders, assuming the posture of a queen as she reached down to take my hand, and instructed me to stand tall. As we walked through the door, I tilted my chin upward to match her chin as she looked the two policemen right in the eye. She spoke to them in a calm, clear voice, explaining that I was not good at reading signs. Then she apologized for any inconvenience I had caused. Her voice didn't sound frightened, but I could feel her hand shaking and the perspiration in her palm.

Suddenly, one of the officers moved close and blocked our

19

way, saying we had to come upstairs for a serious talk. Grandma didn't flinch as he moved too close to her. Instead, she smiled down at me and squeezed my hand. But as he beckoned her to move ahead, I knew we were in more trouble than we'd ever been in before. When she asked where he was taking us, he told her to shut up and do as we were told. Some of the crowd moved with us. When we passed close to Mother Lois, she and Grandma talked to each other with their eyes. I started to speak, but Grandma pinched my arm.

Once inside the upstairs room with the straight-back wooden chairs, long table, and cardboard boxes, both officers lit cigarettes. One of them said we must be part of a communist group from up North, trying to integrate Little Rock's bathrooms. Grandma's voice only cracked once as over and over again she insisted that I had made a mistake. She called them "sir" and "mister" as she protested that we were good Little Rock citizens grateful for the use of our own bathrooms. She said she remembered the time when we couldn't even enter the front door of the store and she was humbly grateful for that privilege.

Finally, after an hour, the older policeman said he'd let us go, calling us harmless niggers gone astray. But he warned if we were ever again caught being curious about what belonged to white folks, we'd be behind bars wearing stripes, or even worse, wearing ropes around our necks.

As we climbed into the car, Grandmother India warned me that curiosity killed the cat and it was going to be my undoing. As punishment for my bad deed, she made me read the Twenty-Third Psalm every day for a month. I also had to look up "patience" in the dictionary and write down the definition.

In a way, she was right—patience was slowly bringing changes. As I celebrated several birthdays, growing into double digits, the one major change I could see was Mother Lois's attending still more classes at the white people's university. I was so fascinated with the idea that I had to see this school; so she began driving the whole family past the university extension on Sunday afternoon rides. It was located in the kind of all-white neighborhood we only dared travel through during the day. I craned my neck to look at the pretty houses and manicured lawns.

Sometimes, on our way there, we passed Central High School, so tall, so majestic, like a European castle I'd seen in history books. "Wow, that's a lot bigger than our high school," I said one Sunday. "I want to go there."

"May Brown cooks there," Grandma said. "She tells me that's where the richest white families send their children. Folks up North know about Central High School. They know it's a good school."

"I wish I could see what's inside," I said.

"Don't you dare even say that, girl; curiosity gets a body in a whole lot of trouble. Be patient," Grandma commanded once more as she smiled at me. "Be patient, and one day, God willing, you'll see inside that school, I promise."

3

How could I ever forget May 17, 1954, the day the Supreme Court ruled in *Brown* v. *Board of Education of Topeka, Kansas,* that separate public schools for whites and blacks were illegal? The adults around me behaved so strangely that their images became a freeze-frame, forever preserved in my mind. I learned lessons on that day that I will remember for the rest of my life.

I was twelve years old. That afternoon, I sat at my desk in my seventh-grade class at Dunbar Junior High, copying from the blackboard. My teacher had been called outside. When she returned, she appeared frightened and nervous. Erasing the blackboard before we could finish our copying, she spoke breathlessly about *Brown* v. *Board of Education.*

"Does that mean we have to go to school with white people?" my friend Carl asked as a chorus of voices echoed his question.

"Yes, maybe. But you needn't concern yourself with that. Collect your things. You'all are dismissed early today." Although she said the Brown case was something we should be proud of, something to celebrate, her face didn't look at all happy. I didn't understand why she was in such a big rush to dismiss us that way, but I didn't ask. Going home to be with my grandmother India was something I looked forward to every day. Peering over the book or newspaper she was reading, she would always greet me the same way: "And what did you learn today?" She hadn't finished high school, but she had read lots of books, and she studied everything and everybody all the time. Over an after-school snack of warm gingerbread and milk, the two of us would talk and laugh until it was time for me to start my chores and homework.

Now as we left school I heard my teacher's quivering voice: "Pay attention to where you're walking. Walk in groups, don't walk alone." She stood at the top of the steps, telling us to hurry.

Once outside, I realized I had forgotten a math book, but when I tried to get it, she blocked my way, telling me that I should go on with the others. I couldn't imagine why she was so insistent that I hurry home. She even said she would excuse my homework assignment the next day. She had never excused undone homework for any reason before. *Maybe they are having the class checked*

I trailed behind the others as I pondered her strange behavior. *or* I paid little attention to where I was going. It was, after all, a *some* familiar route, one I had walked since age six. I usually took a *thing* shortcut across a vacant block, through a grassy field filled with persimmon trees. In spring, ripened fruit littered the ground to make walking a hazardous, slippery adventure.

Sometimes it wasn't always safe to take that shortcut because of Marissa. She was an older girl who frightened us. She would suddenly become very mean, striking out for no reason. I would be walking along that path, and all at once I'd be attacked by a shower of overripe persimmons. There was no way I could protect myself or fight back because Marissa was so big and overpowering. At twelve, I was considered tall for my age; most folks thought I was fifteen. But Marissa was even bigger. Nobody knew how old she was—we thought she was about sixteen—much too old to be in our class.

Marissa was different; the teachers called her "retarded." Even though she often misbehaved, adults never did anything about it, maybe because her father was a rich minister in our community. As I crossed the field, I knew that I risked having

23

Marissa rush out of the bushes at any moment. But I also knew I could get past her if I gave her my lunch apple or my allowance money. Otherwise, I felt I was pretty safe in that field—safe enough to lapse into my daydreams. This was my special time of the day—when I could sing as loud as I wanted and make up new daydreams about being a movie star or moving North to New York or out West to California.

I didn't agree with the radio announcers who described Little Rock as a nice, clean Southern town, a place where my people and whites got along peacefully. City officials boasted there hadn't been a Klan hanging of one of our people in at least ten years. They called our citizens forward-thinking because they were completing construction of the Strategic Air Command military base nearby that brought in lots of different races of people. But I didn't think we were so progressive because I still couldn't eat at the lunch counter at the five-and-dime, go to a movie unless I sat in the balcony, ride the merry-go-round at Fair Park, or go into the white ladies' bathroom.

The city fathers bragged about the way our people and white folks were working "side by side." Of the 107,300 Little Rock citizens, blacks numbered about 30,000. They said blacks earned good wages, but that wasn't true. Most of my people who earned tolerable salaries were either teachers, preachers, or doctors. For us, there were very few jobs as clerks, policemen, bus drivers, or insurance salesmen.

My mother had long ago grown weary of trying to get Daddy to finish up his university courses. In fact, she had given up on him by the time I was seven. That's when they divorced. Even though he had been gone from the house almost five years, I still missed him, most often at dinnertime and on those evenings when we gathered in the dining room for family games. It made Conrad and me sad not to have him there. At first, when Grandmother told me to set the dinner table, I would fix a place for him. Then I would remember he wouldn't be coming home, he wouldn't be eating with us, maybe not ever. Often on those walks home from school, I daydreamed that we were a family again—that Daddy finished school to make Mother happy and she canceled the divorce to let him come back home.

As I entered the persimmon field, I sank deep into my thoughts, but a few steps past the big tree at the front of the path, I heard a rustling sound. I stood perfectly still, looking all around. I didn't see a soul. Suddenly, as I came near to the end of the field, a man's gravel voice snatched me from the secret place in my head.

"You want a ride, girl?" He didn't sound at all like anybody I knew. There it was again, that stranger's voice calling out to me. "Want a ride?"

"Who is it?" I asked, barely able to squeeze the words out.

"I got candy in the car. Lots of candy." I crept forward, and then I saw him—a big white man, even taller than my father, broad and huge, like a wrestler. He was coming toward me fast. I turned on my heels and fled in the opposite direction, back the way I had come.

"You better come on and take a ride home. You hear me, girl?"

"No, sir," I yelled, "no thank you." But he kept coming. My heart was racing almost as fast as my feet. I couldn't hear anything except for the sound of my saddle shoes pounding the ground and the thud of his feet close behind me. That's when he started talking about "niggers" wanting to go to school with his children and how he wasn't going to stand for it. My cries for help drowned out the sound of his words, but he laughed and said it was no use because nobody would hear me.

I was running as fast as I could. The lace on my shoe came untied. My feet got tangled. As I hit the ground, I bit down hard on my tongue. I felt his strong hands clutch my back. I bolted up, struggling to get away. He pulled me down and turned me on my back. I looked up into his face, looming close above me like the monster on a movie screen. I struggled against him, but he was too strong.

He slapped me hard across the face. I covered my eyes with my hands and waited for him to strike me again. Instead, I felt him squirm against me, and then I saw him taking his pants down. In my house, private parts were always kept private. I couldn't figure out what he was doing, but I knew it had to be bad. I scratched and kicked and thrashed against him with every ounce of strength I could muster. His huge fist smashed hard against my face. I struggled to push him back and to keep the dark curtain of unconsciousness from descending over me.

"I'll show you niggers the Supreme Court can't run my life," he said as his hand ripped at my underpants. A voice inside my head told me I was going to die, that there was nothing I could do about it. White men were in charge. But then I could hear Grandma India saying over and over again, "God is always with you." I fought to keep my underpants, and to roll the man off of me.

All at once, he frowned and let out an awful moan, and grabbed for the back of his head. It was Marissa banging on his head with her leather book bag. "Melba . . . Melba, . . . run," she shouted. When he rolled off me, I scrambled free. He reached out for Marissa, but she kicked him in the shoulder. That's when I managed to get to my feet and move away from him. He was still on his knees struggling to untangle himself, his legs caught up in his unzipped pants.

Marissa shouted to me to run faster. She let go of her book bag and dragged me by my arm. If we didn't hurry, we'd get raped, she said over and over. Raped? What's raped? I asked as we scurried across the field and back into the street. We raced up the middle of the street, not stopping to talk to anybody, not even the people we knew who tried to say hello. Breathless and shaken, we finally reached my backyard.

My brother, Conrad, braked his bicycle to question me. What was the matter with my face? Why were my clothes torn? I felt ashamed as I wondered if he and his playmate Clark could guess that a strange man had touched me. Just then Grandma India opened the back door. As soon as she looked at me she frowned and sent Conrad and Clark away.

Marissa explained what had happened to us, and she repeated the word "rape." "But he didn't do it all the way," she said. By then, I had figured out it was something awful and dirty.

[handwritten margin note: Good thing Marisa was there or else Melba would have gotten raped]

Before I could ask Grandma more about it, she put a cold cloth to my face and rushed me into the bathtub.

"Now you soak a while, child. When the water goes down the drain, it will take away all that white man's evil with it." She had a curious look on her face, one I'd never seen before. Then she said something that made me realize just how awful things really were. "We'll burn the clothes you took off. I got your fresh clothing on a stool, just outside the door."

I couldn't believe my ears! "Waste not, want not" had always been her rule. What had happened must have been truly disgusting to make her destroy my good clothing. I sat in silence wondering if I could ever redeem myself in the eyes of the Lord.

Later, I heard Grandma talking to my father on the telephone as Mother Lois came in the back door with her usual cheerful greetings. I didn't climb out of the tub. Instead I scrubbed myself in those hot suds to wash away my shame. When Grandma came to check on me, she must have seen the distress in my expression, because she promised the Lord would still count me as one of his good girls because I hadn't done anything wrong.

I listened for so long while the grown-ups argued in loud whispers about calling the police that my bath water turned cold. As I climbed out of the tub and got dressed, I heard Daddy's voice. When I walked into the kitchen, for the first time ever I saw tears in my father's eyes. As he reached to hug me, he said, "We ain't gonna call the law. Those white police are liable to do something worse to her than what already happened."

Grandma told me not to talk about what had happened with anyone, especially not Conrad. She said I had to pray for that evil white man, pray every day for twenty-one days, asking God to forgive him and teach him right. That way, she promised I'd get over the feelings of shame.

I wore my knees out praying night after night—I even got up early to get in extra prayers. Grandma was right. By the time my bruises went away, I didn't feel ashamed anymore.

In my diary I wrote:

*It's important for me to read the newspaper, every single day God
sends, even if I have to spend my own nickel to buy it. I have to
keep up with what the men on the Supreme Court are doing. That
way I can stay home on the day the justices vote decisions that
make white men want to rape me.*

The daily papers were full of news about the *Brown v. Board
of Education* case. Little Rock's white people were saying the
same things as the "raping" man had said. I couldn't imagine
they would ever change their minds and allow their children to
go to school with me, no matter what laws those men on the
Supreme Court made. But on May 24, 1955, the newspapers
said the Little Rock school board had adopted a plan to limit
integration to Central High School. They weren't going to allow
it to actually begin, however, for two years—not till September, 1957.

When my teacher asked if anyone who lived within the Central High School district wanted to attend school with white
people, I raised my hand. As I signed my name on the paper
they passed around, I thought about all those times I'd gone
past Central High wanting to see inside. I was certain it would
take a miracle to integrate Little Rock's schools. But I reasoned
that if schools were open to my people, I would also get access
to other opportunities I had been denied, like going to shows
at Robinson Auditorium, or sitting on the first floor of the
movie theater.

By December 1, 1955, I began to realize that Grandma was
right. Our people were stretching out to knock down the fences
of segregation. I read in the newspaper that one of our people,
a woman named Rosa Parks, had refused to give up her seat to
a white man on an Alabama bus. Her willingness to be arrested
rather than give in one more time led to the Montgomery, Alabama, bus boycott. I felt such a surge of pride when I thought
about how my people had banded together to force a change.
It gave me hope that maybe things in Little Rock could change.
In January 1956, my hopes were dashed when NAACP offi-

cials tried to register a few of our children in several white high schools in Little Rock and were turned back. Grandma India and Mother Lois followed the story closely; but when we discussed it over dinner, the talk about white people doing bad things to us kept me from telling them I had signed the list to go to Central High.

On February 8, 1956, the NAACP filed suit in Federal District Court to make the schools integrate immediately. Referring to a poll that said 85 percent of all Arkansas's people opposed integration, Governor Orval Faubus announced his refusal to support the integration of our state's schools.

In the spring of 1956, I read that Elvis Presley was coming downtown to Little Rock's Robinson Auditorium. As I sat in the middle of my bed among my stuffed animals looking at his picture in the ad, I was heartbroken that I couldn't go. Our people were not even allowed to sit in the balcony during such social events. How many times had I asked my parents, "Why? Why can't I go everywhere whites can go?"

And I was really disappointed when I read that some of the city's prominent white citizens were threatening lawsuits to delay the Little Rock school board's integration plan until 1970. I was certain they'd succeed. They always had things their way.

On August 27, 1956, Federal Judge John Miller dismissed the NAACP suit for immediate school integration, saying it was all right for the school board to integrate gradually. I knew that meant very, very slowly, or not at all. Later, there was an appeal supported by NAACP Attorney Thurgood Marshall, but the appeal was lost, and the school board's stingy plan to integrate only a little bit was deemed "deliberate and speedy." During the summer of 1957, Central High seemed to be just one more place I wasn't going to see the inside of.

In early August of 1957, Johnny Mathis had his first big song, "Chances Are," on the hit parade. That month, a Mrs. Clyde Thomason, secretary of a new group called the League of Central

High Mothers, filed a petition for an injunction to keep the Little Rock school board from carrying out its gradual integration plan.

About that time, I decided to quit worrying about whether I should tell my parents I had signed up to go to Central. After all, if white mothers were fighting integration, it had little chance of success. I knew very well the power of my own mother and grandmother. Besides, I needed all my mind's space for living my daydreams, since Conrad, Mother, Grandma, and I were about to go North. We were driving to Cincinnati, Ohio, to visit my great-uncle Clancey, on mother's side of the family. He was an Episcopalian priest, and his wife, Julie, was a music teacher.

As we pulled into the circular drive, their spacious, fancy house reminded me of the kinds of places I'd seen in the movies. It resembled our Little Rock bank in size and was surrounded by hedges with planned shapes, like an artist had sculpted them.

For me, Cincinnati was the promised land. After a few days there, I lost that Little Rock feeling of being choked and kept in "my place" by white people. They weren't in charge of me and my family in Cincinnati. I felt free, as though I could soar above the clouds. I was both frightened and excited when the white neighbors who lived across the street invited me for dinner. It was the first time white people had ever wanted to eat with me or talk to me about ordinary things. Over the dinner table, I found out they were people just like me. They used the same blue linen dinner napkins that Grandma India favored. They treated me like I was an equal, like I belonged with them.

Afterward, we went to a drive-in movie. The neighbor's daughter, Cindy, who was exactly my age, stood beside me as I walked right up to the concession stand to buy popcorn. No one even looked at me with evil eyes or called me a name! Still, my heart was pounding and my palms were wet as I squeezed through that big crowd of white people to get back to the car.

Right in the middle of downtown Cincinnati, we walked with our heads held high, acting as proud as could be. Neither Mother nor Grandmother ever once stepped aside to let a white person pass. Sometimes we held our ground and white people walked around us, and even smiled hello as they did so. We sauntered through all the big department stores, touching expensive things without the white clerks giving us a second look. I even used the rest room, and the white ladies smiled and said hello. Later, as I sat at the lunch counter in the five-and-dime to have a root beer, I could hardly eat for keeping watch all around me. But no white person so much as frowned at me. That evening, Uncle Clancey took us to a fancy restaurant where white waiters smiled and bowed, and asked if I wanted anything.

"Melba will be hard to get along with after all this spoiled treatment," Mama said as we ate, laughed, and talked. I'd never had lobster or cottage fries before, or had a white man play the piano just to make my meal go down easy.

It was mid August and we'd been in paradise for more than a week. I was wondering how I could tell Mama I wasn't ever going back to Little Rock. I planned to beg and plead with Uncle Clancey to let me live with them and finish high school in Cincinnati. I thought I had a pretty good chance of having things go my way until one evening when we sat watching the national news.

"That was your father on the phone." Mother appeared to be annoyed as she spoke. "He said to pay close attention to the news because he got a call today saying Melba's been assigned to go to Central High with the white people."

All ears perked up when the announcer started talking about Little Rock. He said seventeen children from my community had been selected to enter the all-white Central High School in the 1957 fall term.

Grandma stood and walked over to the television set, signaling us to be silent. The announcer talked about Thurgood Marshall and the NAACP asking the Federal District Court to start integration immediately. A judge had agreed and issued an order preventing Mrs. Thomason and her mothers' group from interfering.

We all stood like statues as the newsman talked about Little Rock's segregationists, who were determined to stop our children from entering white schools at any cost. I couldn't make myself stand still; an awful fear vibrated through my body.

Conrad asked if he could go, too. Grandma India said an emphatic "No." By then Mother was pale, her lips drawn tight as she glared at me. All of them circled around me, like the covered wagons I'd seen in Western movies, when settlers wanted to fend off an Indian attack. With horrified expressions, they looked at me as though I had lied, or sassed Grandma, or grown a second nose. I stood in the middle of the room, hoping the floor would swallow me up as they grilled me.

When had I planned on telling them? Why did I sign my name to the paper saying I lived near Central and wanted to go, without asking their permission? Did I consider that my decision might endanger our family? All the while I was trying to back away from their harsh inquisition. I no longer cared the least bit about Little Rock; I just wanted to live right there in Cincinnati.

It was like a nightmare—suddenly my joy and freedom ended. All night they yelled and paced and discussed. By morning, Mama wasn't talking to me. She ate breakfast with a frown on her face. Grandma's mouth was poked out, but she talked to me, saying over and over again that I was too smart for my britches.

That was the end of my vacation. We hurried home to begin living a life I had never imagined in my wildest dreams. Grandma called it "all Hades breaking loose."

4

BY THE TIME WE ARRIVED HOME FROM CINCINNATI, MY LIFE WAS already upside down. I was living with one concern—preparing to take part in the integration of Central High School. It consumed much of the time and energy of my entire family. I could see it was consuming the energy of the entire city. Nobody I spoke with or watched on local television or heard on the radio talked of anything else.

I was drowning in unfamiliar activities and sounds—the sound of the constantly ringing telephone, of people talking loud in my ear and expressing their views about integration, of reporters' urgent voices describing what integration might do to the city and the South, and of official-looking adults lecturing me about integration for hours in closed meetings.

Meetings—my life was filled with meetings, boring meetings with the white superintendent of schools, the school board, with Central High School officials, with NAACP officials. For the first time, I met Mrs. Daisy Bates, a petite and smartly dressed, steely-eyed woman who was the Arkansas state president of the NAACP. She seemed very calm and brave considering the caravans of segregationists said to be driving past her house and tossing firebombs and rocks through her windows. They saw her as their enemy not only because of her position but because she and her husband owned the *Arkansas State Press,* a newspaper that was the sole voice for our community.

I watched her in action as she spoke up on our behalf during one of those first meetings with members of the school administration. They made it clear they were not our friends and that it would be better if we changed our minds and returned to our own school. Right away they warned us that we would not be permitted to participate in any extracurricular activities. Absolutely not, voices chimed in in unison, and their collective heads shook no. Would we like to withdraw because of that fact, they asked. Although we all were startled by their declaration and their question, we took only a moment to reply. We would continue no matter what.

The only good thing about the meetings was that they allowed me to visit with my friends—the other students who would be integrating Central. I had known most of them all my life. At one point there had been sixteen others, but some of them chose not to participate because of the threats of violence. It frightened me to see our number dwindling. Still, I was delighted with those I knew were definitely going.

In the end, there were nine of us. Ernest Green, the oldest and a senior, was a member of my church. His warm eyes and quick smile greeted me each week at Sunday School. His aunt, Mrs. Gravely, had taught me history in junior high.

Tall, thin Terrence Roberts was a junior like me, and a friend since first grade. He was a very verbal person who could be counted on to give the funniest, most intelligent analysis of any situation. I adored his way of always humming a cheerful tune when he wasn't talking.

Jefferson Thomas was a quiet, soft-spoken athlete—tops in his class. His sense of humor was subtle, the kind that makes you giggle aloud when you're not supposed to.

Elizabeth Eckford was petite, a very quiet, private person who had smiled and waved at me across the hallway at our old school. She was regal in her bearing and, like all of us, very serious about her studies.

Thelma Mothershed and I were friends who saw each other

frequently. Small like Elizabeth, but with a very pale complexion, her wise eyes peered through thick-lensed horn-rimmed glasses. She had a heart problem that, at times, changed her pallor to a purplish hue and forced her to rest on her haunches to catch her breath.

Best of all, my special friend Minnijean Brown was going. Since she lived only a block away from me, we saw each other almost every day. We had much in common; both of us were tall for our age, and we shared daydreams—our worship of Johnny Mathis and Nat Cole, and our desire to sing.

Carlotta Walls was an athlete, very sleek and wonderfully energetic. Everything she said or did was quickly executed. She was a girl-next-door type, always in a good mood, always ready to try something new.

Gloria Ray was another member of my Sunday School class. Delicate in stature, she was as meticulous about her attire as she was about her studies. Her all-knowing eyes grew even more intense as she spoke in softly measured words.

We integrating students shared many things in common. All of our parents were strict, no-nonsense types. Several of them were teachers and preachers, or held well-established positions in other professions. All our folks were hardworking people who had struggled to own their homes, to provide a stable life for their families. We shared many of the same family values traditional to all small-town Americans.

Our parents demanded that we behave appropriately at home and in public. I couldn't imagine that any one of us would ever talk back to our folks or other adults. All of us were church-going; all our parents demanded good grades in school. Although none of us had a lot of money, we had pride in our appearance. Most of all, we were individualists with strong opinions. Each of us planned to go to college.

I felt comfortable being with them, because they were the kind of people my mother allowed me to associate with. And after a period of being together so much, I began to feel as though we had formed some kind of group—an odd family of

35

people with one goal: to get inside Central High and stay there for the school year.

All my friends, adults and children alike, developed some strange need to discuss their feelings about integration. Even strangers stopped me on the street. The opinions weren't always positive, even among my own people, as I discovered at my church one Sunday.

I was startled when a woman I'd seen often enough but didn't really know began lecturing me. For a moment I feared she was going to haul off and hit me. She was beside herself with anger. I could barely get my good morning in because she was talking very loud, attracting attention as she told me I was too fancy for my britches and that other people in our community would pay for my uppity need to be with white folks.

Taken aback by her anger, I stood perfectly still, stunned. I knew very well I couldn't talk back to adults, so I kept my mouth shut even though I wanted to tell her a thing or two. Just as I thought I couldn't hold my words in a moment longer, a family friend walked by and grabbed hold of her arm. He wouldn't let her get another word in edgewise as he explained that he believed Little Rock white folks were ready for a change, and we were just reminding them it was time by registering at Central High.

I hoped he was right about whites being ready for change. At first it seemed they had accepted the limited integration plan. I had heard only a few of my people say they expected a big problem. Oh, sure, nobody said it would be easy, but most thought it would be like integrating the buses; there would be quiet fussing and complaining and a few threats from the white folks, then things would settle down. But just before school started, we noticed in the newspaper half-page invitations to big "states' rights" rallies where important white people urged everybody to fight integration.

At one such rally, Georgia Governor Marvin Griffin addressed a statewide meeting of about four hundred people who came for a dinner. He attacked the Supreme Court decision favoring integration, saying it took away the rights of states to govern themselves. The newspaper said Arkansas Governor Orval Faubus would have breakfast with Griffin the next morning. I worried about that meeting because I thought he would sway Faubus to do things his way. That could change our plans again. One more change and I'd be ready to pack and move to anywhere, USA.

Since I had arrived home from vacation, I didn't know from minute to minute or day to day where I would be starting my school year. The on-again, off-again calls from the NAACP were beginning to make me nervous, even though I knew they were doing their best to help us.

On Thursday, August 29, 1957, just five days before school started, a headline in the *Arkansas Gazette* read:

STATE COURT RULES AGAINST INTEGRATION

Peering above the newspaper, Grandma sighed as she told me I'd better get ready to go back to my old school because it seemed as if Mrs. Thomason's segregationist group had convinced Judge Reed that kids from our community and white students were buying guns. Governor Faubus backed up Mrs. Thomason's testimony, saying he knew personally she was telling the truth. So Reed believed her and ruled against integration, saying it would cause violence.

I felt sad and angry that there was no hope things would ever get any better. I called my friends and got set for a year I assumed would be kind of okay because of the added privileges and respect granted a junior. I figured integration had been put off for that school year and maybe forever. Meanwhile, I was rethinking my plan to entice my family to move to Cincinnati. But on Sunday evening, September 1, two days before school was to start, word came from the NAACP not to register at our regular high school. NAACP lawyers had already gone to federal court to get us into Central High. They expected a favorable ruling.

*   *   *

On Monday, September 2, Labor Day, our family gathered at Auntie Mae's house for the last picnic of the summer. She was mother's sister, a wonderfully round, cuddly woman with flowing wavy hair and a warm smile. A real live wire, she liked to play pranks on people and tell the kind of naughty jokes that made Mother blush and cover my ears.

Her laughter and upbeat attitude always cheered me up. People said I had some of her feisty ways in me. I was certain my Auntie Mae could do just about anything. "Rules are made to be broken," she said. "If there's anyone who can integrate that school, it's you. You're just sassy enough to pull it off."

"Although I don't know why you'd want to go where you're not wanted," said Uncle Charlie, Mother's brother, puffing on his cigar as he hung his fedora on the hat rack by the front door.

"To heck with them," said Auntie Mae. "Besides, I heard a rumor that Governor Faubus is gonna send the National Guard over to the school."

"How do you know that?"

"Mamie Johnson's cousin cooks for that school. They called to tell her where she has to check in tomorrow morning to get past the soldiers." That began a free-for-all about integration. It was just what I didn't want to hear. So I drifted off into my daydreams about Vince, the cute boy I liked. I pictured what it might have been like to have him pick me up in his new car at our old school where everybody could see.

Later on that night, Grandma thought we should listen to the governor's speech on television. To our amazement, he announced he had sent troops to Central. And then he said, "They will not act as segregationists or integrationists, but as soldiers called to active duty to carry out their assigned tasks." Then he spoke the words that made chills creep up and down my spine. ". . . But I must state here in all sincerity that it is my opinion, yes, even a conviction, that it will not be possible to restore or maintain order and protect the lives and property of the citizens if forcible integration is carried out tomorrow in the schools of this community."

"The governor has finally flipped his wig," Mother Lois said, glaring at the moon-faced man on the TV screen.

"He's stirring up trouble by talking about trouble," Grandma added. She was right, as usual. Following that speech, calls from telephone hecklers began to drive us wild. Several times during the days and nights before school opened, those voices had growled at me. "Niggers don't belong in our schools. You-all are made for hanging," one harsh voice shouted the first time I picked up the receiver.

On the night of the governor's speech, the phone didn't stop ringing. One caller said he knew our address and would be right over to bomb the house. Grandma went directly to her room, where she took the shotgun she called Mr. Higgenbottom from its leather case in the back of her closet. That night, she set up her guard post near the window to the side yard where she thought we were most vulnerable. She sat in her rocking chair beside the antique mahogany end table given her by her mother.

After a moment for contemplation and prayer, she stretched her embroidery work tightly over its hoop. With her needles and threads, she settled down for the night with Mr. Higgenbottom across her lap. She sat as erect as those heroic soldiers I'd seen in magazine pictures.

When Mother offered to spell her, she told her to get a good night's sleep so she could be fresh for her teaching job. As I tried to fall asleep, I could hear Grandma rocking back and forth in her chair, singing hymns that must have given her the strength to stay alert all night.

That night in my diary I wrote to God:

Maybe going to Central High isn't such a good idea after all. It is costing my family a lot of agony and energy, and I haven't even attended one day yet. Will Grandma always have to sit up guarding us. She can't go on sitting there forever. What will become of us. Maybe I should start my plan for moving to Cincinnati. Please give me some sign of what I am to do.

Late Monday evening, the shrill ring of the phone awakened me. Mother took the call from the NAACP telling us not to attend school the next day, Tuesday. We were to wait until we were notified before going to Central. Early the next morning I caught Grandmother nodding at her guard post as I went out to pick up the newspaper. The headlines told the story:

FAUBUS CALLS NATIONAL GUARD
TO KEEP SCHOOL SEGREGATED
Troops Take Over at Central High;
Negroes Told to Wait
—*Arkansas Gazette*, Tuesday, September 3, 1957

I wondered why some news reports said Faubus called the troops to keep us away from school. He had said in his speech they weren't there to enforce segregation. Nevertheless, the word came once more that under no circumstances were we to go near Central High. The governor had officially forbidden us to go to Central, and whites were forbidden to go to Horace Mann, our school. Both places were officially off limits.

At breakfast, Grandma India said she couldn't for the life of her figure out why he'd make our school off limits to whites, but it was an intriguing thing to do. I could see the relief in her weary face when we knew I wouldn't be going to school. She said it was a perfectly good idea to pause and take stock. We were in no rush to get into that school.

So all day Tuesday we did just that—we took stock. Lots of people in our community figured they should get a word in, and they did, by telephone and in person. A few even had the nerve to drop over without calling to give us their opinions.

My father dropped by and caused quite an uproar. He stormed into the house demanding that I stay away from Central because his boss was threatening to take his job away. Grandma India quieted him. "Maybe our children getting a good education is much more important than your job." He rolled his eyes at her but left after that. On the way out he was shouting he'd

40

be back to take me away from Mother Lois if there was any trouble.

I guess Grandma saw I had hurt feelings because she put her arms around my shoulders and said, "I figure the vote is running half and half. But you're in luck—God's voting on your side—so march forward, girl, and don't look back."

Tuesday afternoon, School Superintendent Virgil Blossom called a meeting of the nine of us students and our folks. During that meeting, the tall, stocky, grim-faced Blossom breathlessly instructed our parents not to come with us to school the next day. "It will be easier to protect the children if adults aren't there," he said.

The looks on the faces of the adults told me they all were frightened. Not one among them seemed certain of what they were doing.

As we arrived home, the man on the radio explained Federal Judge Ronald Davies's ruling, ordering integrated classes to begin on Wednesday. The phone was ringing off the hook. Our minister said some of the church members were forming a group made up of people from several churches. They would pray and work for peace in the city. At the same time, he said, they would be ready to help us if we needed it.

The call just after midnight from the NAACP didn't really disturb us because we were already receiving a series of late night calls from segregationists who were loud and vulgar in their views. Mrs. Bates said we would meet at Twelfth and Park. The school was between Fourteenth and Sixteenth on Park. Perhaps we would be accompanied by several ministers; some of them would be white. She named Reverend Dunbar Ogden, Jr., the white president of the interracial Ministerial Alliance, and two of our ministers, Reverend Z. Z. Driver of the African Methodist Episcopal Church and Reverend Harry Bass of the Methodist Episcopal Church.

By Wednesday morning, September 4, I could hardly believe it was really happening—I was going to Central High School. As I prepared breakfast before leaving home on that first morning,

41

Grandmother India stood over my shoulder watching while I cracked the breakfast eggs for poaching.

Every radio in the house was tuned to the stations that gave frequent news reports. The urgent voices grabbed our attention whether we wanted them to or not. I'd never heard the news read that often, except when there was a tornado.

Hundreds of Little Rock citizens are gathered in front of Central High School awaiting the arrival of the Negro children. We're told people have come from as far away as Mississippi, Louisiana, and Georgia to join forces to halt integration.

Governor Faubus continues to predict that blood will run in the streets if Negroes force integration in this peaceful capital city of just over a hundred thousand citizens.

Grandma India said seeing as how Federal Judge Davies had ruled for integration, the governor was forced to listen. She was certain Governor Faubus was a God-fearing man who would not defy federal law. I smiled agreement, nodding my head, but I wasn't as confident as she was that Governor Faubus was going to follow the rules. She always saw the good in everybody. It made me feel so proud when people said I behaved and looked like her. There were happy lines around her mouth that made her face always appear as though she were about to break into a sweet smile, even when her words told me she was displeased with my behavior. "You're not gonna let white people make you nervous, are you? They're the same as us, God's children."

"It's not only being with the whites. Central isn't just any school, you know, Grandma." I wondered what it would be like to attend school inside that gigantic brick building that looked so much like a big Eastern university. Rumor had it that Central students enjoyed several fancy kitchens set up just for home economics class, as well as the latest projectors for showing movies and all sorts of science laboratory equipment. The newspaper said it had the highest ranking given by the North Central

Association of Colleges and Secondary Schools. I had read that two of its graduates had become Rhodes scholars.

The building was seven stories high, stretching along two extra-long city blocks. It must have been eight times the size of Horace Mann, my old high school. It was surrounded by manicured lawns and trees, with a pond in front. It had the kind of look I had only seen in movies, the kind that tells you folks have budgeted lots of money to keep things nice.

Grandma reassured me that although Central High was a special place, I deserved to be there as much as anyone. She said I would not have been chosen if school officials didn't think I could measure up to the course work. But there were lots of my own people giving me the kind of advice that made me think they didn't have faith in me. They didn't think my brain or my manners were good enough to be with white people.

My friend Marsha, for one. She had lectured me on the evils of perspiration. She said white people didn't perspire, so I had to be certain I didn't let them see me perspire. I was petrified on that first morning I was to go to school, because standing over the kitchen stove, helping Grandma with breakfast, was making me perspire. I was also afraid of ruining the blouse Mother Lois had sewn for me to wear. But Grandma consoled me by saying there was nothing wrong with perspiration. No matter what, I had to be myself, she chided. I shouldn't ever change myself to try and become like the white people.

The ring of the phone jarred us both. The furrow in Grandma's brow showed her annoyance; nevertheless, she padded down the hall to answer once more. The hecklers should be tired by now, I thought. After all, they had been up all night calling me.

"God hears you talking this way," Grandma shouted into the receiver before she slammed it down. Charging back to the kitchen, she was wearing a pretend smile so I wouldn't know how upset she was. I busied myself basting the eggs, hoping she wouldn't see I'd overcooked them. There was a long silence before either of us spoke.

I said that maybe we ought to change our phone number. But

Grandma said she wouldn't give them the satisfaction. Pulling out the special pocket watch given her by Grandpa, who had been a railroad man, she paused for a moment to be certain of the time. It was on time to the tenth of a second. She directed me to pay attention to what I was doing, reminding me that I was supposed to meet the others at eight. The last thing I wanted was to face the 1,950 white students at Central High all by myself. That was three times as many students as attended Horace Mann.

"Don't look 'em in the eye, Sis," my younger brother, Conrad, said. Tossing his satchel on the table, he continued. "Remember what happened to Emmitt Till?" His expression changed as his eyes lit up with monstrous delight. I thought about Mr. Till, who had been hanged and tossed in the Mississippi River because he looked white folks in the eye. Grandma must have noticed how upset I was getting because she said that was in Mississippi and Little Rock's white people were more civilized. She grabbed Conrad and chastised him for not being more loving when I most needed it. When Mother Lois entered the room smiling her good mornings, I noticed she seemed deep in her own thoughts. I couldn't help thinking if I were as beautiful as she I'd be a real hit at Central High.

Grandma took my hand as she started the blessing, asking the Lord to protect me. I closed my eyes, but not even the breakfast blessing could halt the thoughts buzzing through my mind. As we ate, I hoped no one noticed that I pushed my food about my plate because my stomach didn't want breakfast. Mother spoke my name softly, and I looked up at her. "You don't have to integrate this school. Your grandmother and I will love you, no matter what you decide."

"But I have no choice if we're gonna stay in Little Rock," I said. I couldn't stop hoping that integrating Central High School was the first step to making Little Rock just like Cincinnati, Ohio. Besides, we had been told students of Little Rock's richest and most important white families attended there. They were also probably very smart. As soon as those students got to know

44

us, I had total faith they would realize how wrong they had been about our people.

"A lot has changed in the two years since you signed up to go to Central. You were younger then," Mother said with a frown on her face. "Maybe it was a hasty decision—a decision we'll all regret."

"I have to go," I said. "I've given my word to the others. They'll be waiting for me."

"You have my permission to change your mind at any time. This has got to be your decision. No one can go into that school each day for you. You're on your own."

Before Mama Lois could say another word, the phone rang. Conrad raced to answer, but Mother was there first. "Keep your seat, young man." As she held the phone to her ear, she stood motionless and silent and her face grew ashen and drawn. Then she slowly replaced the receiver in its cradle and said, "It's time to go!"

Maybe the call was from another white person saying to not integrate central high.

5

JUDGE ORDERS INTEGRATION
—*Arkansas Gazette*, Tuesday, September 3, 1957

Dear Diary,
It's happening today. What I'm afraid of most is that they won't like
me and integration won't work and Little Rock won't become like
Cincinnati, Ohio.

AS WE WALKED DOWN THE FRONT STEPS, MOTHER PAUSED AND
turned to look back at Grandma, who was standing at the edge
of the porch. In their glance I saw the fear they had never voiced
in front of me. Grandma lingered for a moment and then rushed
to encircle me in her arms once more. "God is always with
you," she whispered as she blinked back tears.

Trailing behind Mother, I made my way down the concrete
path as she climbed into the driver's seat behind the wheel of
our green Pontiac. I don't know why I veered off the sidewalk,
taking the shortcut through the wet grass that would make
damp stains on my saddle shoes. Perhaps I wanted some reason
not to go to the integration. I knew if Grandma noticed, she
would force me to go back and polish my shoes all over again.
But she was so preoccupied she didn't say a word. As I climbed

into the passenger's seat, I looked back to see her leaning against the porch column, her face weary, her eyes filled with tears.

Mother pressed the gas pedal, and we gained speed. I always watched closely because I wanted my license by my sixteenth birthday—only three months away. I knew the process well by now. She had guided me through practice sessions in the parking lot next to the grocery store often enough.

We moved through the streets in silence, listening to the newsman's descriptions of the crowds gathering at Central High. I noticed some of our neighbors standing on the sidewalk, many more than were usually out this time of day.

"That's strange," Mama mumbled as she waved to people who didn't bother waving back. "No matter, maybe they didn't see me." Our neighbors had always been so friendly, but now they peered at us without their usual smiles. Then I saw Kathy and Ronda, two of my school friends, standing with their mothers. Anxious to catch their attention, I waved out the window with a loud "Hi." Their disapproving glances matched those of the adults.

"I didn't do anything to them," I said, not understanding their reason.

"Then you don't have anything to be concerned about." Mother Lois maneuvered through the unusually heavy traffic. "I don't know where all the cars could have come from," she said. We both craned our necks, curious about all the unfamiliar cars and people. Certainly there had never before been so many white people driving down the streets of our quiet, tree-lined neighborhood.

The voice on the radio grew more urgent as the announcer described the ranks of Arkansas National Guardsmen who ringed Central High School. Hearing the news as we drew near our destination, Mother said, "I think I'll park here. The meeting place is quite a ways away, but from the looks of things we won't get any closer."

The announcer said it was 7:55 as Mama squeezed into a parking space, and we settled ourselves quietly for a moment, trying

47

to identify the buzzing noise that seemed as if it were all around us. It resembled the sound of crowds at my high school football games. But how could that be? The announcer said there was a crowd, but surely it couldn't be that big.

"Well, I guess we'd better get going." Mother was squinting, cupping her hands 'over her eyes to protect them against the glare of sunlight. A stream of white people were hurrying past us in the direction of Central High, so many that some had to walk on the grass and in the street. We stepped out of the car and into their strange parade, walking in silence in the midst of their whispers and glares.

Anxious to see the familiar faces of our friends or some of our own people, we hurried up the block lined with wood-frame houses and screened-in porches. I strained to see what lay ahead of us. In the distance, large crowds of white people were lining the curb directly across from the front of Central High. As we approached behind them, we could see only the clusters of white people that stretched for a distance of two blocks along the entire span of the school building. My mind could take in the sights and sounds only one by one: flashing cameras, voices shouting in my ears, men and women jostling each other, old people, young people, people running, uniformed police officers walking, men standing still, men and women waving their fists, and then the long line of uniformed soldiers carrying weapons just like in the war movies I had seen.

Everyone's attention seemed riveted on the center of the line of soldiers where a big commotion was taking place. At first we couldn't see what they were looking at. People were shouting and pointing, and the noise hurt my ears and muffled the words. We couldn't understand what they were saying. As we drew near, the angry outbursts became even more intense, and we began to hear their words more clearly. "Niggers, go home! Niggers, go back where you belong!"

I stood motionless, stunned by the hurtful words. I searched for something to hang on to, something familiar that would comfort me or make sense, but there was nothing.

"Two, four, six, eight, we ain't gonna integrate!" Over and

over, the words rang out. The terrifying frenzy of the crowd was building like steam in an erupting volcano.

"We have to find the others," Mama yelled in my ear. "We'll be safer with the group." She grabbed my arm to pull me forward, out of my trance. The look on her face mirrored the terror I felt. Some of the white men and women standing around us seemed to be observing anxiously. Others with angry faces and wide-open mouths were screaming their rage. Their words were becoming increasingly vile, fueled by whatever was happening directly in front of the school.

The sun beat down on our heads as we made our way through the crowd searching for our friends. Most people ignored us, jostling each other and craning their necks to see whatever was at the center of the furor. Finally, we got closer to the hub of activity. Standing on our toes, we stretched as tall as we could to see what everyone was watching.

"Oh, my Lord," Mother said.

It was my friend Elizabeth they were watching. The anger of that huge crowd was directed toward Elizabeth Eckford as she stood alone, in front of Central High, facing the long line of soldiers, with a huge crowd of white people screeching at her back. Barely five feet tall, Elizabeth cradled her books in her arms as she desperately searched for the right place to enter. Soldiers in uniforms and helmets, cradling their rifles, towered over her. Slowly, she walked first to one and then another opening in their line. Each time she approached, the soldiers closed ranks, shutting her out. As she turned toward us, her eyes hidden by dark glasses, we could see how erect and proud she stood despite the fear she must have been feeling.

As Elizabeth walked along the line of guardsmen, they did nothing to protect her from her stalkers. When a crowd of fifty or more closed in like diving vultures, the soldiers stared straight ahead, as if posing for a photograph. Once more, Elizabeth stood still, stunned, not knowing what to do. The people surrounding us shouted, stomped, and whistled as though her awful predicament were a triumph for them.

I wanted to help her, but the human wall in front of us would not be moved. We could only wedge through partway. Finally, we realized our efforts were futile; we could only pray as we watched her struggle to survive. People began to applaud and shout, "Get her, get the nigger out of there. Hang her black ass!" Not one of those white adults attempted to rescue Elizabeth. The hulking soldiers continued to observe her peril like spectators enjoying a sport.

Under siege, Elizabeth slowly made her way toward the bench at the bus stop. Looking straight ahead as she walked, she did not acknowledge the people yelping at her heels, like mad dogs. Mother and I looked at one another, suddenly conscious that we, too, were trapped by a violent mob.

Ever so slowly, we eased our way backward through the crowd, being careful not to attract attention. But a white man clawed at me, grabbing my sleeve and yelling, "We got us a nigger right here!" Just then another man tugged at his arm distracting him. Somehow I managed to scramble away. As a commotion began building around us, Mother took my arm, and we moved fast, sometimes crouching to avoid attracting more attention.

We gained some distance from the center of the crowd and made our way down the block. But when I looked back, I saw a man following us, yelling, "They're getting away! Those niggers are getting away!" Pointing to us, he enlisted others to join him. Now we were being chased by four men, and their number was growing.

We scurried down the sidewalk, bumping into people. Most of the crowd was still preoccupied watching Elizabeth. Panic-stricken, I wanted to shout for help. But I knew it would do no good. Policemen stood by watching Elizabeth being accosted. Why would they help us?

"Melba, . . . take these keys," Mother commanded as she tossed them at me. "Get to the car. Leave without me if you have to."

I plucked the car keys from the air. "No, Mama, I won't go without you." Suddenly I felt the sting of her hand as it struck the side of my face. She had never slapped me before. "Do what I say!" she shouted. Still, I knew I couldn't leave her there. I reached back to take her arm. Her pace was slowing, and I tried to pull her forward. The men were gaining on us. If we yelled for help or made any fuss, others might join our attackers. Running faster, I felt myself begin to wear out. I didn't have enough breath to keep moving so fast. My knees hurt, my calves were aching, but the car was just around the next corner.

The men chasing us were joined by another carrying a rope. At times, our pursuers were so close I could look back and see the anger in their eyes. Mama's pace slowed, and one man came close enough to touch her. He grabbed for her arm but instead tugged at her blouse. The fabric ripped, and he fell backward. Mama stepped out of her high-heeled shoes, leaving them behind, her pace quickening in stocking feet.

One of the men closest to me swung at me with a large tree branch but missed. I felt even more panic rise up in my throat. If he hit me hard enough to knock me over, I would be at his mercy. I could hear Grandma India's voice saying, God is always with you, even when things seem awful. I felt a surge of strength and a new wind. As I turned the corner, our car came into sight. I ran hard—faster than ever before—unlocked the door, and jumped in.

Mother was struggling, barely able to keep ahead of her attackers. I could see them turning the corner close on her heels, moving fast toward us. I swung open the passenger door for Mother and revved the engine. Barely waiting for her to shut the door, I shoved the gearshift into reverse and backed down the street with more speed than I'd ever driven forward. I slowed to back around the corner. One of the men caught up and pounded his fists on the hood of our car, while another threw a brick at the windshield.

Turning left, we gained speed as we drove through a hail of shouts and stones and glaring faces. But I knew I would make it because the car was moving fast and Mama was with me. *What about Elizabeth?*

6

We sped away from Central High School's neighborhood and into more familiar streets where we should have felt safe. Mother directed me not to drive straight home but to circle around until we knew for certain that the men from the mob weren't chasing us. Even though I didn't have a license and had only practiced driving in the parking lot, she wouldn't allow me to stop so we could switch places. Her face was drained and her eyes haunted by a kind of fear I had not seen in her before.

Again and again, she urged me to keep moving while she frantically searched the radio dial for word of Elizabeth. We tried desperately to think of whom we could call to rescue her. We couldn't call the police. We couldn't call her parents; they didn't have a telephone. And Mrs. Bates and the NAACP folks were at Central High waiting with my friends.

As I drove, I couldn't help noticing that the streets were clogged with cars and people that did not belong in our neighborhood. There were dust-covered trucks full of tobacco-chewing white men, their naked arms and shoulders sporting tattoos. When we pulled into our backyard, Grandmother India was waiting for us with an anxious expression. "Thank God, you made it home," she gasped.

. So is Melba going to school? Sep 4?

"What about Elizabeth and the others? Have you heard anything?"

"Yes, yes, but let's get inside."

"We've got to call the ministers at the church," Mother said, scrambling up the back stairs.

"Morning," hollered our next-door neighbor, Mrs. Convers, over the backyard fence. "Morning, child. I heard about you on the radio. I think you'all better back off them white people and stay home before we all get hurt."

"Hurry, child. Hurry." Grandma India ushered us through the back door. In her face I saw reason to be even more frightened. There were no smiles, only a furrowed brow and terrified eyes. As we entered the house, I saw that she had locked all the doors and windows and pulled all of the shades. As soon as we were safely inside, she piled chairs against the locked back door.

"So what about Elizabeth?" I said.

"I think she's safe. A white woman and man sat with her on the bus bench, protecting her from those awful people clawing at her. Then they got on the bus with her and rode away, so she's okay."

"That's a real miracle," Mother said.

"And the others—Terry and Ernie and those guys?"

"The soldiers turned them away from that school just like they did Elizabeth. They're safe. They didn't catch as much trouble, because they were in a large group with Mrs. Bates and some of those ministers. But still they didn't have no Sunday picnic; they had to get out of there real fast."

Even though Mother looked exhausted, nothing would do for her but to get dressed and go to work. "We've got to lead as normal a life as possible," she argued as we described to Grandma what had happened to us.

"One report said those troops were armed with rifles, nightsticks, and bayonets. Did you see any of that, Melba?"

"Uh, yes, ma'am. I think I saw guns."

"Maybe things got mixed up. Perhaps the governor had them

there to keep peace, and they mixed up their orders," Grandma mused.

"Seems to me they had ample opportunity to keep peace by protecting Elizabeth." Mother Lois sounded very angry. "I think this situation is different than what we bargained for. We'd better let things cool off a bit. You can go back to Horace Mann for now."

Grandma squared her shoulders and said, "I don't see how that will solve anything. Pretty soon, white folks will think it's as okay to enslave us as it is to use soldiers to keep our kids out of school."

Mother stood in silence, pondering Grandma's words for a long moment. Her expression reflected the painful realization that maybe what Grandma said was true. And then suddenly she said, "I had almost forgotten; I have to speak to you, Melba, and I want you to listen closely to every word and obey. Under no circumstances must you ever mention to anyone what happened to us this morning. Even if you have to tell a white lie and say we didn't go to Central, we have to keep this our secret."

Telling a white lie was something she'd never before given me permission to do. She swore me to absolute silence, saying above all else those men must not connect us with their ugly deed. If we told the story and they found out who they were chasing, they might come after us to finish the job. As she spoke, her voice quivered and her hands shook. I had never seen her so uncontrolled. She looked the way I felt, battered and weary. Finally, she instructed, "Melba, don't you dare go outside, girl. I want to know where you are every moment." She pulled on her jacket, peeked through the glass in the front door, then hurried out onto the porch, almost running around the house to the car.

I resigned myself to the fact that Grandma wouldn't allow me to visit Thelma or Minnijean or any other friends who lived nearby. I wanted to call them for more news of what happened to them, but before I could pick up the receiver, the phone began to ring off the hook.

"Don't you dare answer," Grandma shouted to me from the kitchen.

I plopped down at the dining room table and watched her hop up and down for what seemed like a thousand times to answer the phone. It didn't stop all morning. First, it was the call from the NAACP, then the ministers. There were our frightened neighbors and friends who said they really cared about me but insisted they have answers to a string of their nosy questions. And then there were more hecklers threatening death. Our family minister called and promised to send menfolk to protect us. Grandma said one of the would-be protectors had already phoned saying he wasn't certain whether he wanted to be seen at our house at the cost of endangering his own family and job.

By noon, I was saturated with all the news reports and anxious to have some word from the others. I felt restless, trapped. I had helped Grandma with all the chores she'd allow, and I offered to help her with those she insisted she'd do alone. I had played all my Nat King Cole and Johnny Mathis records for romantic daydreaming. I had read through the latest issue of *Seventeen* magazine and sneaked through the pages of my secret copy of *True Romance;* I was so bored I thought I'd keel over.

"I think I want to go back to Horace Mann," I told my grandmother. "At least I'll have assignments and friends and all sorts of wonderful first school day things to do."

"One little setback—and you want out," she said. "Naw, you're not a quitter."

In my diary I wrote:

I was disappointed not to see what is inside Central High School. I don't understand why the governor sent grown-up soldiers to keep us out.

I don't know if I should go back.

But Grandma is right, if I don't go back, they will think they have won. They will think they can use soldiers to frighten us, and

*we'll always have to obey them. They'll always be in charge if I
don't go back to Central and make the integration happen.*

By late afternoon the ringing phone, the hot weather, and my
confinement were driving me nuts, so when the phone rang, I
grabbed for it.

"Where were you?" I could hear annoyance in Minnijean's
voice.

"I was there," I said. "Across the street. I saw Elizabeth being
chased by those ugly people. Why was she alone?"

"Remember, she doesn't have a phone, so she didn't get that
midnight call. She didn't know where or when to meet us."

"Mama and I barely made it out of there!" I said, being cau-
tious not to tell all.

"We got outta there as fast as we could. First we went to the
superintendent's office. We waited there for an hour, sitting on
those hard benches. Then Mrs. Bates dragged us on to the
United States Attorney's office, to see a Mr. Cobb."

"Why?"

"She said since Judge Davies made a federal order, we should
go there, but Cobb sent us on to the FBI office. That was kind
of secret and fun. Those guys look just the way they do on
television, like they know something but they won't tell."

"Yeah, but what did they do?"

"Asked a lot of questions and wrote the answers down."

"Questions?"

"Yeah, all about where we stood and who did what to us.
Took hours and I was sweating so bad I thought I would die."

"Well, are they gonna do anything?"

"Investigate, they said they'd investigate."

"Sure, by that time we could be dead."

"You ain't kidding. That mob was outright nasty. I gotta go
now, but can you meet me in fifteen minutes and we'll go to
the Community Center?"

"The Community Center," I whispered. It seemed like forever
since I'd had an ordinary afternoon there listening to records
and talking to friends who didn't use the word "integration." I

thought about the wonderful times Minnijean and I had shared—times when our greatest concern was saving enough allowance to buy a new record or praying to be asked to walk to the cafeteria with the right boy. Maybe our lives could be that way again. I tiptoed past Grandma, peacefully snoozing in her rocking chair. Suddenly she was awake. "Just where do you think you're going, Missy?"

"Uh, to the Community Center. I didn't want to disturb you. I thought you were sleeping."

"Uh, huh. Have a seat. The best you can do is let up a window. But you ain't going to no Community Center."

I couldn't stop the rush of tears. I ran to my room and fell onto the bed, burying my face in the pillow to hide the sobs that wrenched my insides. All my disappointment over not getting into Central High and the mob chase as well as the big sudden changes in my life over the past few weeks came crashing in on me.

Then I heard Grandma India padding across the room and felt the weight of her body shift the plane of the mattress as she sat down.

"You had a good cry, girl?" Her voice was sympathetic but also one sliver away from being angry.

"Yes, ma'am."

"You'll make this your last cry. You're a warrior on the battlefield for your Lord. God's warriors don't cry, 'cause they trust that he's always by their side. The women of this family don't break down in the face of trouble. We act with courage, and with God's help, we ship trouble right on out."

"But I . . ." I tried to explain.

"But nothing. Now, you get yourself together, read the Twenty-Third Psalm, and don't ever let me see you behave this way again."

"Yes, ma'am." The anger in her voice hurt my feelings, but her warm hand patted my arm to reassure me of her love. From then on, I knew I could only cry when no one would hear me.

I became very anxious as I watched the curtain of dusk shadow the sun. Although I relished the protective veil of night,

I feared the men who had chased us earlier might use the cover of darkness to hurt us. For much of the early evening, my family hovered in the living room reading newspapers, listening to the radio, and watching the news. There were the ever-present phone calls to frighten us. Sometimes they even entertained us, as when we heard Grandma give them her call-to-worship, reading Bible verses and asking them if they had found the Lord.

"Whew, that was quite a workout," she said, fanning herself with a folded newspaper and settling down into her favorite chair. "White ministers have their work cut out for them."

Turning away from the television, Mother said, "Yeah, but I'm not certain those ministers will get their work done before we're driven out of our minds by the phone calls. I think we'll have to get another telephone number. We can't go on this way."

"Give it a few more days," Grandma said. "Surely . . . surely they'll get tired and go away."

"You know the effort they made to integrate over in North Little Rock failed dismally," Mother Lois said. She went on to explain to us how the attempt to integrate North Little Rock's white high school had also been met with a violent and angry crowd.

And then she told us of a frightening talk she had had with one of the administrators at the school where she taught seventh-grade English.

"He started the conversation innocently enough, but then he asked me why I would subject my daughter to being the first to integrate. I told him if nobody takes responsibility for being the first, it will never get done. On and on he went, asking questions and describing the worst possible outcomes. Then he warned that some North Little Rock white school officials might take it personally that I allowed Melba to go to Central."

"I think this might be a time when we have to keep our business close to our chests," Mother cautioned. "I didn't give him any details of our encounter this morning. He asked me point-blank if I would take you out of school, and I said we'd have to see how things worked out."

"Sounds as though they are threatening you a little." Grandma's face showed anguish as she spoke.

The thought of Mother not having that teaching job upset me. Before she was hired, we had little food on the table, and Grandma had to make most of my dresses from bleached flour sacks. Mother had worked so hard for it. Besides, she was now our sole support. Daddy gave us money only now and then. I decided I had to change the thoughts running through my mind. They frightened me too much. I was ready to see something other than integration on the news, so I began flipping channels, looking for *Lucy*, *Sid Caesar*, or *The Hit Parade*.

Just then Grandma India raised the newspaper to show me headlines: RING OF TROOPS BLOCK INTEGRATION HERE. NO INCIDENTS REPORTED, OFFICIALS HUDDLE. The article said that the Arkansas National Guardsmen were indeed armed with rifles, bayonets, and nightsticks to keep us out of the school, and that troopers from the Arkansas State Police had joined them. The official total was 270 guards posted to fend us off, but folks who had driven around the school said it was more like five hundred.

I took heart from another headline: IKE ORDERS BROWNELL TO LOOK INTO FAUBUS ACT. Then I spotted another story farther down the page that said Wiley Branton, legal counsel for the local NAACP, had officially announced that our parents would not allow us to return to school. We breathed a sigh of relief. The question of what I would do the following morning had definitely been settled.

Our usual household routine was stalled, however, as we dealt with threats from callers. No matter how many times we vowed we'd have a normal evening, somehow we always ended up turning back to the news to keep up with what was going on. Radio reports said the crowd gathered outside Central earlier had broken into splinter groups and now roamed the city terrorizing our people wherever they found them.

The news reports were all the same:

Gangs of gun-toting renegades are reportedly arriving from surrounding states to join segregationists' fight to halt integration.

Meanwhile, Governor Faubus continues to predict blood will run in the streets if the federal order to integrate schools is enforced.

"I don't see why we should allow these silly white people to frighten us into giving up our lives. I'll start dinner, and I expect you'all to help." Grandma gathered up the paper and headed for the kitchen.

The shrill ring of the telephone upset me even more now that I had seen my enemies. I imagined the callers to resemble those men who had chased, me. It felt as though they were entering my home each time they called. I could tell Mother felt the same way. With each ring, her expression turned grimmer.

"I'll get it." Conrad's voice was less enthusiastic than usual, but still he made his chase for the phone until he was ordered to halt. Grandma had interrupted her cooking to hurry to the phone.

She called to me from the hallway. "Sounds like maybe that boy Vince. You know, the polite one from church that we usually see at the wrestling matches." Grandma beckoned me to take the receiver.

Vince, I thought to myself as my heart leaped with joy. Sure, I knew very well who Vince was. He attended high school in a neighboring town, but he was in my Sunday School class. It was Grandma who didn't really know that Vince was my secret, pretend dreamboat boyfriend. I wasn't at all certain he knew it. He was at least two years older than me and drove a new Chevy and looked sort of like a caramel-colored James Darren.

"Make this conversation brief, honey," Grandma said as she handed me the phone.

"Hello . . . ," I said, using the sexy whisper dictated by romance magazines.

"Melba?" It wasn't Vince's voice saying my name.

"Yes," I answered in a polite tone, dropping my pretense. The voice wasn't at all familiar to me.

"Melba, nigger, I know where you live . . . Twelfth and Cross. We gonna get you tonight . . . 'long about midnight.'" I heard the receiver click, and he was gone. Did he know where my bedroom was? Would he come over now? Did he have a bomb? I couldn't tell Mama and the others that he knew so much about us, so I choked back my tears.

As I entered the living room, faces turned my way in anticipation. I pretended a smile and said it was somebody else, another friend, not Vince.

I thought it was a sign that we were feeling more confident when we turned the television set off right in the middle of all the uproar about Central and took our places at the dinner table. After the blessing, the topic turned to what was really on our minds.

"I'll keep watch again tonight. If I need you, I'll call you," Grandma said.

I could tell Mother was deep in thought; she studied her plate for a long moment before she looked up at Grandma and said, "Maybe you could get some sleep tonight, and I could stand guard?"

"That would be a real good idea except you don't know how to shoot a gun. This is no time for on-the-job training." Grandma was an expert marksman. As a railroad man, Grandpa had spent lots of time away from home. He had insisted Grandma learn to use a gun to protect herself because they had lived in an isolated area in the early years of their marriage.

"May I have on-the-job training?" Conrad asked.

"Not with this job, you can't. God does not forgive those who kill others," Grandma said. "Expert marksmanship is a must because you always got to aim for fingers or toes, and them's small targets."

When the call came from the NAACP saying perhaps we wouldn't be going to school for several days because we'd be in court, we all seemed to relax. But our peace was only for a moment. Later that evening, phone callers told us that the houses of several of our people connected with integration had been attacked. The news reports were revealing our names and addresses. Mother Lois said Conrad couldn't play outside, and she demanded that from now on he walk to school in the company of several other children.

As I stood over the kitchen sink getting ready to wash the dishes, Grandma went about what for the past few nights she had been calling her security walk. She placed a flashlight by the back door near the stack of chairs that blocked it. Then she took Conrad with her as she double-checked the lock on every door and window in the house.

Peering out the window over the sink, I was astonished to see the neighborhood silent, empty, and eerie. Usually, this time of the year, all our windows and doors would stand open, like those of our neighbors. We would go back and forth bearing lemonade, engaged in happy chatter. I could always hear laughter as people gathered on their porches. Sometimes a gospel group or a blues singer practiced songs for everyone to enjoy. But tonight it was dead silent; it appeared everyone had locked their windows and doors.

"Melba." Mother Lois walked up behind me, interrupting my thoughts.

"Yes, ma'am."

"I guess I'd better say this while we're alone and I'm thinking about it. I'm gonna leave a change of clothing hanging outside your bedroom closet door. If somebody ever gets into our house late at night, you grab those clothes, go out the back door, and run as fast as you can down to Ninth Street."

"But, Mama, why Ninth Street? You told me never to go to Ninth Street." It was the roughest area of Little Rock, where all the honky-tonks and sinful people gathered.

"Yes, but no white person would know you there. Those places stay open late at night and are filled with our people. They'll protect you."

"But what about you and Grandma and Conrad? I wouldn't wanna leave you."

"We'll be fine. You could send the menfolk up here to help us. Do you understand what I'm telling you?"

"Yes, ma'am."

"I don't want to frighten you, but we have to take some precautions now." Mama had a sad look in her eyes, although she feigned a smile as she kissed me.

I stood still for a moment, listening to the pounding in my temples. Mama's words really upset me. She must have expected someone to come after me if she was telling me to go to Ninth Street. So I decided I could either frighten myself to death by imagining what might happen to me, or I could think about Vince. I started to spin a happy daydream.

What Melba's mom said would have made me more scared especially after the call.

"Are you deaf, child?" Grandma India was shouting at me from the hall and beckoning me to the phone.

"Hello."

"So, hi. It's me." It was really Vince this time. "Been hearing about you on the news. Are you all right?"

"Yeah. I'm fine." I wanted to appear nonchalant.

"The radio guy said you are being hidden somewhere special to protect you from all the death threats."

"Not me. I'm right here."

Grandma India was hovering over me, pointing to her watch.

"Are you scared? Is anyone there to protect you?"

"Not really, but we're just fine."

"Everybody's talking about you'all. We're so proud of what you're doing."

"Well not everybody's proud."

"Yeah, sure, some folks are afraid of losing their jobs. My mama says some of her creditors told her they'd shut her restaurant down if they ever caught her helping with integration."

"Oh, I'm sorry." I hoped he wouldn't be angry with me and stop calling.

"Lots of white businesses are threatening to lay off our people, and they're gonna squeeze us every way they can, it seems."

"What do you want us to do about it?" I couldn't tell what his position was.

"Nothing you can do. Mama's church is having a secret meeting to kind of lift folks' spirits and give a little help to those that really need it."

"We're not out to hurt anybody, you know that."

"Just ignore our people who bad-mouth you. They got no thoughts about the future. They're waiting for white folks to fix things for them."

"I've got to go."

"I understand—Miss India's right there next to you, isn't she? See you at the wrestling matches."

I ignored Grandma India's questioning eyes as we headed for the living room to join Mama and Conrad, who were watching TV. I pretended I wasn't absolutely overjoyed that Vince cared whether I would be going to the matches with Grandma on Saturday night. It was the one thing in my life that made me feel normal and happy, the way I did before integration took me over.

I settled down into my chair and buried my face in a magazine, refusing to give myself over to television. I wanted to save all of my mind for daydreaming about Vince and me, and how we might actually become real girlfriend and boyfriend. I wanted everybody to know I had a fellow of my own. Suddenly I heard a loud popping sound, like firecrackers on the Fourth of July. Then glass was breaking.

"Get down, now!" Grandma yelled.

I fell forward on my knees, looking at the broken glass. The green vase on top of the television set had shattered into a thousand pieces, spraying slivers all over the walls, the floor, and us. For an instant we were paralyzed, motionless, like people in a snapshot. Everything after that moment seemed to be happening in slow motion, frame by frame. Before we could move, there was another firecracker noise, and more glass fell to the floor.

"We gotta get the lights out," Mama ordered. Each of us moved to shut off the lights nearest us. My hands were shaking as I crawled over to turn off the television. I heard rustling sounds like somebody moving through the bushes just outside the window. Oh, God, I thought, they're gonna come in and shoot all of us, Grandma and Mama and Conrad and me. What if it's those men who chased us this morning. I couldn't help myself; I was so frightened I wet my pants.

Grandma made her way through the broken glass to peek out the window, then looked back and signaled us to lie flat. Without making a sound, she took the rifle, opened the window, and rested the gun barrel on the sill. Slowly she squeezed off a shot. The noise it made was like a big explosion.

Grandma really knows what to do.

"Bingo! I hit it!"

"Hit what?" I whispered.

"The old metal oil can—you know, the trash burner," Grandma said happily. "That might give them something to think about."

As she fired again, we heard people whispering and running along the side of our house, and finally the slamming of car doors.

A few minutes later, Mrs. Convers, our next-door neighbor, called. "You'all got a problem in your backyard," she told us. "After all that noise you'all made over there, three white men scooted out of your yard as fast as flying bullets. Mr. Convers says they were all he could see, but just the same he's got his double-barreled business partner loaded and he's a-fixing to give you'all some backup. A couple of the other neighbors are gonna prowl around to see what they can find."

But, she added, her husband advised us not to call the police. "White cops ain't no help in these kinda situations. Besides, then they'll know exactly where you live and hang your butts for sure."

As I lay in bed that night, I felt so frightened, I couldn't cry. Instead I lay silent for hours listening to noises outside, wondering if the men had really gone away and when they would come back.

I wouldn't be able to go to sleep either.

"YOU'RE ONE OF THOSE PEOPLE INTEGRATING CENTRAL HIGH,"
the man with the scruffy beard said. Bang, bang, bang, his gun
went off. I clutched my chest. I'm dead. I sat straight up in bed,
soaked with perspiration. There it was, the bang, bang again.
Was someone shooting through our window? I jumped out of
bed and ran down the hall. Great! I'm running! Maybe I'm not
dead. I wanted someone to tell me I wasn't dead.

"Grandma, Grandma India!" I called to her as I darted in and
out of every room in the house.

"I'm here, in the living room," she answered. "What's the
matter?" I came to a screeching halt and tried to catch my
breath. There she was, perched on top of a chair, stretching her
arms high above the television set, nailing a picture to the wall.

"Won't do to have bullet holes in the wall," she said. "Somebody will stop by and want us to explain it. We can't make a
big deal of what happened last night, you know."

I gripped the back of the chair she stood on to steady it.

"There, you see. I always liked the sheep in that picture. Their
faces are smiling out at us from a heavenly pasture."

I held her hand as she climbed down from the chair.

"Kind of hard on a girl, getting shot at that way, huh," she
said as she touched my cheek with her forefinger and winked

at me. "But you don't seem none the worse for it. You look like you're full of zest and vinegar this morning."

"I'm frightened," I whispered. I reached out to hug her, seeking the safety of her arms. She was wearing a freshly starched dress and apron, and smelled of vanilla extract. "A little vanilla behind the ear always helps a woman's femininity," she often said. I loved her so much. Just for an instant, I thought how awful it would have been if the gunmen had hit her.

"So, missy, you slept right through your mama and brother leaving for school." She carried the chair back to the dining room, placing it just so. Then she paused and turned to look back at me. "Well, get dressed. I'll make you some hot oatmeal with raisins. After I go to the store for putty, we'll sit and talk a spell until Mr. Claxton gets here to fix the window."

"May I go with you to the store?"

"Absolutely positively not," she said. "You're not going out of this house today for any reason."

As I dressed, I fretted that if Grandma wouldn't allow me to go anywhere today, she might not let me go with her to the wrestling matches. Surely nothing that awful could ever happen to me! I put it right out of my mind.

So there we were, Grandma and me, giggling and talking together over the breakfast table, just like always. It felt like a very normal morning. For a short while I forgot the shots and integration, but as we started cleaning up the breakfast dishes, I saw her favorite green vase now shattered in a thousand pieces in the trash can. It reminded me of the bullets and what might happen come nightfall.

Then the wretched phone calls started. Shaking hands and a pounding pulse were my responses to the ring of the phone, no matter how hard I tried to ignore it. The shrill sound went on forever; Grandma had decided she wasn't going to play phone tag with hecklers.

When the doorbell rang, I jumped, but it was only Mr. Claxton, Grandma's friend. When I teased her about his being her boyfriend, she said I shouldn't be getting into grown-ups' pri-

67

vate business. But I noticed she had put on just a touch of lipstick and a black bow in the back of her hair before he arrived.

All of sudden, I heard loud talking in the front hall. Grandma and Mr. Claxton were exchanging harsh words. I wanted to see what was going on up close, so I tiptoed past, announcing I was going out to get the newspaper. I heard him say the gunshots through our window were a clear sign that I should withdraw from Central, because I would bring the white people's wrath down on our community. In a very loud, strong voice, Grandma said he should mind his own business.

That morning's newspaper showed a picture of Minnijean and Jeff at the Federal Building as they filed reports about our being turned away from Central. Most of the headlines in the *Gazette* were about us and integration.

On the front page a headline stating DECISIONS OF NORTH DAKOTA JUDGE REVERBERATE THROUGH ALL OF DIXIE crowned a picture of Judge Ronald Davies. There he was—the man who had ordered the governor to move ahead with integration was pictured right there on the front page. He had the same huge, kind, all-knowing eyes as Grandma.

"Davies, from Fargo, North Dakota, who described his career as 'humdrum,' had landed in the middle of a racial battle that may have repercussions for the entire South," the article said. "This man who stands 5'1" and ran 100 yards in 10 seconds at the University of North Dakota" had come to Little Rock two weeks earlier to clean up a backlog of cases in the eastern district of Arkansas.

Twice he had interrupted his regular duties to rule on crucial matters pertaining to integration. Two nights before, it had been Davies who heard pleas from the Little Rock School Board's attorney asking what to do, considering that Faubus was ringing Central High with troops. "Move ahead with integration," Davies had said.

Although mild-mannered, the paper said the fifty-two-year-old judge could sometimes be testy and speak brusquely. As I read more about Judge Davies, I didn't think he was "humdrum" at all.

The next article actually made me laugh aloud. Under a head-line that read: SITUATION AT SCHOOL IS GETTING SMELLY, it said the National Guard blockade at Central was creating a smelly situation at homes in the vicinity because the guards weren't allowing nonwhite garbage collectors to get through their barricades.

"You can't live your whole life in that newspaper, girl. Get busy with your day!" With my arms in soapsuds up to my elbows, I could feel pretty ordinary and forget about newspapers and headlines and integration. Washing clothes with Grandma and hanging them on the line was a meditation, she always said.

A little later, unable to take the ringing telephone any longer, I picked up the receiver. It was the NAACP asking me to go to Mrs. Daisy Bates's house that afternoon for a news conference.

I wondered how Grandma would feel about my going. More than once, I had heard her say that giving interviews was just asking for trouble. "You don't wanna be singled out." Still, I was anxious to go because it meant I would get to see the others. I was going stir crazy. I decided to wait to get permission until Grandma was in her very best mood.

By the time Mr. Claxton had finished repairing the window, I noticed that Grandma's anger toward him had cooled consider-ably. He cooed at her as he headed for the front door, and she smiled like a flustered schoolgirl with a crush. After she closed the door behind him, she turned to discover that I was watch-ing, and resumed her "strictly business" manner.

"Did I tell you someone called from your church office? The Negro Interfaith Ministers' organization is speaking out on your behalf, saying Faubus is not living up to his responsibility to all the people he represents."

"Maybe he'll listen," I said.

"They say a dozen or so white ministers in Little Rock are gonna do the same." Great, I thought to myself. Maybe now Governor Faubus will see that he has been unfair and change his ways.

Shortly after Mr. Claxton left, the church ladies arrived with baskets of food. "So's the white people won't catch you'all shopping and chop your heads off," Mrs. Floyd said with an acidic smile as she brushed past me. She was Grandma's very good friend, but she wasn't at all in favor of the integration. "We have our place, and we do the best when we stay in it," she said. Her words made me tense up, but I knew she meant well. She had no way of knowing about last night's shooting and how much the things she said hurt my feelings.

The ladies included bags of store-bought things as well as homemade treats. They uncovered their bowls and heavy metal pots, releasing inviting aromas that made my mouth water.

Right away, I could tell Grandma was getting real impatient with all their talk of whether or not we ought to be stirring up the integration pot. "We're just getting settled on the front of the bus," one of them said.

"Why not wait a while till the white folks get used to having us around, in five years or so," another added.

"Nonsense." I knew I could count on Grandma's feisty friend Mrs. Crae, who shook her finger in their faces. "White folks ain't never given us nothing. Getting from them's been like pulling dinosaur teeth. We gotta grab everything we can, and most times pay for it with our blood. You just move right along, girl, you hear me. You integrate, now!"

And so it went as they scurried about. Grandma was mostly silent, with the kind of expression that let me know she was about to burst from holding in what she really thought. She was polite but firm in explaining we had lots of chores to do and couldn't tarry. They headed for the front door.

"Well," said Mrs. Floyd indignantly, "none of this would be necessary if you'd stayed out of that white school where you're not wanted." I wanted to say something and then remembered what an awful sin Grandma said it was to show disrespect to an adult. I knew for certain I shouldn't be talking back to one of the ladies in our church, whom I would have to see every Sunday for the rest of my life. I walked back into the house without saying a word, feeling as if I had been surrounded by enemies even in my own neighborhood.

*   *   *

"It's like opening day at the rodeo here," Grandma said an hour later, breathlessly racing through the living room to answer the front door once more. I was under strict orders never to answer the door by myself. When the bell rang, I was to move to the center of the house. If the visitor was friendly, I could relax. If it were someone up to no good, I had to hide in the closet, or better still, run for the back door and escape.

"It's your father. Brace yourself. He's not in a great mood," Grandma whispered, hurrying back to the kitchen.

Daddy came storming in, huffing and puffing his anger. "I'm not the kind of man that takes on over his I-told-you-so's, but the fact is, I told you it would be this way!" He shouted loud enough to be heard as far away as Texas. Grandma came rushing back from the kitchen to stand in the doorway. He looked at her with angry eyes, pointing his finger at me and shouting in harsh tones that made my knees shake.

"Sacrificing this child's life and endangering the lives and jobs of kinfolks ain't got nothing to do with freedom! We ain't free if we're hungry, or worse yet, hanging from a tree."

"Shut your mouth, Will Pattillo! Don't make this child doubt her good deed," Grandma shouted back. That was just the beginning of an awful string of mean words Papa and Grandma exchanged about me and the integration. The only good thing about his visit was that he hugged me good-bye.

"You know, don't you, that I'm only thinking of what's best for you? You're too young to be in this kind of mess." He squeezed me hard, pressing my head against his chest with his huge, warm hand. He hadn't hugged me for more years than I could remember. I stayed in his arms for what seemed like a long time, savoring his strength. I wanted him to come back home—to stay with us the way he did before the divorce. I needed him to help make the shooters go away.

"I love you, baby," he said as he walked out the front door. And when I asked if he'd come back later that evening to help us, he answered, "Maybe if you'all get scared enough you'll quit this nonsense." He turned and walked away. I slammed

the front door hard, but I stared after him through the window
for a long, long time.

The home of the NAACP president, Mrs. Bates, stood amid
a pristine row of elegant residences in one of our community's
nicer neighborhoods. This meeting marked the first time all nine
of us had come together since soldiers and the mob turned us
away from Central High. As we drove up to the house, I told
Mother I was curious about whether the others had been shot
at, but she said, "Don't you dare mention one word about the
men chasing, or the shooting in our window, do you hear
me, girl?"

"Yes, ma'am," I said, locking the car door.

"Is this a drag or what?" Minnijean said as she joined us on
the walkway to the front door. I liked her feisty way of putting
things. She always said just exactly what she was thinking as
though she weren't afraid of anything or anybody.

"Are you under lock and key the way I am?"

"Every minute of every day. I feel like a prisoner in my own
house," I said. Mother walked ahead of us, ignoring our gripes.

Mrs. Bates's home, a long, rambling ranch-style house, was
set on the side of a hill. It appeared to be one story high, but
there were rooms snaking down the back of the hill to a second
level. What made it so beautiful was its spaciousness and its
modern decor, the likes of which I had only seen in magazines
or movies before. But despite its grandeur, the huge bay window in the living room made me fret about her safety at night.

The living room was crowded with all kinds of people, most
of them strangers. They were laughing and chatting as though
there were a big celebration going on. It was the first time I'd
seen people of that many different colors and types in the
same room.

As I approached the downstairs rumpus room, I could hear
Ernest Green and Terrence Roberts mimicking the prejudiced
newscasters who'd used the word "negra" for "Negro."

72

"Well, I understand you folks are going to a new school," Ernest quipped.

"I hear the welcoming committee was dressed a little odd. Did you say they were wearing helmets? All of them, wearing uniforms and carrying rifles? I wonder why. Did they offer you a cool lemonade and say they'd carry your books?"

What a relief I felt to laugh aloud, a real deep rumbling belly laugh. I felt my insides loosen up as the two boys continued doing a parody of our dilemma.

Jefferson joined the other boys in their skit, making more fun of our predicament. We girls could not match the boys' humor. They were like three seasoned comics performing at their peak on a nightclub stage.

As we made fun of ourselves and our situation, Elizabeth Eckford, silent and obviously still shaken by her ordeal, arrived with Thelma Mothershed. Down the steps came Gloria Ray, followed by the always good-natured Carlotta. Our giggles got louder and more prolonged. We were happy to see each other, and in no time we were all talking at once. Just for that moment, we were snatching a tiny slice of normalcy for ourselves, although it was apparent all of us had questions about what would come next.

For the first time in many days, I felt my whole self relax. I took a seat and sipped my Grapette cola. Someone turned the music up, and it sounded to me like we had a party going. The sounds coming from the adults upstairs were just as festive. I was feeling okay—safe and very normal—until I noticed that a man with a shotgun resting on his shoulder was strolling back and forth outside the rumpus room window. The fear knot in my stomach tightened. For me, the party was over.

Not long after that, Mrs. Bates called us to come upstairs. "We'll get started now, if you kids will quiet down and take a seat," said the slender, stylishly dressed NAACP president. Two very dignified and important-looking men sat at the center of the room. I recognized one of them as Arkansas NAACP attorney Wiley Branton, a man of average height with milky skin, hazel eyes, and auburn hair. He could easily have been mistaken for one of the white men who opposed us.

He explained that we were smack dab in the middle of what was fast becoming a major historical fight involving the governor of Arkansas, the U.S. courts, and President Eisenhower. "What we're in now is a waiting game," he said, "waiting while everybody squares off and chooses up sides. We're all rooting for Judge Davies and the federal law to prevail." say yes.

He went on to say that Central High was off limits to us, but not for long. He advised us to keep close to home and let someone know where we were at all times. Two women from our community had been pulled out of their cars the night before and beaten. Several of our people had been attacked in broad daylight. He warned us that this was not the time for socializing, and especially not for being out at night.

We also learned that one of us might be required to testify in a federal court hearing about what happened on the day we tried to enter Central High.

"All that means is telling the truth," he said.

"Truth?" I whispered. But I had sworn to Grandma and Mama not to tell the whole truth. I'd have to put my hand on the Bible. I hoped and prayed I wouldn't be the one chosen to testify. I also wondered if I should tell him about Mama and me being chased that day at Central, and about the gunshots into our windows. Maybe if he knew about that he wouldn't call on me to testify. But I could hear Grandma India's voice in my head saying if we made a big thing of it and our names got in the papers, those segregationists might feel compelled to come back and finish the job, just to prove a point. I kept my mouth shut.

"It appears that the segregationists are prepared to resist our school registration harder than we'd anticipated," Branton said. "But we're doing everything we can to get you into the school. We need your cooperation. It's going to take time and energy." He asked us not to register at another school and to make sure we kept up with our classwork until the issue was resolved in the court.

"For how long?" I asked. All nine of us were good students. I was worrying about measuring up to those white kids in Central who'd had better books and equipment all through school. Central was supposed to be one of the top high schools in the nation. "How long can we afford to stay out of school?" a chorus of voices chimed.

"For as long as it takes," Branton replied.

Dear Diary,
The two days since I first went to Central felt like I was living in
some stranger's life. Today I won't think of integration, I won't
think of Central High, and I won't think of the white people. I
will spend the whole day finding the perfect disguise to wear to
the wrestling matches.

No matter what, I'm gonna be a regular person. I'm gonna have
my usual date with Grandma and my secret, pretend date with
Vince at the matches.

As hard as I tried not to care, I couldn't start my morning
without knowing what the governor, his National Guard, and
the school board were up to. I had to face the awful truth.
Grandma was right, I was letting those people determine how
I felt, and how I lived a great part of my day. I brushed my
hair back into a ponytail and headed for the front porch. As I
picked up the newspaper, headlines leaped out at me.

HALT IN INTEGRATION ASKED:
BOARD SEEKS SUSPENSION OF U.S. ORDER

The Little Rock School Board was asking Judge Davies to suspend temporarily the plan for integrating Central High. He would be holding a hearing on their petition on Friday, September 6, today.

I took a deep breath, preparing myself to digest the words I didn't want to see. School Superintendent Blossom was wimping out. After several years of selling his integration plan to the public, he was now asking the courts to suspend integration. He didn't say for how long. But even if it was for only a month, his asking would make segregationists think they were winning. They would surely know the next step would be to stop it altogether. I felt betrayed.

The article reported that the board filed the delay petition after a meeting on Thursday morning where a crowd of four hundred circulated a petition demanding the resignation of Blossom and other school board members.

As I read on, I wondered whether my eight friends had seen this same article and gotten as discouraged as I was. Would they abandon ship and go back to our old high school where life was at least tolerable? I was sinking deeper into a dreary mood, when I saw the good news.

IKE SAYS HE WILL USE LAW.
TELLS FAUBUS: COOPERATE WITH US

"The federal Constitution will be upheld by every legal means at my command," President Eisenhower had told Governor Faubus. The President had sent a telegram to Governor Faubus saying he was sure the governor, the National Guard, and other state officials would give full cooperation to the United States Supreme Court. The President also reassured the governor that rumors of federal authorities waiting to arrest him were untrue.

"I think the school board's backing off having the integration," I told my mother as she prepared to leave for school. "Besides, the fight between the President and the governor is getting worse."

"Your faith is sagging. We live in a country where the law

and the Constitution prevail." She smiled at me as she tossed her papers into her briefcase.

"Now, if only somebody would tell Mr. Faubus that."

"Be patient," Mother said, heading toward the car. "By the way, I'm counting on you to give your grandmother extra special help today. She's a bit weary."

Oh, no, I especially didn't want Grandmother India to be weary. I was counting on her to take me to the wrestling matches. For the rest of the day, I devoted myself to doing more than my share of the chores. I would do anything to keep her able-bodied and fit.

As Friday evening descended upon me, I noticed the phone wasn't ringing. I had no invitations from school friends, no talk of what the boys were doing, no talk of meeting at the Community Center. I began feeling sad and lonely. Mother must have noticed because she said, "Why don't you call some of your other friends and make a date for a little fun? I'll drive you."

"Can I make fun plans, too?" Conrad asked. "I'm tired of this integration thing. Integration is no fun."

"I know it seems that way, son, but you'll see, soon things will be back to normal," Grandma told him.

As I dialed my friend Marsha on the phone, I tried to remember how it felt to be normal. By this time of the year, had I been in my own school, my friends would have begun to form cliques. I counted myself in the middle-of-the-road, good-girl group. We made good grades and behaved like ladies. We didn't meet with boys alone. We invested endless hours in planning for the time when we would date or listening to details from those who already were. Every now and then, we sneaked an "accidental" group date. That meant we happened to go to the same place at the same time as a group of boys we knew.

The music and laughter in the background almost drowned out the sound of Marsha's voice as she answered the phone. Her voice was a little strange as she explained that several of our old friends were having dinner, and they were going to have a pajama party. I waited for her to invite me, to say she'd forgotten and I should come right over. Instead, she explained that they didn't want me there because they feared segregationists would attack or bomb their homes to get at me.

I stood for a long moment, holding the receiver to my ear, listening to the dial tone, blinking back tears. Mother came over to comfort me, but I felt as though it were the end of the world—at least the end of my own social world. I was no longer somebody people wanted to be with. I couldn't help saying aloud how I felt. Here I was willing to face mean men with hanging ropes, give up my junior year among friends, and all the parties and fun, to integrate—to make things better for everybody. But Marsha and the gang didn't see it that way. What I was doing wasn't important at all to them. Instead I was someone to avoid.

"Some people are short-sighted, sweetheart. They can't see the future, they can only live for today. In the long run, you have to do this thing because you are convinced it is right for you, not for what others will think."

"But I don't want to lose all my friends."

"Well, let's not dwell on it. Marsha's not your only friend. Call a few others."

"I can't. They're mostly all at Marsha's house."

"Then we'll have a family date, right here at home. We'll pop corn and watch TV and play games."

Swell, I thought as I dialed Minnijean, who was feeling the same as me—like she didn't know where she really belonged any more, either. As that boring evening wore on, the one thought that put a smile in my heart was the wrestling matches—Grandma and me—we'd be sitting right in the middle of all that fun in less than twenty-four hours.

GOVERNMENT MAY TRY FOR AN INJUNCTION
AGAINST FAUBUS
—*Arkansas Gazette*, Saturday, September 7, 1957

Governor Faubus had written a long telegram to President Eisenhower, asking for understanding and support. He was also complaining that he had not had his day in court to show that he had been forced to call out the National Guard to prevent integration because the threat of violence was so great.

I spent Saturday morning worrying that Eisenhower would take Faubus's side and school integration would be swept beneath some carpet for my grandchildren to retrieve. Between my dish-washing, reading the homework assignments Mother gave me, and answering hate phone calls, I managed to restyle my hair, and try on everything in my closet, searching for a proper disguise. I was consumed with only one thought: Grandma, the wrestling matches, and my sneak date with Vince. I worried about leaving Mother Lois and Conrad home alone at night; maybe the shooter would come again. But that worry was erased when Mother's sister, Auntie Mae, and her husband, Uncle Morris, said they'd come for dinner and stay late.

As the morning turned into afternoon, I was busy keeping to myself so I could apply my grown-up makeup. It was an art I had not yet acquired since I wasn't allowed to wear makeup. Even by the third try I resembled a circus clown. But as I looked in the mirror for a final check, I was proud of the job I had done. I was a new person.

Promptly at five, Grandma breezed into the front hall. She was dressed in churchgoing clothes, her Ladies Day outfit, a blue suit with a matching hat that swooped down from its mischievous perch on the side of her head.

"Well, don't just stand there, child, help me find my parasol." I couldn't help smiling. The frantic search for the umbrella was a familiar scene. It made me feel that at least some part of my life was left intact.

"We'd better go without it," I said. We were running late, and if we didn't hurry, the bus would leave us behind. I had been patiently waiting, hoping that at any moment my grandmother would signal her approval of my grown-up outfit, upswept hairdo, and high-heeled black patent shoes. Layers of forbidden makeup and dark glasses completed what I thought was the perfect disguise. The white people would never, ever recognize me from any picture they might have seen. Of course, my one big worry was that Grandma might say it was too grown-up, but she only peered at me with a strange and lingering expression.

"Let's go, Grandma, we're gonna be late," I said, trying to coax her toward the front door. I was praying Vince wouldn't grow impatient waiting for me and leave, or, worse yet, allow himself to be talked into spending the evening with one of the other girls.

"Why don't you take a seat. I'll be back in a moment," Grandma said, sounding quite strange, beckoning me to remain there in the hallway by the door. I heard her and Mama whispering in the other room. As I settled into a chair, I thought about all the earlier times when we had gone together to the wrestling matches.

Those matches were big events in my life because we traveled downtown to the Robinson Auditorium, a place usually reserved for white people only. Those were the times when I got to go outside my neighborhood, outside the world where I spent most of my life. We sat in the same room with white folks, able to observe them close up. I wanted to get to know them better, to see what it was they had that put them in charge.

Besides, the wrestling matches had always been just plain fun. Sure, we suspected it was 30 percent wrestling and 70 percent make-believe. We couldn't have enjoyed it if we'd thought the wrestlers were really in pain, bleeding real blood and breaking real arms.

Grandma India would adjust her hat, and then we would both strut down the aisle to the seats that Mr. Claxton had saved for us. He would always be there waiting for us with the best balcony seats our people were allowed to have.

After we got settled, I would complain about my thirst, and Grandma would grant permission for a trip to the soft-drink stand. There I would meet Vince, as we'd planned, and take him to join Grandma and Mr. Claxton, explaining that our meeting had been accidental. I had enjoyed eight evenings of double-dating with Grandma and Vince, and she didn't even realize it. I knew full well my family would never have allowed me to date. They had said all along that when I was eighteen and going to college, I could go out with boys, and then only in the company of a chaperon.

As the evening wore on and the matches got really heated, Grandma India and I would behave as we behaved nowhere else. She would pound the floor with her parasol and shout and wave her fist until her hat was twisted on her head and her churchgoing outfit was rumpled. Once she had even dropped her glasses and broken them in a fit of rage when her tag-team favorites, Mud Mountain and Blue Moon Hog, were counted out by the referee.

When it was all over, she would revert to her quietest and most cultured tone, speaking barely above a whisper. "Magnificent, child. That's the way a body gets rid of aggression without misbehaving. Now, Melba, straighten yourself up, honey, time to present ourselves as the ladies we are."

"Sorry, child, you can't go with me to the matches, not tonight," said Grandma, grabbing me from my happy recollections. "Maybe next time, when the integration settles down."

"But why?" I felt tears coming, but I had promised Grandma I wouldn't cry.

"It's just too dangerous for you to go there amongst all those white people."

"They'll never recognize me—see, see!" I twirled about to show her that I was really a new person.

Grandma India moved closer to me and cupped my face in her hands. "You're staying home, baby. It's for your own good."

"Everything's being taken from me!" I cried.

"Your grandmother's right, honey." Mother Lois put her arm around my waist, trying to convince me it was not the end of the world. "Suppose one of those people who saw us at Central recognizes you and tries to pick a fight? What about the risk to your grandmother?"

"I'll never go back to Central!" I ran from the room and locked my bedroom door, burying my face in the pillow so no one could hear me cry. Later, I wrote in my diary:

Freedom is not integration.

Freedom is being able to go with Grandma to the wrestling matches.

The next day, in the Sunday paper, I saw a pitiful closeup photograph of Elizabeth, walking alone in front of Central on that first day of integration. It pained my insides to see, once again, the twisted, scowling white faces with open mouths jeering, clustered about my friend's head like bouquets of grotesque flowers. It was an ad paid for by a white man from a small town in Arkansas. "If you live in Arkansas," the ad read, "study this picture and know shame. When hate is unleashed and bigotry finds a voice, God help us all."

I felt a kind of joy and hope in the thought that one white man was willing to use his own money to call attention to the injustice we were facing. Maybe the picture would help others realize that what they were doing was hurting everybody.

Seeing that ad was the beginning of a wonderful Sunday. Just before church started, Vince walked right up and said to me flat-out, "I want you to be my girlfriend."

"Girlfriend?" I repeated the word, desperately groping to find just the right response. I'd never been asked before.

As the organ music began, we found our usual seats in the pews to the right of center. From the pulpit, the minister looked down on us, two hundred or so parishioners seated in that magnificently spacious room with a ceiling that rose two stories above us. The choir began with "The Old Rugged Cross," followed by "Were You There"—familiar hymns that were supposed to settle us into a state of grateful worship.

As the sermon began, I felt guilty that I didn't have my mind on prayer. Instead, I was wondering whether Vince would give me a friendship ring or the letter from his sweater. It pushed all thoughts of Central High, Governor Faubus, and integration into the back of my mind.

The minister was urging us to pray for Governor Faubus and do whatever was necessary to heal any sour feelings we had against white people. He had been organizing other ministers in Little Rock to speak out and condemn the governor for dispatching the troops. He said we should pray for the judges and city officials and the President to make the right decisions—to let us into Central High.

Suddenly, my attention was drawn to what the prayer ladies were saying. They were calling my name, asking God to protect me when I walked into the lion's den at Central. I remembered what Grandma had said: "Church is the life's blood of our folks' community."

I knew very well that without the church and the help of the people sitting around me, I had little chance of making it through that school year. Certainly I couldn't count on the police. If I got into trouble and really needed protection, it would probably be the network of phone calls initiated by Reverend Young that would set off a rescue and construct a web of safety.

Church was also the place where we exchanged the real news of what was going on within our community. It was the way we fit together the bits and pieces of information we got from our limited relations with whites. First one and then another would recount what they overheard in white ladies' kitchens, on their other jobs, or maybe on a bus. Already, we knew that the stories of our people buying up guns and knives were untrue. We didn't have that kind of money. Instead, one man said, some of our folks were digging in attics and closets, dusting off rusty hardware.

"Reasonable folks smell trouble. There's too many strangers in town, too many people with Mississippi attitudes," he continued. "Ain't no way we're out there buying hardware like the governor is saying. He's a stone-faced liar."

The big discussion on the lawn after church was all the questions white folks were asking our people about who was and was not planning to send their children to Central and who was in favor of our going there. I heard rumors that two people were fired as maids at a local hotel because their answers weren't acceptable.

"You're doing the right thing, girl; we're proud of you!"

"It might hurt a little while, but when it stops we're all gonna feel real good."

"You're making a mistake, but you're making it for all of us." Those were some of the whispered good-byes after church. Lingering among the crowd as I always did, I discovered things weren't exactly normal, not even at church. Several people stood back and stared at me in silence. When I returned their gazes, some of them smiled, but others frowned.

"Smile, no matter what," Mother said. "Remember, not everyone approved of what Jesus did, but that didn't stop him."

U.S. COURT SUMMONS SERVED ON GOVERNOR
—*Arkansas Gazette*, Wednesday, September 11, 1957

A week after our first attempt to get into Central, I was still rushing to get each morning's newspaper to read about the people who gathered daily in front of the school to see that we didn't get in. The President had agreed to give the governor a ten-day respite to sort out his response to the court order. There would be a meeting at Eisenhower's vacation spot in Rhode Island after that.

The next day we learned that Representative Brooks Hays would go with Governor Faubus to a five-man conference that included the President, Attorney General Herbert Brownell, Jr., and Sherman Adams, Chief White House Assistant. I couldn't stop worrying that they were going to make a decision that could affect the rest of my life, and I wasn't getting to tell my side. What was worse was there was nobody invited who could say what was best for us.

"Did you really think they'd invite any of our people?" Grandma India said, as she stood tending her backyard garden.

"At least they could have had somebody like NAACP President Roy Wilkins, or Mr. Marshall, or some person of color."

She laid down the shears, pulled off her work gloves, and peered above her glasses as she said, "Dream on, child. But don't lose faith. You've got the most important representative of all attending that meeting—your heavenly Father."

I read and listened to every word of news about that meeting. I saw that Grandma did, too. We all felt the suspense, waiting to see whether or not Governor Faubus would convince the President to allow him to stop integration. Newspaper pages were filled with stories of their talk. Faubus wanted Eisenhower to delay integration for at least a year. Back and forth they went with hopes for an agreement running high one day, rock-bottom the next.

Meanwhile, we nine students were forced by circumstance to look to each other for social activities; our lives were being totally dictated by preparations for what lay ahead at Central High. We were no longer a part of all those activities we had formerly excelled in, like after-school sports, student council, or choir and band rehearsals. Few of my old school friends telephoned, and when they did, they asked lots of questions about the integration, questions I couldn't answer.

On September 15, the *Arkansas Gazette* headlines read:

FAUBUS ASKING COMPROMISE, IKE REFUSES COMMITMENT;
STATUS OF TROOPS STILL UNANSWERED

Realizing that the dilemma of integration wasn't going to be resolved quickly, everybody seemed to be concerned about our falling behind in our schoolwork. Teachers from our community along with other professionals were offering to give us books and to tutor us. Dr. Lorch and his wife, Grace, the couple who had helped Elizabeth escape the mob, organized tutoring sessions and structured them along the lines of regular classes. It felt good to dress in school clothes and go to Philander Smith, our community's college. For part of each day, I studied schoolwork and spent time with my eight friends, enjoying a thimbleful of normality.

Being together in those classes, the nine of us were developing a true friendship—becoming closer knit than we might have been under other circumstances. We talked about our fears, what we missed at our old school, and our hopes that the integration issues would soon be resolved. While I regretted the friendships I was losing, I cherished the growing ties to the eight.

Just before the court hearing where Governor Faubus would be called to account, the nine of us were summoned to Mrs. Bates's house to meet with the press. Nothing had changed since our last meeting. The troops were still in place around the school, and every morning the crowd of segregationists grew larger. Governor Faubus was still predicting violence.

Several very dignified and important-looking men sat in her living room. One was the NAACP attorney, Wiley Branton. I recognized another man whose picture I'd seen in the newspapers: the famous lawyer Thurgood Marshall, the man who had delivered the argument that resulted in the Supreme Court's 1954 school integration ruling.

Judging by my father's height, I figured Mr. Marshall was more than six feet tall, with a commanding presence, fair skin, and brown hair and mustache. He spoke like somebody on television, his sharp, quick New York accent overlaying a slight Southern drawl. "At the same time we are petitioning for a court order to force your governor to move his troops away from Central's front door, we'll be planning other options. Meanwhile we are asking that you be patient. Justice will prevail." He spoke confidently, in a way that made me feel that I deserved to be admitted to Central High.

I looked at this man who seemed to have none of the fears and hesitation of my parents or the other adults around us. Instead he had a self-assured air about him as though he had seen the promised land and knew for certain we could get there. We had only heard rumors of freedom, but he had lived it, and it showed in his every word, his every movement, in the way he sat tall in his seat.

He urged us to prepare ourselves to testify in federal court, if need be. Right then and there I began to fret about the truth I couldn't tell. If I testified in court about what really happened to me, it would get printed in the newspapers, and those men would come after us again. But now I knew that, worst of all, it would give the governor yet another excuse to keep us out of school. The very basis of his argument against our integrating was that it would cause so much violence that blood would run in the streets. If I told the judge about the men chasing us and shooting through our windows, the governor could use my words as weapons against us.

But as I listened to Mr. Marshall speak, I felt much better. His positive attitude gave me hope that even if I couldn't speak my truth, the scales of justice were weighted on our side. I had read that he had faced up to other Southern segregationists and forced them to let my people run for public office. He had also fought for equal rights for women. I felt honored that he would take the time and energy to fight for our rights. There was no doubt in my mind that if any soul on this earth could get us into Central High, this great man, Mr. Thurgood Marshall, was the one.

During the meeting, the upstairs had filled with a throng of news people, most of them white, with just a sprinkling of our people. We students were directed to take our seats and to answer questions as clearly and briefly as possible. For the first time, we were introduced as the "Little Rock Nine."

Cameras flashed, bright lights stung my eyes, and reporters asked lots of questions for the next half hour. Many of the reporters asked the attorneys what they planned to do to get rid of the troops. And questions were directed to Elizabeth. She seemed shy about answering, but with Mrs. Bates's help, she forced herself to say a few words. Eventually, however, questions were directed to all of us. My heart raced with fear and anticipation as I observed the process. I was almost hypnotized by the wonder of it all.

"Miss Pattillo, how do you feel about going back to Central High?"

"Miss," I whispered as my hands perspired and my knees shook. Thoughts buzzed inside my head like bees disturbed in their hive. It was the first time anybody white had ever called me Miss. They cared what I thought. I struggled to find a suitable answer.

"We have a right to go to that school, and I'm certain our governor, who was elected to govern all the people, will decide to do what is just." I felt myself speak aloud before I was ready. Who said that? It sounded like me, but the words . . . where had they come from? The white reporters wrote my words down and behaved as if what I said was very important. Pride welled up inside me, and for the first time, I knew that working for integration was the right thing for me to be doing.

"Mrs. Pattillo, how does a mother decide to send her daughter into such a dangerous situation?" Mother Lois was sitting, shy and quiet, in a shadowed corner of the room. I could tell she was startled by the question; nevertheless she stood and said, "Indeed it is a hard decision—but we are a Christian family, with absolute faith that God will protect her, no matter what."

After the main session, reporters pulled each one of us students aside for what they called one-on-one interviews. Listening to all the talk about our being heroes and heroines made me proud of Mama and Grandma and all of us. I wished Grandma could tell the reporters how she stood guard and made the shooters go away. Then they would know she was a heroine, too.

When the conference broke up, I lingered in a quiet corner, soaking up the sights and sounds around me. I was fascinated by the way the reporters wrote so fast in their narrow notebooks and spoke into their hand-held tape recorders. Their confident way of moving about and their quick, sharp talk made them appear as though they knew they were free—at the very least they were in charge of their own lives.

The way they responded to me made me feel equal to the white reporters. They looked me directly in the eye. I never saw any sign they were thinking of calling me a "nigger." Some of them looked at me with admiring eyes and answered all my questions about their work without making me feel silly for asking. They also behaved as though they were genuine friends with the people of color among their ranks, sharing work and laughter.

I felt a new fountain of hope rise up inside me. Just maybe,

I thought to myself, just maybe this is what I want to be when I grow up. If I were a news reporter, I could be in charge of a few things.

That night I wrote in my diary:

> Today is the first time in my life I felt equal to white people. I want more of that feeling. I'll do whatever I have to do to keep feeling equal all the time.
>
> I apologize, God, for thinking you had taken away all my normal life. Maybe you're just exchanging it for a new life.

HOPE OF SETTLEMENT FADES AS GOVERNOR
FACES DAY IN COURT
—*Arkansas Gazette*, Thursday, September 19, 1957

The town was crowded with journalists from around the world. Their frantic phone calls asking for interviews before the hearing only added to the anxiety we felt because hecklers continued ringing our phones off the hook. I was relieved when we were told to refer all requests to the NAACP office.

The federal court hearing would be one of the most significant in history—a precedent-setting decision could be made that affected the whole country. That's what all the newspaper reporters and radio announcers said over and over again. States'-rights advocates from surrounding Southern towns were up in arms. They were headed for Little Rock to add to the incendiary feelings in our town.

The segregationists were doing a lot of newspaper advertising to get people to participate in their rallies. The Arkansas National Guard remained at Central High, and hooligans rampaged through the streets. In particular they preyed on our people walking alone in isolated areas or at night. A new level of tension crept into our own household, nearly overwhelming me. I found it difficult to study, difficult to concentrate. Some days, it was as though someone had put me in Grandma's cake mixer, but I was struggling to be still, not to spin or shudder or shake.

During those rare moments when I sat alone in my room among my stuffed animals, I daydreamed about Vince and what it would be like to be his ordinary girlfriend and have real dates. I had finally gathered the nerve to ask Mother and Grandma for permission to date. After giving me what amounted to a thorough exam with really hard questions about Vince's intentions and character, Mother Lois said, "Have him come to the house." Her expression saddened as she went on: "Now understand, this is not really dating, and you can only see this boy in the presence of another adult. I'm allowing you to do this because integration has taken away so much of your social life."

I had a hard time containing my hallelujah shouts as I started to leave the room. But just as I reached the door, she said, "Of course, you'll wait to exercise this privilege until after the court hearing tomorrow."

On the night before the hearing, I took Grandma's advice and let God worry about what was going to happen in that courtroom.

I wrote in my diary:

Dear God, We can't get along without you. Governor Faubus has lots of attorneys and the paper says they have more than two hundred witnesses. I'm counting on you once and for all to make it clear whether you want me in that school. Thy will be done.

9

FAUBUS, U.S. GOVERNMENT HEAD INTO CRUCIAL
COLLISION IN FEDERAL COURT TODAY
—*Arkansas Gazette*, **Friday, September 20, 1957**

The first clash between the federal government and a state over school integration will reach a crucial stage at 10 A.M. today in Federal District Court at Little Rock. The immediate issue will be whether Governor Faubus and the Arkansas National Guard should be enjoined from further interference with integration at Little Rock Central High School.

The overriding historic issue will be whether the federal government has the constitutional authority to check a state governor when he uses the powers of his office to defy the federal court.

SITTING ALONE IN MY ROOM, I COULDN'T STOP THINKING HOW Governor Faubus would for certain have to be in that courtroom. I couldn't imagine that he wouldn't be there. In my diary I wrote:

This is the day I hope to meet Governor Faubus face to face. I can't decide what to say to him. If only he will listen to me one

92

minute, I know I can make him understand there is nothing so bad about me that he shouldn't allow white children to go to school with me.

The weatherman says it's going to be 85 and up this afternoon. I'll regret wearing my cotton blouse and quilted skirt, but they're new and pretty. I want to look just right so the governor will know who I really am.

The nine of us walked up the sidewalk toward the Federal Building at a brisk pace. Our group included Mrs. Bates, attorneys Thurgood Marshall and Wiley Branton, and a number of people I did not know. I was told they were community ministers and lawyers, coming along to protect us. Between awkward scraps of conversation, I could hear our footsteps on the sidewalk as we moved toward the official-looking building. I had never paid much attention to it before.

It was a muggy day, rather like the inside of a steam room. As we grew closer to our destination, there were more people and more chatter, but my mind was flooded with important things I wanted to say to the governor. One voice inside me said he didn't care what I thought, but the other said I should be prepared just in case.

I was a bit on edge. A small part of me was becoming accustomed to the fact that since the integration had begun, both my people and whites stared at me. Some of the faces lining the streets on that morning had welcome smiles, others were indifferent, while still others were undeniably angry. I wore dark glasses, which allowed me to peer out wherever I wanted without anybody being able to see how fearful I was.

I had never been in court before. I'd only seen pictures of judges. I felt frightened—frightened of the Federal Court, but mostly frightened of all those powerful government men, the governor's lawyers, who could make things happen just as they wanted.

I had read in the newspaper that attorneys for the federal government would be arguing that there was no evidence of the kind of violence that made it necessary to call out troops. Since the governor claimed our going to Central was what caused the trouble, we nine students were subpoenaed to tell that we had seen and experienced on that first day at Central High School. I was afraid of what would happen if we lost. Would that mean we could be sued or arrested? Would the news reporters make fun of us? What would my friends say?

"We're going to have to take the kids in through the side door," a man's voice said. My pace quickened as we were ushered past all the people milling about, through a very narrow, dimly lit marble hall, where our voices and footsteps echoed. We were led to the elevator, walking fast as if we were being chased. The door slid shut, and I stared straight ahead. My knees were trembling, and every inch of my body was perspiring. That elevator was so full that I could hear its guts grinding as it struggled to deliver us to the fourth-floor courtroom.

I hoped the opening elevator doors would admit fresh air. Instead, they revealed a crush of people, jammed body-to-body, shoving each other, desperately trying to get through that narrow hallway to go somewhere or do something. I was blinded by the glaring lights held high over the heads of the sea of people by news photographers trying to get pictures. We could hardly get out of the elevator and into the throng. Like sardines we wiggled and pushed, trying to forge a pathway. I stopped thinking about fresh, cool air, I just wanted to breathe and not be crushed. As we emerged, several reporters started shouting questions at us. I felt as though I were attending one of those Hollywood openings I'd seen on TV.

"What do you think of Governor Faubus?"

"How do you think the white students will treat you if you go back to Central?"

"Why do you want to go to the white school?"

"Are your parents buying knives and guns?"

"No," I shouted. "Nobody's buying weapons."

Mrs. Bates touched my shoulder. "Shhhhhhhhh!" she said. We had been cautioned not to talk back to reporters on this day. We were to say nothing until after the NAACP attorneys had made our case.

Flashing cameras and blinding lights followed as we inched our way through the corridor. The questions continued—rapid-fire, close in our faces. Perspiration trickled down the back of my neck. I could see beads of water on the noses and foreheads of many people crowded around me.

"Smile, kids," Mrs. Bates whispered. "Straighten your shoulders. Stand tall."

It felt as though there were about a hundred people in that hallway, where only half that many should have been squeezed in. Cameramen were perched on chairs and even on each other to get pictures. They must have been real anxious to be there because they were undoubtedly suffering in the sweltering heat and risking bodily injury as well.

"Melba, we're inside now. Take off those dark glasses. Please." I was embarrassed to be singled out that way by Mrs. Bates. The glare of the light hurt my eyes, and I didn't really want to look into the faces of all those people who seemed to be staring at me.

"Some of you'all think we're stars, but really, all these reporters are here to see if we're gonna get killed or not," teased one of the comics from our group.

Step by step, with enormous effort, we managed to get through the crush of human bodies. The courtroom was smaller than I'd imagined, about the size of an average living room, with wooden benches lining either side of a narrow aisle. I had heard someone say the courtroom only held 150 people. It was filled to overflowing. I was glad to see that a good number of the spectators were our people. Sections of the room were roped off. We were squeezed through the crowd and ushered to one of the areas in front, near the bailiff.

Reporters holding their notebooks sat in the jury box and in a small section at the rear of the room. As we took our seats, I noticed the United States and Arkansas flags displayed in the front of the room.

"Niggers stink. The room smells now," a voice called out from somewhere behind us. I turned around to see three white ladies directly behind me.

"I'll bet you don't even know your ABC's, monkeys," one of them said. "You monkeys. What are you looking at?" I glowered at her, trying not to say what I was really thinking. Where I came from adults didn't behave that way.

Suddenly uniformed soldiers were arriving. I turned my attention away from the woman heckling me as the soldiers paraded down the aisle with military precision. So these were the armed men who were keeping us away from school. These were the leaders of the Arkansas National Guard. Up close, they seemed much less intimidating. Some of them were no taller than I was.

Several men and one woman, all wearing business suits and carrying briefcases, were talking to the uniformed men. I figured they were the governor's attorneys. I asked where the governor was, expecting him any moment. That's when one of the attorneys told us that an elected official does not have to appear to answer a summons. Maybe I would not have the privilege of seeing the governor after all. I had hoped that seeing him in person would help me get over my dislike for him.

Suddenly, a whisper of concern made its way through our group. We were all aware that Thelma Mothershed had a heart condition, and now, right before our eyes, her lips and fingertips were turning blue. She struggled to catch her breath. All of us focused our attention on her, and instantly I knew it was a mistake. Not only might it alarm her, but our behavior could also alert school officials to her failing health. I assumed they had never bothered to check her school records; otherwise they might have stopped her going to the integration.

"Shhhh. Thelma will be just fine. Sit up straight. Think about what you'll say if you're called to testify." Mrs. Bates relieved our tension as she moved to sit beside Thelma.

"All rise. The Honorable Judge Ronald Davies presiding." The deep voice sounded like a circus ringmaster announcing the next act. I held my breath. I had read so much about him. What would he be like? A very small man wearing a black robe entered and moved swiftly toward the massive desk. His smooth dark hair was parted in the middle, framing his pleasant round face.

As he climbed up to the imposing leather chair and settled in, what stood out most of all were his huge eyes peering through thick horn-rimmed glasses. From where I sat, I could see only the top part of his black robe, his round face, and those all-seeing, all-knowing eyes.

Shortly after the hearing began, one of the governor's attorneys, Tom Harper, stood and made a motion that Judge Davies disqualify himself because he was biased due to his appointment by the federal government specifically for our case. Judge Davies pounded his gavel and ruled the motion for disqualification was not legally sufficient and not timely.

Next Wiley Branton asked the court's permission to file a supplementary complaint joining us in the government's petition against Faubus and two Arkansas National Guard commanders. Davies ruled it could be filed.

The governor's attorney Tom Harper then asked to have subpoenas withdrawn that had been served on Arkansas National Guard Commander Adjutant General Clinger and his assistant, saying men on military duty are exempt from subpoenas. Again the judge ruled against them.

Meanwhile, there was a commotion at the rear of the room as reporters hustled back and forth, scribbling on note pads and whispering to each other. They behaved as though they had some divine right to do whatever was necessary to get the information they needed. They were an electrifying show unto themselves, separate and apart from the judge and lawyers.

The more I watched them, the more I thought I'd like to become one when I grew up. As a reporter, I would get to observe interesting events and write about them. I'd also get to behave with a know-it-all urgency, as though what I was doing were more important than anything else.

The seats were so hard that I was pleased Judge Davies moved things along swiftly, pounding his gavel, denying motions presented by the governor's attorneys, all the while speaking sternly. Finally, just before noon, Harper, once again speaking for Governor Faubus, asked if preliminary matters were taken care of.

"Well," the judge growled, "I haven't gotten the late mail, but I think so."

Continuing in a matter-of-fact tone, Harper then asked Judge Davies to dismiss the case because it involved constitutional issues that required a three-judge panel. Judge Davies ruled that the case would continue. In response to that ruling, Harper said, "May we be excused?"

Judge Davies spoke emphatically: "You are excused, gentlemen, but you understand that this is a moot question. The hearing will proceed."

Continuing to speak for all the governor's attorneys, Harper began reading a statement. "The position of Governor Faubus and the military officials of the state is that the governor and the state will not concede that the U.S. Court or anyone else can question the authority of the governor to exercise his judgment in administering the affairs of state, and since he does not concede this responsibility, we will not proceed further in this action."

To my amazement, Harper led the way as several men and one woman gathered their papers and followed him out the door. "Is this a protest?" someone asked. Reporters ran for the door like corralled horses through an open gate. I thought they'd hurt themselves. The judge pounded the gavel.

The attorneys for the Department of Justice called themselves "amicus curiae," saying they were prepared to offer more than one hundred witnesses to support the order for integration. Word was whispered down our line that "amicus curiae" meant friend of the court. But surely no real friend would keep us sitting on those hard seats long enough for a hundred people to testify. My heart sank as we nine eyeballed each other with grim expressions.

"We'll be too old for high school if we have to listen to all those people," I whispered aloud. To my delight, the judge announced the hundred witnesses would not begin until after recess.

In order to get to our lunch, we walked through a gauntlet of hot flashing lights and squeezed past people shouting questions.

Once outside, we encountered the problem that had always plagued our people in Little Rock. There were no restaurants that would serve us, at least no decent ones.

The mighty Thurgood Marshall was forced to join us in a greasy joint that served wilted lettuce on overcooked hamburgers in the shabby section of our neighborhood known as Ninth Street. As he ate, he answered our questions. More than anything he seemed to be astonished that the governor's attorneys had walked out of the room so suddenly. "It must have been their plan all along," he said.

That afternoon the parade of witnesses presented by the Justice Department made one major point. They said the threat of violence due to integration was not sufficient for the governor to have called out troops. The mayor of Little Rock, the chairman of the school board, the superintendent of schools, the principal of Central High, and the Little Rock chief of police all testified that they found no threat of violence in Little Rock and had not requested that the governor send troops.

School Superintendent Virgil Blossom testified for a long time about the details of the school board's plan for integration, which had taken two years and two hundred meetings to devise. U.S. District Attorney Orso Cobb asked how many complaints he had gotten. Blossom said the school board had received only a few complaints and suggestions for improving the plan. "As a matter of fact, the plan has been very well received. I'm not saying I believe any majority of the people of Little Rock want integration," he said. "They don't. But they favor this plan as the best answer to a difficult problem." The judge asked the superintendent a question many people had asked me and one I had wondered about myself.

"How were these nine students chosen?"

"The Negroes were selected on the basis of scholarship, personal conduct, and health. We picked those who had the mental ability to do the job and had used it," Blossom answered.

For just a moment, I fretted they would discover Thelma's

secret heart problem. But the fact was they had never had us examined by a doctor and there was no talk of doing so.

Then it was time to present our case. The nagging voice inside my head said how could I put my hand on the Bible and not tell the whole truth. Another voice argued that yes, Mother and I were chased, but in fact we weren't hurt—they didn't really touch us. So the truth was—we weren't injured on that day. Over and over again it had been explained to me that to say we were physically injured or attacked that first day on the school grounds or in the immediate area would be to support the governor's case. We knew he would use the slightest justification to delay integration for all eternity.

First to testify from our group was Ernest Green. He wanted to go to Central, he said, because it was closer to his home and would save time and money. He was asked whether he offered any assault against the troops. "No, sir, I didn't," he said with a broad smile.

Next, Elizabeth Eckford testified. She did not complain about the life-threatening mob that had traumatized her. She sat erect, speaking calmly, saying that a few white people lived not far from her house, yet there had been no racial disputes. I was relieved when the attorney said that there would be no need for the rest of us to testify. Had I been asked to place my hand on the Bible, I don't know what I might have been forced to say, perhaps truths that would have hurt us. I figured it was that divine force again moving us on to integration.

The attorneys for the United States made repeated references to the May 1954 decision. I had to stop listening. The very mention of that decision always made me sad. It brought back the face of the angry white man who had chased me down that day. Panic-filled recollections flooded my mind, blotting out the courtroom proceedings.

"Melba! Melba!" Minnijean was tugging at my arm. The others were excited.

The judge was announcing his decision, saying that the governor had "thwarted" the court-approved plan of integration by means of National Guard troops. The judge's voice was deep, his tone emphatic, as he said, "There is no real evidence here that we shouldn't proceed with the court-ordered integration of Central High School. The order is so entered." He pounded the gavel, stood, and walked out of the room.

"Oh, damn nigger-loving judge!" someone shouted, using all those words that Grandma said would lead a body to hell.

Mrs. Bates told us to remain seated until everyone else left the room. I sat very still for a long moment as everybody around me began moving. So, God, you really do want me to go back to that school. For a time it seemed as if I were all alone in a silent tunnel, and everyone else was way at the other end. I would always remember that judge and his huge, piercing dark eyes. There must be something wonderful in his heart, I thought. I would remember him in my prayers.

As a throng of reporters surged toward us, my heart was pounding, my breath coming in short spurts. I flashed my confident smile, but my knees wobbled. Those reporters went crazy, all shoving and shouting their questions at once. I thought they might injure us and themselves as they climbed over each other and tried to get their cameras into position. It was like nothing I had ever experienced before.

"Come Monday morning you'll be a genuine Central High student. How do you feel about that?" one reporter shouted his question above all others.

"Monday morning," I whispered, "I'm gonna be a Central High student—Monday morning!"

At 6:20 P.M. Friday evening, Governor Faubus made a big deal of removing the Arkansas National Guard from Central High. He appeared on television saying that he would appeal Judge Davies's ruling. He gave a long and impassioned speech, predicting once again that if integration took place, blood would run in the streets of Little Rock.

"You know he's smart like a fox," Grandma said. "He's got something in mind, suddenly moving those troops that way."

"Naw, I think he's just following the judge's orders. Anyhow, he's a defeated man. Let's celebrate." Mother raised her glass of lemonade. Grandma frowned. She disliked any one of us to do with milk or a cola what sinners did with liquor.

"To integration with peace and joy and harmony," Mother said, smiling, and took a sip of her lemonade.

"All right," Grandma said, lifting an imaginary glass into the air. "To life without all this ugliness. Maybe now things will quiet down and get back to normal."

That night I wrote in my diary:

Okay, God, so Grandma is right it's my turn to carry the banner. Please help me do thy will.

Over the weekend, Little Rock became an eerie city. Only those with urgent business walked the streets, with quick nervous strides. People from my community did not gather and visit as they usually would. Like me, they must have been frightened by the news reports that continued to describe roving gangs of segregationists crisscrossing the city, looking to do harm to any of our people they could find. Rumors persisted that various people we knew had been beaten or chased.

It felt awful not to have authorities to turn to in the midst of all the violence. I could see fear in the faces of the adults around me. I could hear it in their whispered conversations. All my life I had felt unprotected by city officials. If some major crisis took place, like a fire in our community, white firemen had always taken their time coming to help. They didn't fight to save our lives and property, as if neither had any value to them, so we had set up our own systems of summoning each other for help.

The integration dispute made me feel as though we were much more vulnerable. Whites had control of the police, the firemen, and the ambulances. They could decide who got help and who didn't. Even if the Ku Klux Klan ravaged one of our homes, we wouldn't call the police for help. None of us was certain which of our city officials wore civic uniforms by day and white sheets at night.

News reports described Governor Faubus as unruffled by all the turmoil. He was living his life and doing business as usual in the face of this crisis. One article said that through the two previous hectic weeks the governor had been sleeping soundly, eating regularly, chatting with his son in college, enjoying his fan mail, and relaxing as he read about his favorite president, Abraham Lincoln. He didn't sound to me like a man who was remorseful or planning to mend his ways, or a man who was suffering the inconvenience of having his normal way of life shattered, as were we.

On Sunday, I thought the news of more violence in the streets might cause Grandma and Mama to forget about church. I should have known better. It was cloudy, with thunderstorms expected, as we cautiously drove our regular route to church. It upset us to see that sidewalks usually filled with families on their way to Sunday service were empty. We heard the church bells toll, their echoing clang a protest to the silence that blanketed our community.

However, a hopeful mood was evident in the church service. The judge's positive decision for integration was God's will, Reverend Young said. And God would give us the strength to go forth. He said we needed to pray and work to heal our divided community.

He spoke of the many God-fearing, reasonable white people who supported our activities and of the white ministers joining forces to help stop the violence. He expressed gratitude and prayed for Mayor Woodrow Mann, who continued to defy Governor Faubus, accusing him of being wrong in opposing integration and the federal government. Our minister urged support for the nine of us who were integrating Central, mentioning the three of us who sat in church, Gloria, Ernie, and me.

Mumbles of "Yes, Lord" and "Amen" made me hope some people had changed their minds and that now most of my church family thought that I was doing the right thing. But nevertheless there were those who disagreed and were willing to show their feelings at every turn. One woman snagged me in the ladies' bathroom, saying, "The nice white lady I work for treated me like family up till now. These days she treats me like I'm just the colored help."

"Look," Mother said, "there's a price to be paid for freedom; we pay it now or we're in 'ball and chain' forever."

"Easy for you to talk, Mrs. Pattillo. You're an educated woman. I ain't got no sheepskin on my wall."

The church service seemed to last longer than usual. Afterward there was so much talk of integration that I felt wrung out. The only bright spot in my Sunday was Vince's offer to drive me home from church. Mother frowned at the suggestion. When I pleaded, she demanded that she trail us in her car. So we formed a two-car caravan, Vince in his brand-new square-back, red-and-white Chevy, and Grandma, Mama, and Conrad following close behind in our car.

"I guess I'd better not speed," he said, grinning that handsome smile. I was craning my neck to look back every now and then. "Yep, they're there," he said. I was embarrassed that Mother was following us so closely. To make things worse, Vince had one thing on his mind—integration, finding out about what we nine were doing, when we got together, how we studied, and what the NAACP said to us in meetings. I began feeling as though I were giving a news report.

"How does it feel to see your name in the paper, to be a celebrity that everybody's talking about?" I glanced at him in his Eisenhower jacket and slick shoes. He was sharp and wonderful. Why couldn't it be another place and time?

"Uncomfortable," I grumbled.

"Hey, there's got to be some good things in all the fuss they're making over you."

"It's all so new that I can't figure it out yet. Right now I'd give anything for just one day of normal school with old friends."

"Too late for that, you're a Central High student."

I had counted on our date as one last opportunity to feel

normal joy before Monday came. Our conversation and his cute charms were supposed to stoke my daydreams so I'd have something to smile about when things went wrong at Central. No such luck. In less than twenty-four hours, I would face my first day inside Central High without this protective veil.

10

CITY AND STATE POLICE TO BE THERE TODAY;
OFFICIALS CONFIDENT. FAUBUS SAYS HE'S HOPING FOR
NO UNREST; U.S. KEEPING CLOSE EYE ON LITTLE ROCK
—*Arkansas Gazette*, Monday, September 23, 1957

AS I READ THE MORNING NEWSPAPER THAT MONDAY, WHAT WITH
all the changes, I thought maybe the headline would read, IN-
TEGRATION HALTED AGAIN. At least this time it seemed
everybody was expecting us to arrive at Central High School
and go inside for classes.

As I walked back to the kitchen, I decided I would begin to
mark off my days at Central High on the big wall calendar that
belonged to Grandma. I longed to see all the cross marks fill
the days that would become weeks and then months. I glanced
at the month of September and picked the spot where I would
put the first cross mark, if I completed the first day. Lord, please
let me be strong enough to fill in this day and all the school
days that follow, I whispered.

It was not yet eight o'clock when Mama and I parked at the
curb, just outside Mrs. Bates's home. I was surprised to see so
many people milling about the yard. There was double the usual
throng of news reporters. Everybody spoke in whispers. We

greeted each other as though there were a compelling reason not to talk in ordinary tones. I was ushered through the crowd and into the living room, where radio and news reports held everyone's attention.

Hundreds are gathered at Central High to await the arrival of nine Negro students who will begin the court-ordered integration. Some believe the governor should have instructed the soldiers to remain at the school to keep order. Assistant Police Chief Gene Smith and a group of officers arrived at 7 A.M. to patrol the area. Fifty state police have joined them.

We nine acknowledged each other with nervous smiles and a very few whispered words. Adults nodded to each other with the kind of glances that seemed to carry secret messages as they periodically looked at their watches. The nervousness grew worse with each passing moment. People were pacing, pretending to smile, sitting a moment, then rising to pace again. After a while, I became one of those people. We were going to be late for school, no doubt—late on the first day. What would everybody think? The phone rang. It was time to be on our way.

Mother Lois looked as though she were on the brink of tears. As we filed silently out of the house, I waved good-bye to her. I wanted to hug her, but I didn't want everyone to think I was a baby. Other parents milled about, looking as if we were being carted off to be hanged. As we started to walk to the cars, they clutched at us as though they weren't completely certain we'd be coming back.

We settled ourselves into two cars. Mrs. Bates was in the first car with four of the nine, and a man introduced as C. C. Mercer. Another NAACP official, Frank Smith, was driving the car I rode in with the remaining four students. We watched the news reporters run to their vehicles and rev their engines. The nonwhite reporters seemed hesitant about getting started. They hovered together. That's when I realized it must be difficult, even dangerous, for our people to cover a story like this.

We seemed at first to be driving in circles. Our driver explained that the police advised we not take the usual route because segregationists might lie in wait for us. I looked at my watch. It was after eight-thirty. We'd be very late arriving—even later than I had feared.

Central High was located on Park Street, stretching a two-block distance between Fourteenth and Sixteenth streets. But the route we took confused my sense of direction. I was surprised when suddenly we pulled up to the side entrance at Sixteenth Street, just beyond Park. Amid noise and confusion, the driver urged us to get out quickly. The white hand of a uniformed officer reached out toward the car, opening the door and pulling me toward him as his urgent voice ordered us to hurry. The roar coming from the front of the building made me glance to my right. Only a half block away, I saw hundreds of white people, their bodies in motion, their mouths wide open as they shouted their anger.

"Get along," the voice beside me said. But I couldn't move; I was frozen by what I saw and heard. Policemen stood in front of wooden sawhorse barricades holding the people back. The rumble of the crowd was like that at a football game when the hero runs the ball to the end zone for a touchdown—only this time, none of the voices were cheering.

"The niggers! Keep the niggers out!" The shouts came closer. The roar swelled, as though their frenzy had been fired up by something. It took a moment to digest the fact that it was the sight of us.

Hustled along, we walked up the few concrete stairs, through the heavy double doors that led inside the school, and then up a few more stairs. It was like entering a darkened movie theater—amid the rush of a crowd eager to get seated before the picture begins. I was barely able to see where we were rushing to. There were blurred images all around me as we moved up more stairs. The sounds of footsteps, ugly words, insulting shouts, and whispered commands formed an echoing clamor.

"Niggers, niggers, the niggers are in." They were talking about me. The shouting wouldn't stop; it got louder as more joined in.

"They're in here! Oh, God, the niggers are in here!" one girl shouted, running ahead of us down the hallway.

"They got in. I smell something. . . ."

"You niggers better turn around and go home."

I was racing to keep pace with a woman who shouted orders over her shoulders to us. Nobody had yet told us she was someone we could trust, someone we should be following. I tried to move among the angry voices, blinking, struggling to accustom my eyes to the very dim light. The unfamiliar surroundings reminded me of the inside of a museum—marble floors and stone walls and long winding hallways that seemed to go on forever. It was a huge, cavernous building, the largest I'd ever been in. Breathless, I made my legs carry me quickly past angry white faces, dodging fists that struck out at me.

"The principal's office is this way," whispered a petite woman with dark hair and glasses. "Hurry, now, hurry." I was walking as fast as I could. Then we were shoved into an office where there was more light. Directly in front of us, behind a long counter, a row of white people, mostly women, stood staring at us as though we were the world's eighth wonder.

In the daylight, I recognized Mrs. Huckaby, Central High's vice-principal for girls, who had been present at several of our earlier meetings with the school board.

"This is Jess Matthews, the principal," she said. "You remember him."

No, I didn't remember. He peered at us with an acknowledging frown and nod, then quickly walked away.

"Here are your class schedules and homeroom assignments. Wait for your guides," Mrs. Huckaby said.

That's when I noticed that just beyond the glass panels in the upper part of the door that led to the office clusters of students stood glaring at us. One boy opened the door and walked in, yelling, "You're not gonna let those niggers stay in here, are you?"

All at once, Thelma Mothershed slumped down on the wooden bench just inside the door of the office. Mrs. Huckaby hustled the boy out and turned her attention to Thelma, as we all did. She was pale, her lips and fingertips blue. Breathless as she was, she mustered a faint smile and tried to reassure us.

None of us wanted to leave her there with those white strangers, but Mrs. Huckaby seemed to be a take-charge person who would look after her. She ushered us out, saying we had to go. Just for an instant, I worried about how Thelma's parents would get through the huge crowd outside to pick her up if she were really ill.

Three thirty-nine, that was the number of the homeroom on my card; I was assigned to the third floor. We quickly compared notes. Each of us was assigned to a different homeroom.

"Why can't any of us be in the same homeroom or take classes together?" I asked. From behind the long desk, a man spoke in an unkind booming voice. "You wanted integration . . . you got integration."

I turned to see the hallway swallow up my friends. None of us had an opportunity to say a real good-bye or make plans to meet. I was alone, in a daze, following a muscular, stocky white woman with closely cropped straight black hair. Up the stairs I went, squeezing my way past those who first blocked my path and then shouted hurtful words at me. "Frightened" did not describe my state; I had moved on to terrified. My body was numb. I was only aware of my head and thoughts and visions.

I had fantasized about how wonderful it would be to get inside the huge beautiful castle I knew as Central High School. But the reality was so much bigger, darker, and more treacherous than I had imagined. I could easily get lost among its spiral staircases. The angry voices shouting at me made it all the more difficult to find my way through these unfamiliar surroundings. I was panic-stricken at the thought of losing sight of my guide. I ran to keep up with her.

"Move it, girlie," she called back at me.

"Pheeew!" one boy said, backing away from me. Others stopped and joined in his ridicule. For an instant, I stood paralyzed.

"Don't stop!" the woman commanded. Her words snapped me into action. I scuffled to move behind her. Suddenly I felt

it—the sting of a hand slapping the side of my cheek, and then
warm slimy saliva on my face, dropping to the collar of my
blouse.

A woman stood toe-to-toe with me, not moving. "Nigger!"
she shouted in my face again and again. She appeared to be a
little older than my mother. Her face was distorted by rage.
"Nigger bitch. Why don't you go home?" she lashed out at me.
"Next thing, you'll want to marry one of our children."

Marry, I thought, as I darted around her. I wasn't even allowed to go on a real date. Grandma wouldn't let me marry.
Besides, why would I choose to marry one of those mean Little
Rock white people? My temples throbbed, my cheek stung, the
spit was still on my face. It was the first time I had ever been
spat upon. I felt hurt, embarrassed. . . . I wondered if I'd catch
her germs. Before I could wipe it off, my guide's harsh command summoned me to move.

"Get going. Now. Do you hear me? Move! Now!" I brushed
the saliva off my nose with my hand.

As I entered the classroom, a hush fell over the students. The
guide pointed me to an empty seat, and I walked toward it.
Students sitting nearby quickly gathered their books and moved
away. I sat down, surrounded by empty seats, feeling unbear-
ably self-conscious. Still, I was relieved to be off my feet. I was
disoriented, as though my world were blurred and leaning to
the left, like a photograph snapped from a twisted angle and
out of focus. A middle-aged woman, whom I assumed to be the
teacher, ignored me.

"Open your book to page twelve," she said, without allowing
her eyes to acknowledge me.

"Are you gonna let that nigger coon sit in our class?" a boy
shouted as he glared at me. I waited for the teacher to say or
do something.

"Now, class, if you've done the homework, then you
know——" A loud voice cut her off, shouting. "We can kick the
crap out of this nigger," the heckler continued. "Look, it's
twenty of us and one of her. They ain't nothing but animals."

Again, I waited for the teacher to speak up, but she said

nothing. Some of the students snickered. The boy took his seat, but he kept shouting ugly words at me throughout the rest of the class. My heart was weeping, but I squeezed back the tears. I squared my shoulders and tried to remember what Grandma had said: "God loves you, child; no matter what, he sees you as his precious idea."

Walking the gauntlet to my next class was even more harrowing. I had to go out behind the school, through the girls' dressing room, down a long concrete walkway, and onto the playing field.

"You'd better watch yourself," the guide warned as we moved at high speed through the hostile students. As we went outside to the walkway in the back of the school, I could hear the roar of the crowd in front of the school. It was even more deafening than the jeers immediately around me.

On the playing field, groups of girls were gathered tossing a volleyball. The teacher appeared to be a no-nonsense person. With a pleasant smile, she pointed me to a spot near the net and warned the other girls not to bother me.

"Let's keep the game going, girls," she said in a matter-of-fact way. The girls paused for a moment, looked at each other, looked at me, and then began tossing the ball back and forth. For just one instant, I was actually concerned about whether or not I could hit the ball and score. It took me a moment to realize it was whizzing awfully close to my head. I ducked, but they hit me real hard, shouting and cheering as they found their target.

And even as I was struggling to escape their cruelty, I was at the same time more terrified by the sound of the angry crowd in the distance. It must be enormous, I thought. How would the police keep them back?

"Get inside, Melba. Now!" The face of the gym teacher showed both compassion and alarm as she quietly pointed to a group of women some distance away, jumping over the rear fence as they shouted obscenities at me. "Hurry!"

I started to run for my life.

"Nigger . . . nigger . . . ," one woman cried, hot on my heels. "Get the nigger." Three of them had broken away from the pack and were gaining on me. I was running at top speed when someone stuck out a foot and tripped me. I fell face forward, cutting my knee and elbow. Several girls moved closer, and for an instant I hoped they were drawing near to extend a hand and ask me if I needed help. "The nigger is down," one shouted. "She's bleeding. What do you know. Niggers bleed red blood. Let's kick the nigger." I saw the foot coming my way and grabbed it before it got to my face. I twisted it at the ankle like I'd seen them do at the wrestling match. The girl fell backward.

As I scrambled to my feet, I looked back to see the brigade of attacking mothers within striking distance, shouting about how they weren't going to have me in school with their kids.

I ran up the stairs, hoping I could find my way back to the office. With the mothers close on my heels, shouting their threats, the twisted maze of the hallway seemed even more menacing. I felt I could have gotten lost forever as I struggled to find the door that led to the office and safety, opening first one, then another. I raced through a honeycomb of locker rooms and dead-end hallways.

After several minutes of opening the wrong doors and bumping into people who hit me or called me names, I was in tears, ready to give up, paralyzed by my fear. Suddenly Grandma's voice came into my head: "God never loses one of His flock." Shepherd, show me how to go, I said. I stood still and repeated those words over and over again until I gained some composure. I wiped my eyes, and then I saw blood running down my leg and onto my saddle shoe. It was too much! I pressed my thumb to the wounded area to try and stop the bleeding.

"I've been looking for you." The stocky guide's voice was angry, but I was so glad to see her I almost forgot myself and reached to hug her. "And just where do you think you are going? You are only supposed to travel through the school with me." She looked at my leg, but said nothing, then looked away.

"Yes, ma'am, but . . ."

"But nothing. Let's go to shorthand class." She didn't know it, but she was the answer to my prayer. I was so grateful for her being there. I looked over my shoulder to see the group of mothers standing still, obviously unwilling to come after me with a school official at my side. I choked back tears and speeded my steps.

"Hello, honey, welcome. We're just beginning. I'm Mrs. Pickwick." The warm voice of the tiny dark-haired woman comforted me. Although she was petite, I quickly discovered that my shorthand teacher was definitely not one to tolerate any hanky-panky. When students moved away from me, hurling insults, she gave them a stern reprimand. "If you move, you move to the office and see the principal," she said without so much as a hint of compromise in her voice.

As I headed for the last row of empty seats by the window, she called out to me, "Melba, stay away from the window." Her voice was sympathetic, as though she really cared what happened to me. As I turned back to follow her orders, I caught a glimpse of the crowd across the street from the front of the school. I was so transfixed by the sight, I couldn't move. The ocean of people stretched farther than I could see—waves of people ebbing and flowing, shoving the sawhorses and the policemen who were trying to keep them in place. There were lots of uniformed policemen, but the crowd must have outnumbered them a hundredfold. Every now and then, three or four people broke through and dashed across the street toward the front of the school. The police would run after them.

"Melba, please take your seat."

Slowly, reluctantly, I turned away and stumbled to my seat. As I sat there, trying to focus on the shorthand book before me, I could hear some of the things the crowd was shouting. "Get the niggers," and "Two, four, six, eight, we ain't gonna integrate."

Although I could not erase the images or the sounds of those people outside, somehow Mrs. Pickwick was so sincere and determined to be as normal as possible that I actually listened to what she had to say about shorthand. I even managed to draw several shorthand characters on my tablet as the noise got louder and louder. I looked up from my notes to see my guide entering

114

the door. She wore a frown and was red-faced and perspiring. Something was awfully wrong. It was written all over her face.

"Come with me, now. To the principal's office," she called out nervously. This time she collected my books and shoved them into my arms. I walked even faster than before. We were almost running. "Don't stop for anything," she shouted at me over the noise.

As I followed her through an inner office past very official-looking white men, I was alarmed by the anxious expressions on their faces. I was led to an adjoining anteroom—a smaller office, where some of the eight had gathered. Two of the girls were crying. I stood near the door, which was ajar enough so that although I could not see who was speaking, I could hear much of the men's conversations. I heard their frantic tone of voice, heard them say the mob was out of control, that they would have to call for help. "What are we gonna do about the nigger children?" asked one.

"The crowd is moving fast. They've broken the barricades. These kids are trapped in here."

"Good Lord, you're right," another voice said. "We may have to let the mob have one of these kids, so's we can distract them long enough to get the others out."

· whos gona be the distracter?

11

"LET ONE OF THOSE KIDS HANG? HOW'S THAT GONNA LOOK? NIG-
gers or not, they're children, and we got a job to do."

Hang one of us? They were talking about hanging one of my
friends, or maybe even me. My knees were shaking so badly I
thought I would fall over. I held my breath, trying not to make
any noise. The two men discussing our fate were just on the
other side of the door. I turned my back to the partially opened
door, at the same time moving closer to it so I could hear more.
I tried to look unconcerned so as not to frighten the others.
Already some of them were crying, and Thelma's face was blue.
I moved even closer to hear a man's voice say, "They're children. What'll we do, have them draw straws to see which one
gets a rope around their neck?"

"It may be the only way out. There must be a thousand people out there, armed and coming this way."

"Some of these patrolmen are throwing down their badges,"
another breathless voice said. "We gotta get them out of here."

I heard footsteps coming closer. I moved to the center of the
room, closer to where my friends stood surrounding Thelma,
who sat on her haunches.

A tall, raw-boned, dark-haired man came toward us. "I'm
Gene Smith, Assistant Chief of the Little Rock Police Depart-

116

ment." He spoke in a calm tone. "It's time for you to leave for today. Come with me, now." Right away, I had a good feeling about him because of the way he introduced himself and took charge. He urged us to move faster, acting as though it mattered to him whether or not we got out. "It's eleven-thirty. I want you out of here before noon."

Gene Smith. His was the voice I had heard in the next room, saying he would rather get all of us out than hang one to save the others. I decided to forever remember this man in my prayers. I scrambled to keep up with the others as we moved at a quick pace toward the Fourteenth Street side of Central High. It was almost a block away, but suddenly Smith and the other men turned from the main hallway and began descending stairs into passageways that became more and more dim.

What if they were going to kill us? I didn't really know these men, yet I had no choice but to trust them. I focused on speeding down the narrow concrete passageway, down the stairs into a dark cellar, where one of the men walking ahead of us switched on a flashlight. We were inside some kind of basement garage. In the distance was a huge door that appeared to lift upward with chain pulleys. It resembled a loading dock of some kind. Two cars were sitting with engines running, lights on, hoods pointing toward the door.

"Hurry, now . . . get in," Smith said, as he held open one of the doors. I looked at the others getting into the second car. Thelma, Minnijean, and Ernie were in the car with me. A white man sat behind the wheel. He had an absolutely terrified expression on his face and was busy looking all around us, his eyes darting back and forth.

"Roll your windows up, lock your doors, keep your faces away from the windows. Put your heads down when we start to move." His voice quivered. He hunched over to secure something on the floor, and that's when I saw the gun strapped to his side in a leather holster.

Smith leaned down to talk through the open window to the driver. "Move fast and don't stop no matter what." Then he looked at us and said, "Listen to your driver's instructions and do exactly what he says. Your lives depend on it."

We were surrounded by white men in suits speaking in frightened tones. Their expressions told me we were in the kind of trouble I hadn't even imagined before. The enormous roaring sound coming from the crowd just beyond the door made me wonder whether or not they had waited too long to get us into these cars. Just for one instant I tried to imagine what would happen if the mob got hold of us.

"Now!" Smith shouted. "Let 'er roll."

The driver shifted gears and gunned the engine as I crouched down in the back seat. Suddenly I heard the loud sound of what must have been a heavy chain, dragging. The door was opening, letting streaks of sunlight in. I scooted farther down in my seat, hiding my face. But I decided I had to keep my eyes open. I wanted to know what was happening to me. At least that way I'd know what to pray for.

I felt the car surge ahead. We were climbing upward, out of the basement toward bright sunlight. I could hear the tires spin onto a gravel driveway just beyond the door. The car gained momentum, lunging forward. As the full light of day crept into the windows, the deafening noise of the mob engulfed us.

"Get the niggers! Hang those niggers! Stop those cars," I heard somebody shout. Then I saw wave after wave of white faces, angry white faces, everywhere. Their mouths were open shouting threats. Clusters of white hands with fingers extended seemed for a moment to envelop us . . . clutching, grabbing at us. Some of the faces were moving along with us, coming closer to the car windows.

"Hold on and keep your heads down," the driver shouted. I heard the engine grind and felt us go faster. The people running beside us accelerated their pace, hurling rocks and sticks at the car.

That's when the car really began moving fast, faster than I'd ever ridden before. Finally, there were fewer hands and faces on the car windows, the noises were subsiding. I took a deep breath.

"You'all can sit up now. But keep an eye out." I could see that the others in the car behind us were safe. We were mostly silent on our journey, craning our necks, keeping watch in every direction.

"Thank you for the ride home," I said to the driver as I climbed out of the car. He cast a pleasant but impatient glance my way. I wanted to say, "Thanks for risking your life to save mine," but I didn't know how it would sound to the others. It was an awkward moment with a stranger, a decent white man.

"Get in the house now—go," he said, pausing for an instant, then gunning his engine and pulling away. I waved good-bye to my friends. Standing at the curb for a moment, I peered after the car as it drove away, wondering if he would get into trouble with the segregationists when they found out he was the one who rescued us from the mob. He was the second white man I would pray for God to protect.

I turned to see that some of my neighbors had gathered, a few sitting in our lawn chairs, a few standing around talking. I wondered what they were doing there. Then Grandma India rushed out the front door, her arms open to receive me.

"Thank God you're safe. Your mama is on her way home."

She was shoving me, both her hands at my back, not letting me pause to say hello to the alarmed neighbors who kept asking if I was all right.

"Now you've had your lesson. You don't have to go back to that awful school anymore," our neighbor Mrs. Floyd said, as Grandma ushered me past her.

I settled down on the couch in front of the television with the radio blasting loud from the hallway. I sipped the Grapette soda Grandma had given me and thought about what the mob might have done to us. I worried that they would come looking for us at our homes.

Although we had left shortly after noon, word came that the mob continued its rampage. Even after the Central High School registrar came out to announce on a microphone that we had been removed, not everyone believed her. Instead, they surged forward, threatening to overrun the barricades and the police, demanding to see for themselves that only white students remained. A police official convinced them to send representatives inside the school to check. When three women returned to report we were not there, the mob cheered but continued the siege.

Armed with guns, ropes, and clubs, the report said, they surged toward the school, in the doors and through the halls, dancing and shouting, "Two, four, six, eight, we ain't gonna integrate."

"Melba, where's Melba? Is she all right?" Mother Lois came rushing into the living room, disheveled and frantic. "I got here as soon as I could. Those newsmen said you were trapped by the mob."

"I'm fine, Mama." I stood to embrace her.

"We've made a mistake. You're definitely not going back to that school."

"What's that on your knee?" Grandma India asked.

"I fell." I decided I didn't need to add to Mother's nervousness. I would wait until she calmed down to explain the details of my day.

"I heard they passed the hat and collected a hundred and forty dollars to encourage those policemen to abandon their duties," Grandma added.

"You must have been scared to death. I'm sorry," Mother said.

We all listened as the newscast continued airing sounds of the angry mob taking over the school. I discovered that one reason we were able to slip into the school that morning was that the mob had been preoccupied chasing and beating three black reporters, James Hicks, Alex Wilson, and Moses Newsom, whom they had accused of purposely distracting the crowd in order to allow us time to get in the side door. Mr. Wilson was hit on the head with a brick, and even as he lay wounded on the ground, they continued to kick and beat him.

The mob had then turned to beat up white reporters. Several members of the *Life* magazine staff were beaten. Other newspeople and out-of-towners were chased and beaten until they reached police lines. Even after they were inside police cars, they were showered with rocks.

A concerned and flustered Conrad rushed into the house to greet me. His friend Clark had told him I was dead. In order to settle him down, Grandma busied him with helping her fix lunch. I remained glued to the news, mulling over whether or not I should tell them what really happened to me that day. I decided it would only make things worse, and maybe it would make them decide I could never go back to the integration.

Later on, we got hold of a copy of the evening newspaper, the *Arkansas Democrat*. The headlines read: GROWING VIOLENCE FORCES WITHDRAWAL OF NEGRO STUDENTS AT CENTRAL HIGH. CROWD'S YELL TOUCHES OFF BRUTAL BEATING.

"These pictures are enough to curdle your blood," Grandma said, pointing to the one of reporter Alex Wilson being beaten. There was another showing a white man riding on him piggy-back. The paper was filled with pictures of the crowd and the police trying desperately to control it. Only by looking at those pictures did I begin to understand the real danger of that mob.

In my diary I wrote:

> There seems to be no space for me at Central High. I don't want integration to be like the merry-go-round. Please, God, make space for me.

The phone started to ring nonstop with calls from angry strangers spewing hatred and threats. There were also calls from our family and friends inquiring about my safety and warning us that the mob was continuing to search out and beat up people in our neighborhood. One phone call came from a news reporter who asked what I felt about the situation. Before Mother or Grandma caught on to what I was doing, I told him. He complimented me, saying I was articulate and asked if I could write. I said yes, and he asked if I would write an article about my first morning at Central. Right there I just jotted down a few notes and started dictating the article to him as it came into my head, the way I wrote letters to God every night in my diary. All the while I was talking to the reporter, I kept our instructions in mind: Accentuate the positive—don't complain too much. He said my story would appear in newspapers everywhere just as I had written it because it was on the Associated Press wire. Sure enough, the next day I saw it on the front page:

Would you have exchanged places with me and entered Central as I did this morning? I went, and I am glad.

Previous to making actual entrance into Central I had feelings that I'm sure have never been experienced by a child of 15 years. Sensations of courage, fear, and challenge haunted me. With the morning, came my definite decision: I must go.

"The Lord is my strength and my shield; my heart trusted in Him, and I am helped." With this verse in mind and a hopeful prayer in my heart I entered the halls of Central High. The spacious halls brought again the school feeling, however the atmosphere was not conducive to study but one of uneasiness.

The sea of faces represented no special personality to me. Although some were kind, many showed contempt, especially some boys gathered in the halls.

I was beginning to believe that the long hard fight was over, that finally this American way of life was going to pay off. As I walked through the halls alone it seemed as if I were lost on an island, an island of strange people, having no way of communicating with them. I longed to tell them, "I won't hurt you, honest, give me a chance, come on. How about it? I'm an average teenager, just like yourself, with the same aspirations and heartaches." But it was useless, only a few facial expressions told me I had gotten through.

Each time as I was about to give up, exhausted from the jeers and insulting remarks, some kind face would come up and say: "I want you here" or "You're pretty" or "Won't you stay and fight it out?"

This above all made all the "Go home, nigger" and "I'm gonna get you before the day is over" fade into the background.

There were a few trying experiences such as being blocked from passage to class by a few rough, tough-looking sideburners, boys who I'm sure if separated would not attack a mouse. Then, there were the three women who jumped the fence and attempted to "get me."

A favorite activity of the kids was to form a group in a circle and scream: "Two, four, six, eight, we ain't gonna integrate." I know of no physical injury to any of the nine students. I was slapped by one girl. I turned and said "Thank you" and continued on my journey to class.

I did not realize the size or the intentions of the crowd outside until I was told for my safety I had to leave Central High. This hurt me deeper than I can ever express. I'm glad I went, Oh, so glad I went, for now I know without out-of-school interference integration is possible in Little Rock, Arkansas.

When I finished the article I realized it was not the whole truth but a version that wouldn't jeopardize the integration. If I had told what really happened, one of the officials might say we couldn't go back. I composed the story in a way that would make my day sound okay. Maybe in a few days if I remained patient and prayed it would really be that way—white students would welcome me and smile and treat me like an ordinary human being.

All that evening we continued our vigilance on the couch in front of the television. Mother seemed to relax a bit, and Grandma settled down with her almanac and handiwork. The newsmen reported more roving gangs of hooligans doing their evil deeds throughout the city.

From his Sea Island, Georgia, retreat, Governor Faubus urged our leaders and school officials to allow a cooling-off period before resuming integration.

President Eisenhower had earlier complimented us on our

bravery in a radio message, saying all parents must have sympathetic understanding for the ordeal to which we nine children had been subjected. Now he issued a warning statement:

> I want to make several things very clear in connection with the disgraceful occurrences today at Central High School in the city of Little Rock. I will use the full power of the United States, including whatever force may be necessary, to prevent any obstruction of the law and to carry out the orders of the Federal Court.

He ended his long statement by demanding that all persons engaged in obstruction of justice "cease and desist."

"At least we've got a President who respects the law," Grandma said, applauding.

"There will be no school for you tomorrow, Melba," Mother Lois said.

"But I'm going to school tomorrow, aren't I?" Conrad asked.

"Perhaps. We'll have to see how things go," Mother Lois said.

"I'll bet that mob will heed the President's words," Grandma said. "Things will be back to normal tomorrow."

But this time Grandma was wrong. After a restless night, we awoke on Tuesday to find the mob had not heeded the warning of the President. As early as 7:30 A.M. more than two hundred people had gathered in front of Central High to protest our arrival. The headlines read:

IKE CLEARS WAY TO SEND TROOPS:
COMMANDS CEASE AND DESIST IN LEGAL MOVE
—*Arkansas Gazette*, Tuesday, September 24, 1957

The article said that President Eisenhower signed a history-making proclamation clearing the way for possible use of federal troops to quash any further school integration violence in Little Rock.

But next I read: FAUBUS CHALLENGES IKE ON USING TROOPS. From Sea Island, Georgia, on September 23, Governor

Faubus had declared that the President couldn't use federal troops to combat the Little Rock integration violence unless he, as governor, requested him to do so. And he added, "I don't plan to make any such request."

And even as I read those headlines, the announcer on the radio said the unruly crowd surrounding Central High was larger than it had been the day before.

12

"GOVERNOR FAUBUS DIDN'T ASK FOR FEDERAL TROOPS, BUT they're up in his face anyhow," Grandma said as we sat watching the arrival of the 101st Airborne Division early Tuesday evening. We were transfixed as we listened to newsmen describe the power of that very special military unit.

> Fifty-two planeloads—C123's and C130's have brought 1200 battle-equipped paratroopers to Little Rock to see that integration is carried out at Central High School without further violence.
> Planeloads of the men of the 101st Airborne Division stationed at Fort Campbell, Kentucky, started landing at Little Rock Air Force Base at 3:30 P.M. this afternoon, at half-hour intervals. The troop convoy is entering Little Rock to take up positions at Central High school.

I sat perfectly still, my attention riveted on the television screen, where the most wonderful pictures moved before my eyes. Silhouetted against the slate gray sky, jeep headlights cast halos in the evening light as the mighty 101st Airborne Division rolled across the Broadway Bridge into Little Rock. It was a caravan of army vehicles that seemed to go on forever.

"More of God's handiwork," Grandma said, her eyes brimming with tears. "Who'd a thought Mr. Faubus's mistreatment of our nine little children would bring the President and the 101st down on his head."

The arrival of the troops made me feel hopeful that I had protection from the mob. But it also made me feel even more frightened because President Eisenhower hadn't chosen to send just any old military unit. The men of the 101st were famous heroes, combat specialists, the newsman said. If we needed such brave soldiers, the President and those powerful men in his cabinet must have agreed that the integration was as dangerous as a hostile enemy in war.

It felt to me as though the nine of us were expected to wage ·In some kind of war to make integration happen. The thought was upset me. I knew Mother was alarmed as well when she sug- some gested I leave the next day for Cincinnati to live with Uncle body Clancey and attend school there. I didn't want to go away be- always cause I knew it would get printed in the newspapers and the hurt. segregationists would think I was afraid. They would think they had won. Why couldn't she have made this offer earlier? It would have been so much easier then.

For the first time ever, Grandma placed dinner on trays in front of the television so we could hear President Eisenhower speak to the nation. "Let's put things into perspective. He is our President, and he happens to be talking about us. The whole world's watching, why shouldn't we," she said.

Speaking from the White House, President Eisenhower said he sent troops because "Mob rule in Little Rock menaces the very safety of the United States and the free world." This was so, he said, because gloating communists abroad were using school integration riots to misrepresent the United States and undermine its prestige and influence around the globe. And then he looked straight into the camera and said, "Mob rule cannot be allowed to override the decision of the courts."

Later Governor Faubus came on television to give what one reporter described as a pleading speech. "We are now an occupied territory. In the name of God, whom we all revere, in the

name of liberty we hold so dear, in the name of decency which
we all cherish, what's happening in America?"

"I can help you figure this out, Mr. Faubus," Mother Lois
shouted at the screen. "The President has called your bluff."

Later that night as my head was swimming with news reports
and questions about whether or not to go back to Central High,
I wrote in my diary:

> Everything in my life is so new. Could I please do some of the old
> things that I know how to do again. I don't know how to go to
> school with soldiers. Please show me.
>
> P.S. Please help the soldiers to keep the mobs away from me.

Instead of going to sleep in my clothing, as I had for several
nights before, I put on my pajamas. With the soldiers in town,
I felt safe enough to have a deep sleep, something I hadn't done
for a long time. I figured the segregationists wouldn't dare do
their late-night raids on our house with the President watching
so closely.

It was very quiet as I turned out the light. With the 101st in
town, we didn't hear as many sirens going off. Later, when I
woke up thirsty and went to get water, I found Grandma snor-
ing with the rifle lying across her lap. Maybe she felt safer, too.

I don't know how long I'd been asleep when I was jolted
awake. I sat straight up in bed. The doorbell was ringing, and
I heard voices on the front porch. Mama was standing over me.
She put her hand over my mouth and motioned me to get up.
The doorbell kept ringing over and over again. We moved
toward the living room. Sleepy-eyed, Conrad met us in the hallway with a confused expression, asking, "Is somebody shooting
at us again?"

"Who is it?" Grandma yelled through the door as she peeked
through the covered glass inset. "White men. It's white men
wearing black hats. What are they doing on our front porch at
this time of night?" Grandma said as she picked up the shotgun.

Then she shouted through the door again: "State your business, gentlemen, or I'll be forced to do mine."

"We're from the Office of the President of the United States; please open your door," they called back. "We have a message from your President."

Grandma opened the door ever so slightly and demanded that they show proof of who they were. They passed their identification through the half-opened door. Mother Lois examined the writing closely and nodded a yes.

"How can we help you?" Grandma lowered the gun to her side, keeping it hidden as she opened the front door a bit more. Mother Lois stood beside her. I thought it was funny as I looked around and noticed we were all wearing our nightgowns and pajamas to greet the messengers from the President of the United States.

"Let your daughter go back to school, and she will be protected," one of the men said, handing Mother Lois an envelope.

The next morning, Wednesday, September 25, at 8 AM. as we turned the corner near the Bates's home, I saw them, about fifty uniformed soldiers of the 101st. Some stood tall with their rifles at their sides, while others manned the jeeps parked at the curb. Still other troops walked about holding walkie-talkies to their ears. As I drew nearer to them I was fascinated by their well-shined boots. Grandma had always said that well-kept shoes were the mark of a disciplined individual. Their guns were also glistening as though they had been polished, and the creases were sharp in the pant legs of their uniforms.

I had heard all those newsmen say "Screaming Eagle Division of the 101st," but those were just words. I was seeing human beings, flesh-and-blood men with eyes that looked back at me. They resembled the men I'd seen in army pictures on TV and on the movie screen. Their faces were white, their expressions blank.

There were lots of people of both races standing around, talking to each other in whispers. I recognized some of the ministers from our churches. Several of them nodded or smiled at me. I was a little concerned because many people, even those who knew me well, were staring as though I were different from them.

Thelma and Minnijean stood together inspecting the soldiers close up while the other students milled about. I wondered what we were waiting for. I was told there was an assembly at Central with the military briefing the students.

Reporters hung from trees, perched on fences, stood on cars, and darted about with their usual urgency. Cameras were flashing on all sides. There was an eerie hush over the crowd, not unlike the way I'd seen folks behave outside the home of the deceased just before a funeral.

From time to time, as we walked about, we nine students acknowledged each other with nods and smiles. Like the others, I felt compelled to stare at the uniformed men. Walking up close to them, I saw that some weren't much older than I was. I had been told that only white soldiers would be allowed at Central, because the presence of nonwhites would inflame segregationists. Nonwhites were sent to the Armory, where they would be used as support teams or to guard our homes in case of a dire emergency.

There were tears in Mother's eyes as she whispered good-bye. "Make this day the best you can," she said.

"Let's bow our heads for a word of prayer." One of our ministers stepped from among the others and began to say comforting words. I noticed tears were streaming down the faces of many of the adults. I wondered why they were crying just at that moment when I had more hope of staying alive and keeping safe than I had since the integration began.

"Protect these youngsters and bring them home. Flood the Holy Spirit into the hearts and minds of those who would attack our children."

"Yes, Lord," several voices echoed.

One of the soldiers stepped forward and beckoned the driver of a station wagon to move it closer to the driveway. Two jeeps moved forward, one in front of the station wagon, one behind. Guns were mounted on the hoods of the jeeps.

· More security

130

We were already a half hour late for school when we heard the order "Move out," and the leader motioned us to get into the station wagon. As we collected ourselves and walked toward the caravan, many of the adults were crying openly. When I turned to wave to Mother Lois, I saw tears in her eyes. I couldn't go back to comfort her.

Suddenly, all the soldiers went into action, moving about with precise steps. I hoped I would be allowed to ride in the jeep, although it occurred to me that it didn't have a top so it wouldn't be as safe. Sure enough, all nine of us were directed to sit in the station wagon.

Sarge, our driver, was friendly and pleasant. He had a Southern accent, different from ours, different even from the one Arkansas whites had. We rolled away from the curb lined with people waving to us. Mama looked even more distraught. I remembered I hadn't kissed her good-bye.

The driver explained that we were not riding in a caravan but a jeep convoy. I could hear helicopters roaring in the distance. Sarge said they were following us to keep watch. We nine said very little to each other, we were too busy asking Sarge about the soldiers. At times the car was so silent I could hear my stomach growl. It was particularly loud because nervousness had caused me to get rid of my breakfast only moments after I'd eaten it.

Our convoy moved through streets lined with people on both sides, who stood as though they were waiting for a parade. A few friendly folks from our community waved as we passed by. Some of the white people looked totally horrified, while others raised their fists to us. Others shouted ugly words.

As we neared the school, I could hear the roar of a helicopter directly overhead. Our convoy was joined by more jeeps. I could see that armed soldiers and jeeps had already blocked off certain intersections approaching the school. Closer to the school, we saw more soldiers and many more hostile white people with scowls on their faces, lining the sidewalk and shaking their fists. But for the first time I wasn't afraid of them.

We pulled up to the front of the school. Groups of soldiers

on guard were lined at intervals several feet apart. A group of twenty or more was running at breakneck speed up and down the street in front of Central High School, their rifles with bayonets pointed straight ahead. Sarge said they were doing crowd control—keeping the mob away from us.

Sarge said we should wait in the station wagon because the soldiers would come for us. As I looked around, I saw a group of uniformed men walking toward us, their bayonets pointed straight up. Their leader beckoned to us as one of them held open the car door. As I stepped outside the car, I heard a noise behind me. In the distance, there was that chillingly familiar but now muffled chant, "Two, four, six, eight. We ain't gonna integrate." I turned to see reporters swarming about across the street from the school. I looked up to see the helicopters hovering overhead, hanging in midair with their blades whirring. The military leader motioned us to stand still.

About twenty soldiers moved toward us, forming an olive-drab square with one end open. I glanced at the faces of my friends. Like me, they appeared to be impressed by the imposing sight of military power. There was so much to see, and everything was happening so quickly. We walked through the open end of the square. Erect, rifles at their sides, their faces stern, the soldiers did not make eye contact as they surrounded us in a protective cocoon. After a long moment, the leader motioned us to move forward.

Hundreds of Central High students milled about. I could see their astonishment. Some were peering out of windows high above us, some were watching from the yard, others were on the landing. Some were tearful, others angry.

I felt proud and sad at the same time. Proud that I lived in a country that would go this far to bring justice to a Little Rock girl like me, but sad that they had to go to such great lengths. Yes, this is the United States, I thought to myself. There is a reason that I salute the flag. If these guys just go with us this first time, everything's going to be okay.

We began moving forward. The eerie silence of that moment

132

would forever be etched in my memory. All I could hear was my own heartbeat and the sound of boots clicking on the stone.

Everyone seemed to be moving in slow motion as I peered past the raised bayonets of the 101st soldiers. I walked on the concrete path toward the front door of the school, the same path the Arkansas National Guard had blocked us from days before. We approached the stairs, our feet moving in unison to the rhythm of the marching click-clack sound of the Screaming Eagles. Step by step we climbed upward—where none of my people had ever before walked as a student. We stepped up to the front door of Central High School and crossed the threshold into that place where angry segregationist mobs had forbidden us to go.

13

— Figurative Language

THE SCREAMING EAGLES HAD DELIVERED US SAFELY INSIDE THE front door of Central High School. The soldiers, we nine students, white school officials—all of us were standing absolutely still as though under a spell. It seemed no one knew what to do next.

Without any warning, a uniformed soldier stepped out of nowhere with an enormous old-fashioned camera. He pointed it toward us and snapped a picture.

The commander of the troops spoke a few words, and our military protectors fell into formation and marched away. I felt naked without that blanket of safety. An alarm warning surged through my body.

Principal Jess Matthews greeted us with a forced smile on his face and directed us to our classrooms. It was then that I saw the other group of soldiers. They were wearing a different uniform from the combat soldiers outside, but they carried the same hardware and had the same placid expressions. As the nine of us turned to go our separate ways, one by one a soldier followed each of us.

Along the winding hallway, near the door we had entered, I passed several clusters of students who stared at me, whispered obscenities, and pointed. They hurled insults at the soldier as well, but he seemed not to pay attention. My class was more than a block away from the front door, near the Fourteenth Street entry to the school. I saw other 101st soldiers standing at intervals along the hall. I turned back to make sure there really was a soldier following me. He was there, all right. As I approached the classroom, he speeded up, coming closer to me.

"Melba, my name is Danny." He looked me directly in the eye. He was slight of build, about five feet ten inches tall, with dark hair and deep-set brown eyes. "I'll be waiting for you here. We're not allowed to go inside the classrooms. If you need me, holler."

My heart skipped a beat as the classroom door closed behind me. I looked back once more and saw Danny's eyes peering through the square glass inset in the door.

The teacher beckoned me to take a seat near the door, where I was in full view of the soldier. I was one of about twenty students.

"You'all just gonna sit still and let this nigger come in here like this? I'm leaving. Who's coming with me?" A tall dark-haired boy paused for a moment, looking around the room. At first, there was silence, but no one left. I took my seat, hoping to settle down and focus on the classwork. Sunlight flooded into the room through a full bank of windows along the far wall. It was a beautiful morning. I tried hard to concentrate, tuning myself in to what the teacher was saying as she continued her discussion of diagramming sentences.

What a stroke of luck. Mother had played a game with Conrad and me, teaching us diagramming at an early age. It's convenient to have a mom who is an English teacher. I tried hard to ignore the boy, who had now begun a scathing dialogue with one of his companions. He carried on in a low tone, just above a whisper, which everyone could hear, but the teacher could legitimately ignore.

"You ugly niggers think just because you got those army boys following you around you gonna stay here."

I swallowed a sadness lump in the back of my throat. I wondered whether or not I should press the teacher to stop him. I

[handwritten margin note:] I wouldn't tell the teacher because that would show that I can't work things out by my self + also the teacher may be against int.

from treating me that way. I decided against it because I thought she must be well aware of what he was doing. Besides, we had been instructed not to make a big deal of reporting things in front of other students, lest we be labeled tattletales.

The boy continued his taunting throughout the period. At the end of class, I spoke to the teacher to get a list of back assignments, and during the conversation, I asked if she could do something to calm people down.

"I hope you don't think we're gonna browbeat our students to please you'all," she said. I pushed down my anger and walked out.

Danny followed, walking far enough behind so that some students got between him and me. As I walked through the crowded spaces, I felt almost singed by their hostile words and glares. Occasionally students moved in close to elbow me in my side or shove me. That's when Danny would step closer to make certain they saw him. When one boy walked up to try to push me down the stairs, Danny stared him down. The boy backed away, but he shouted at Danny, "Are you proud of protecting a nigger?"

When I entered Mrs. Pickwick's shorthand class things improved decidedly. It was like being on a peaceful island. She remained ever in control. There were a few whispered nasty remarks but no outbursts. Her no-nonsense attitude didn't leave room for unruly behavior.

I had been there about thirty minutes when I realized I was feeling kind of normal, enjoying the classwork and learning the shorthand characters. My stomach muscles let go a little, and I drew a long, deep breath. I didn't know Mrs. Pickwick, but I liked her and felt safe in her presence. I knew I would always be grateful to her for the moments of peace her class provided.

En route to the next class, I had to use the rest room. I had put it off as long as I could. I had hoped I could put it off until I went home. It was what I dreaded most because the girls' rest rooms were so isolated.

Danny leaned against the wall, across from the bathroom

door, quite a distance away. I hurried inside. The students appeared astonished at the sight of me.

"There ain't no sign marked 'Colored' on this door, girl," one of them said as I whizzed past.

I couldn't respond or even stop to listen to her. I was desperate to find an empty stall. Once inside, with the door closed, I felt alarmed at their whispering and scrambling about, but I couldn't make out exactly what they were saying.

I wanted to get out of there as quickly as possible. I promised myself I would drink much less water so I wouldn't have to take that risk so often. The scratching and giggling frightened me. Just as I started to step outside the stall, one of the chorus said, "Nigger. Ain't no soldier in here. . . . We got you all to ourselves. You just wait."

I ran out like a shot, pausing only a second to get a few drops of water to clean my hands. That's when I noticed it—written all over the mirror with lipstick was "Nigger, go home."

Midway through my next class the bells began ringing in a way I'd never heard before. "Fire drill!" students shouted as they rushed out of the classrooms, gleefully chattering. I was terrified. Waves and waves of white faces rushed toward me, some sneering, some smiling, some angry; still others took the opportunity to shower me with ugly words.

Outside, I was happy to see all those wonderful soldiers parading with precision, going through a kind of changing of the guard with helicopters roaring overhead. It was a real military show, and one that made me feel safe. Even though Danny was only a short distance away, I began to feel uneasy, exposed to so many angry white students. Minnijean and Thelma were nearby, and I spoke with them. To our surprise, two or three white students actually exchanged pleasantries with us, but just beyond, a group of whites began whispering hurtful words. After a while, we were left alone while everyone became fascinated with watching the 101st.

Despite the entrancing military activities, time began to drag. At our former school, fire drills had always been brief, three to five minutes, but now twenty-five minutes later we remained outside Central. I was getting antsy, feeling even more vulnerable standing out in the open that way. There was still a rather large, unhappy crowd gathered across from the school. Photographers and news reporters scrambled about, taking pictures and vying for scraps of information about how we were being received in class. Finally a bell rang, signaling our return to class.

I hesitated as the throng of students made its way back up the front staircase. When the bottom of the stairway had cleared, Danny motioned me to move ahead. By then I was anxious to go to the cafeteria. I was looking forward to being with my friends, with people I could talk to and laugh with, but Danny said we had been summoned to the vice-principal's office.

He walked only a few steps behind me as I moved cautiously through the clogged hallway avoiding close contact with hecklers wherever I could. We moved up to the second floor and into the office, where I was met by Carlotta, Thelma, and Mrs. Huckaby, the girls' vice-principal. She was hard to read. I felt neither wrath nor warmth from her. She seemed a woman determined to carry out her duties and keep things going as smoothly as possible. She insisted on escorting us to the rest room and the cafeteria, and we thanked her.

The four of us walked to the lower level and into a wider hallway, a brightly lit area of what appeared to be a basement corridor leading to the biggest cafeteria I had ever seen.

Danny trailed behind me, taking up a station across from the entry to the cafeteria. I turned to glance at the sea of white faces that stretched before me. The cafeteria seemed to be half the size of a football field, filled with long tables. There was a roar of noise from the hundreds of chatting, laughing students and the clang of utensils. The line of people waiting to pick up their food appeared to go on forever. Many of the students in that room turned to stare at us. All at once I caught a glimpse of nonwhite faces—my people serving food behind the counter. I didn't feel the same twinge of painful embarrassment I sometimes felt when I saw my people in service positions in public places. Instead, I was thrilled to see them smiling back at me.

The cafeteria line was treacherous, but I survived with my tray of food intact. Over lunch, Carlotta, Thelma, and I were joined by a couple of friendly white girls. For a brief moment, we laughed and talked about ordinary things as though it were a typical school day. Indeed, a few white students were trying to reach out to us. They explained that many of their friends would stay away because they feared segregationists who warned them against any show of kindness toward us.

After lunch, as I headed for gym class, I had two more reasons to hope integration could work. Amid all the hecklers taunting me, two girls had smiled and waved a welcome. Danny and I parted company at the door that led to the girls' dressing room. We agreed to meet after I changed into my gym uniform. He would wait near the head of the narrow corridor that led to gym class. I was frightened as I looked down at the bandage on my knee from the last time I had walked those isolated corridors to gym class. I got out of there as fast as I could.

I entered the dressing room and changed my clothing, going about my business briskly, even when someone tried to block my way. The stares and name-calling hurt, but I was growing accustomed to coping with it. With surprising speed, I had changed into my uniform and was on my way out to meet Danny.

He pointed me toward the concrete stairs that led down to the first-level playing field. Several hundred yards beneath us on what had been an enormous playing field, there was now a huge city. Hundreds of olive-drab tents stood in meticulous rows. There were jeeps and larger trucks with tarpaulins. It was an absolute beehive of activity. Several soldiers were posted directly below us in the field where my class would be. The sight of pristine lines of marching soldiers going back and forth in the distance calmed my nerves.

I walked down the steps to where the class would be playing volleyball and joined the others as they divided themselves into teams. But before we could start playing, a girl called out to Danny.

"You like protecting nigger bitches?" She smiled sweetly and fluttered her eyelashes at him. "Wouldn't you rather be following me around instead of her?"

Danny's facial muscles tightened, but he said nothing as she continued to spew insults at both of us. The gym teacher was quite a distance away, blowing her whistle and refereeing the game. Occasionally she would look back, but I wasn't at all certain she could hear the heckling. I joined the game and tried to be as cooperative as possible.

When class ended, I played a game with myself. I would earn a world record for getting dressed at the fastest speed known to mankind. When Danny greeted me, he confirmed I had far exceeded his expectations. As he trailed me through an isolated passage to the open hallway, we were confronted by a chorus of chants from sideburners. Copying their hairstyle from James Dean and Elvis, they fancied themselves to be "bad boys."

"Hut, one two three, march . . . march company . . . march to the beat of the nigger drum," the choir of boys chanted as we walked past. Suddenly, one of them came up to me and slammed my books out of my hand onto the floor. We were surrounded by thugs, many much bigger than Danny.

"Don't move," Danny whispered. "Stand absolutely still." His words stopped me from running for my life. At that moment it was hard to remain still; my knees were shaking as the group closed in on us. All at once, from nowhere, other soldiers appeared and made their presence known by holding on to their nightsticks and moving toward us slowly. I wondered where they had come from so quickly. Then I looked behind me and there were still more, standing against the walls, erect and silent, as though steeled to go into action at any moment.

Reluctantly, the hooligans dispersed, leaving a trail of insults in their wake. The soldiers withdrew as quickly and quietly as they had appeared, out of sight in an instant.

There was no harsh greeting or heckling as I entered French class. In fact, some of the students wore pleasant expressions. It took a while to realize they had a different kind of unwelcome mat for me. I was excited about French class. Mother Lois spoke fluent French; she often gave Conrad and me lessons over the dinner table. I was anxious to get started because I could see that Central had tape recorders and special headphones, things I hadn't had in my French classes before.

The students spent the entire hour speaking in French about suntanning. I understood the language, and I didn't know what to do as one student spoke in French about not wanting to get too dark "for fear of being taken for a . . . Uh, well, you know, a 'nigger.' " I blinked back tears of disappointment.

A serious headache was overtaking me by the time I headed for study hall with Danny tagging behind. Entering the door was like walking into a zoo with the animals outside their cages. The room was double the size of the largest classroom in my old school. I'd never seen anything like it or imagined in my wildest dreams that an important school like Central could allow such outrageous behavior. Stomping, walking, shouting, sailing paper airplanes through the air, students were milling about as though they were having a wild party. The teacher sat meekly behind his desk, a spectator stripped of the desire or power to make them behave.

I took five steps into the room, and everybody fell silent, abandoning their activities to glare at me.

"Take that seat over there," the study hall teacher said.

"But I need—" I wanted to ask him for a seat near the door where I could see Danny, but he cut me off.

"Did you hear me? I said take the seat over there or see the principal."

The teacher returned to reading his newspaper while the students threw spitballs. They directed only a few at me; mostly they were involved in their own little games. At one point, they started passing notes back and forth. When one was passed to me, I opened it. "Nigger go home," it read. I looked at it without emotion, folded it neatly, and put it aside.

"The helicopters are coming to pick up the nigger," someone shouted. Thank God, I thought. I had lived through the wildest hour where nobody did anything major to me, but their threats, near misses, and flying paper airplanes and pencils had shattered my nerves. "Helicopters. Home," I whispered. It seemed like a lifetime since I had been home and comfortable and safe. Just then Danny opened the door and beckoned to me. "Let's move out for home!" he said.

The whirring sound of the helicopter overhead drowned out some of the shouted insults as I made my way out of the study hall. Danny and I headed to the principal's office, where I was to connect with the other students and soldiers for the trip home. I had made it through my first day at Central High.

"Readin', writin', and riotin'." The comedic dialogue of our group had already begun before we left the building. What I needed most was the kind of laughter that would take my headache away. There we were, the nine of us, smiling, chatting, and behaving as though we were normal teenagers ending a normal school day. At the same time, uniformed and armed soldiers with bayonets held high were gathering around us for the trip out of the building. Nestled within the same protective cocoon that had enveloped us on our way into school, we made our exit through the front door. I looked back to see a group of white students trailing behind us, their hostile feelings painted on their faces.

The engine of the helicopter roared louder as we descended the stairs. Protected by the mighty power of the Screaming Eagles, we walked to the army staff car waiting at the curb. Once again, a group of soldiers was galloping back and forth. Even the chants of "Two, four, six, eight, we ain't gonna integrate!" could not dispel my joy. I was going home. As I stepped into the car, a wave of peace washed over me.

"Relax, we're on the move," Sarge, our driver, said as we snuggled down into our seats. The convoy was the same as it had been that morning; in front, the open jeep filled with soldiers, a machine gun mounted on its hood, with a similar vehicle behind us. As we pulled away from Central High, I looked back to see students gathered on the school lawn, staring at us as though they were watching a parade they hadn't known was coming their way. For just one tiny instant, I even felt a twinge of sympathy for them.

"You'all have a good day, did you?" Sarge said, making polite conversation. We all gave our different versions of the same answer:

"Good isn't exactly the word to describe my day."

"All right."

"Depends on what you mean by good."

"My mama never told me there'd be days like this one."

That was the beginning of a funny round-robin to see who could describe their experience in the most colorful language. The ride home brought the joyful relief I had awaited all day. At times, our stories halted all laughter as we noticed someone's eyes filled with tears. There were tales of flying books and pencils and words that pierce the soul. But there were also descriptions of polite students who volunteered to sit beside us or offered to lend back homework assignments or flashed a warm smile just when we needed it most.

Our respite was over all too soon. As we approached Mrs. Bates's home, I saw news reporters. My headache started up again. The cameras began to flash even before Sarge could get the car parked. We said our "thank-you's" to him and turned to face the bombardment of questions as we made our way to Mrs. Bates's front door.

"What was it like inside the school? Were you frightened? How were you treated? Did anybody hit you? Did they call you names? What classes are you taking?" Over and over again the same questions. Then there was one that stuck in my mind and made me tighten my jaw. "Are you going back tomorrow?"

I wasn't ready to think of another tomorrow at Central High. I sat quietly and pondered the question as I glanced out the front window at the few soldiers standing at attention. But they were there for only a brief moment before they climbed into the jeeps and the station wagon and rolled away. And then my attention was quickly brought inside by the rude question being asked.

"Would you like to be white?" I scowled at the reporter, and he must have understood my irritation. "Uh, I mean, does all this trouble make you'all wish you were white instead of Negro?" he amended his question.

"Do you wish you were Negro?" I heard the angry words roll out of my mouth. "I'm proud of who I am. My color is inconvenient right now, but it won't always be like this." I'd said what I felt, despite the fear that it would be considered talking back to an adult.

"Can you write as well as you can speak?" a slender dark-haired man asked.

"I don't know," I answered.

"Why don't you try it? I'm Stan Opotowiski of the *New York Post*, and this is Ted Posten. Here's my card. I would like you to write what you're thinking, and I'll see to it that it's printed." I looked at them. Posten was the same race as me.

"Yeah, sure, I can try." I took the card from him. I had always written. It was the first thing I remembered about life, writing my thoughts down in letters to God on the pages of the orange-covered tablet with the black ink drawing of an Indian head on the cover. Besides, I was very flattered that he would ask me. I told myself I owed him a favor. If reporters hadn't been covering our story, we might have been hanged. News of our demise would be a three-line notation buried on the back page of a white newspaper were it not for the Northern reporters' nosy persistence in getting the facts and dogging the trail of segregationists.

"We're off to the Dunbar Community Center for another news conference." I couldn't believe my ears, but off we went—once more answering questions in a more formal setting. It was quite a while after dark before we called Thelma's father to pick us up. It felt as if the news conference had gone on forever. Reporters from all the major periodicals I'd read in the library were there asking questions.

As we rode home I looked forward to shedding my day like soiled clothing. But the first thing I saw as I rounded the corner to my house was reporters sitting in the green lawn chairs on my front porch holding cameras and notebooks, and a few neighbors gathered in front of my house talking to them. I can't face them, I thought to myself. But I did—I got through it. I smiled, I said the right things, I pretended to be interested in the questions.

By 9 P.M., I was so tired that I only wanted my pillow and dreams—sweet, happy dreams with no white people and no Central High. The next thing I heard was the song on my radio as the alarm went off, waking me out of a cold, sweaty dream. "Peggy . . . Peggy Sue-ue-ue . . ." Buddy Holly was singing. It took me a minute to realize where I was and what I had to do. How I hated that song, hated, hated it! They played it over and over every morning at that time. I picked up my diary and started to write:

It's Thursday, September 26, 1957. Now I have a bodyguard. I know very well that the President didn't send those soldiers just to protect me but to show support for an idea—the idea that a governor can't ignore federal laws. Still, I feel specially cared about because the guard is there. If he wasn't there, I'd hear more of the voices of those people who say I'm a nigger . . . that I'm not valuable, that I have no right to be alive.

Thank you, Danny.

14

OVERHEAD, THE HELICOPTER WAS ENGAGED IN ITS ROARING FLUT-
ter. I relaxed a bit because I was, by the second day, familiar
with the military routine of our ride to Central. I allowed myself
to become hypnotized by the sight of soldiers executing their
duties. Disciplined, crisp, precise, confident, and powerful—
those were the words that came to mind. Sarge was even more
talkative, explaining that the 101st had earned its reputation for
bravery during World War II by stopping the German attack at
the Battle of the Bulge.

I asked Sarge if our escorts in the jeeps felt as odd as we did
about being propped up there with those big guns mounted in
front of them just to take us to school.

"Nope," he said. "We do what we're told."

I couldn't help thinking about the *Gazette* morning headlines,
which read: "TROOPS ROUT MOB; IKE TO SEE GOVERNORS,
TALK OF REMOVING ARMY." Already Southern governors
were joining forces to press for the withdrawal of the 101st soldiers from Central High. They were to meet the following week.

"Whatcha wanna bet we'll be making this trip alone, come
next week," Ernie said with his usual grin. Even though he was
laughing and teasing, I knew his words held a very painful
truth. But I couldn't even think of the troops leaving.

146

"School days, school days, dear old Golden Rule days." To block any thoughts of the troops leaving, I began to sing. The others were chiming in as we pulled up to the curb to join the soldiers for our walk to class. I was rather dismayed to see that a complement of only six soldiers surrounded us as we ascended the stairs to the front door. The helicopter hovered, while perhaps two hundred soldiers stood at attention in clusters nearby.

This time as we moved forward I was frightened because classes had not yet begun and students hovered all around us. About three hundred refused to clear a path to the front door. As they stood their ground, it was obvious that they must be part of a planned protest against us. Finally, when the soldiers bristled, they moved away. But as we climbed to the top of the middle staircase, a boy cried out "Boooooooo," holding the sound for longer than I thought humanly possible. He sounded the way a crowd does when visiting players beat the home team. Enthusiastic applause and laughter followed. I felt embarrassed and very unwelcome.

I glanced back over my shoulder to see whether any of the mob was left across the street and whether any of those persistent reporters were standing by. Sure enough, both groups were manning their posts. We could hear the muffled voices chanting in the distance: "Two, four, six, eight. We ain't gonna integrate."

"Four, six, eight, ten, we're already in," Terry whispered.

Danny was waiting for me near the front door. We nodded to each other as I began the long trip up to my homeroom. The early-morning hecklers were full of energy. One girl walked up close behind me, getting between Danny and me. I didn't look back; instead I quickened my pace. She started walking on my heels, and when I turned to face her, she spit at me. I ducked and scampered out of her way. To keep my focus, I began saying the Lord's Prayer. I continued to whisper the words under my breath as I approached the door to my homeroom at the top of the third-floor stairs.

"Hey, Melba, pay attention to what you're doing. Watch out!" Danny shouted as a group of boys bumped straight into me.

147

One of them kicked me in the shins so hard I fell to the floor. A second kick was delivered to my stomach. Danny stood over me, motioning them to move away. Other soldiers made their presence known, although they kept their distance. I struggled to my feet. More white students gathered around and taunted me, applauding and cheering: "The nigger's down."

"Stand tall," Danny whispered. "Let's move out."

"Why didn't you do something?" I asked him.

"I'm here for one thing," he said impatiently. "To keep you alive. I'm not allowed to get into verbal or physical battles with these students."

As some of the students continued their catcalls, I fought back tears and headed down the stairs to the principal's office.

"Did any adult witness this incident?" the woman clerk behind the desk asked in an unsympathetic tone. "I mean, did any teacher see these people do what you said?"

"Yes, ma'am, the soldiers."

"They don't count. Besides, they can't identify the people you're accusing."

"No. I didn't see any adults other than the soldiers," I answered, feeling the pain in my shin and my stomach.

"Well, in order to do anything, we need an adult witness."

"Yes, ma'am." Those were the words my mouth said because that's what I had been told was appropriate to say. But another part of me wanted to shout at her and ask why she didn't believe me or care enough to ask whether or not I needed medical help.

"I think you'd better get to class, unless you want us to call an ambulance," she said in a sarcastic tone.

I turned to walk out the door. It had hurt my feelings as much to report the incident to her as to live through it. I could see Danny's face, his expression was blank. But his posture was so erect and his stance so commanding that no one would dare to challenge him. Seeing that made me think about my own posture. I had to appear confident and alert. I squared my shoulders, trying not to show how frightened and timid I really felt.

I told myself I had to be like a soldier in battle. I couldn't imagine a 101st trooper crying or moping when he got hurt.

As I approached my homeroom class, I could hear the students yelling football cheers. Their loud voices, the pounding, their enthusiasm frightened me. It could so easily be a cover for whatever they wanted to do to me. I didn't know any of the cheers. There was no one to teach me. All around me they were laughing and talking of things I had no part in. I felt invisible, excluded, and once again as though there were no space for me.

For a while I sat perfectly still in the middle of all the fuss, and then, feeling awkward, I decided to try and join in. I clapped my hands and swayed back and forth to the rhythm, even though what was their fun was my terror. I felt a haunting aloneness; I yearned for someone, anyone, to say a friendly word to me. I kept a smile on my face and my posture erect. Afterward, I realized that the prospect of their attacking me had coiled my stomach into knots. Ideas in my mind were frightening me— rather than any reality. I would have to take control of my mind as Grandma said Gandhi had done.

I made my way to my next class, where Danny stood patiently outside the glass peephole in the door, watching boys throw pencils at me. Every time the teacher looked the other way, I was the target of yet another airborne object. But I was trapped. If I raised my hand to report their behavior, I might have to endure even worse treatment. The teacher wouldn't do anything to protect me. I already knew that. So I decided the best plan was simply to ignore them. If they got no satisfaction from their activities, perhaps they would stop. Partway through the class they stopped throwing things at me, but they didn't stop hurling whispered insults.

During the rest of the day, I forced myself to endure annoying little pranks that distracted me and made me nervous but did not really hurt me. After the ride home in the convoy with a fun game of verbal Ping-Pong with my friends, the usual group of news reporters once again greeted us at Mrs. Bates's house. That night I wrote in my diary:

It's hard being with Little Rock white people. I don't know if I can do this integration thing forever. It feels like this is something people do for only a little while. I want to run away now. I want a happy day.

The next morning, after a full night's sleep, I felt fresh and new, and the ride with Sarge and the others was a real tonic to start my day.

"Smile, it's Friday," Danny said, greeting me at the front door of the school. I was in an almost chipper mood as I walked up the stairs to my homeroom, even though I knew I had to be extra careful because of that morning's *Gazette* headline:

GOVERNOR CALLS FOR CALM, ORDER—
BUT VOICES RESENTMENT OF OCCUPATION

Grandma had told me the governor had given a speech the night before in which he talked at length about his anger that Little Rock was "an occupied city." He also talked of people being injured by soldiers' bayonets. But worst of all he showed a photograph of two Central High School girls being hustled along by soldiers with bayonets extended at their backs. A caller from the NAACP said to expect trouble because Faubus's speech was inflammatory.

There had been fewer soldiers accompanying us up the front stairs. Their absence meant the defiant chants and hateful words grew much louder. When I stepped inside the school, the soldiers were not as visible as they had been the day before, but I thanked God that they were still there.

"I'm gonna be in the background today. They're trying to figure how you'all will get along without us being up real close," Danny said.

I nodded to him as though I felt okay with his announcement. I wanted to say, "Please, please don't leave my side," but I didn't. I felt myself beginning to rely on him, but I didn't know what else to do. I had never before felt such fear. It was an unfamiliar position—me, counting on a white man to defend me against other white people determined to hurt me. And yet I was resigning myself to the fact that, for the moment, I had no choice but to depend on Danny, and God.

As I drew near the classroom, I was very apprehensive because this time I was entering my homeroom before class officially got under way. Everybody would be free to laugh and taunt or even hurt me. But I had no place else to go.

One girl with short red hair, freckles, and a pixie smile was being especially attentive. She invited me to accompany her to the window that overlooked the school yard. I was suspicious of her kindness, but I wanted to believe someone was having a change of heart. As I stood beside her chatting about the bright day and the activity of soldiers on the grounds beneath us, I felt a twinge of joy. Maybe I wasn't batting my head against a stone wall after all.

"Stand right here. We're gonna salute the flag now," she said. I raised my hand to my chest and smiled as the flag was hoisted up in front of the classroom.

"Aren't you gonna take my picture saluting the American flag with this famous nigger," she suddenly shouted to a boy who was focusing his camera. "Snap it, you idiot . . . now! I wanna get into *Life* magazine like the niggers are."

My heart sank. What should I do? Everyone was looking at me. The teacher arrived, and chiding the girl briefly, she halted the flag salute and instructed the class to maintain reverence for the flag. I turned away from the girl to walk to the opposite side of the room, and that's when I felt a stabbing blow that pierced my blouse and my skin. I lunged forward to escape the thrust, for a moment stunned by the pain. When I turned around, I saw the red-haired girl was holding a slender wrought-iron flagpole about twice as long as a chopstick with a very sharp point on one end. A Confederate flag was attached to it. I had seen other students carrying those flags in school and letting out the rebel yell. Now it had become her weapon.

The teacher either didn't see, or pretended she didn't. She resumed the salute to the flag. The puncture wound throbbed, and I could feel the blood trickling down my back as I held

[handwritten margin note: After that I think I wouldn't be able to trust a white person.]

151

my hand over my heart and wondered whether I should go for first aid, tell the teacher, or stay in class. I decided I wouldn't rush to report what had happened. I wouldn't give my classmates the satisfaction of knowing how much pain they had inflicted on me. And I wasn't sure any of the adults would do anything to tend my wound in any case, so I took my seat. I thought class would never end; the hands of the clock seemed frozen. When the break finally came, I raced for the bathroom to tend my wound while Danny trailed behind me asking questions about the blood on the back of my blouse.

As with any high school on Friday, the anticipation of the weekend brought excitement, and this was a special Friday for Central High's student body. The occasion for all the hoopla was a big football game that night with Baton Rouge, their arch-rival. People had been lingering about the stairwells, cheering, and waving pom-poms, making those areas particularly hazardous for the nine of us.

The stairwells were huge, open caverns that spiraled upward for several floors, providing ample opportunity to hurl flying objects, dump liquids, or entrap us in dark corners. As I descended the stairwell, it dawned on me that except for Danny, I was almost alone. There should have been many more people around because it was a class break.

"Look out, Melba, now!" Danny's voice was so loud that I flinched. "Get down!" he shouted again as what appeared to be a flaming stick of dynamite whizzed past and landed on the stair just below me. Danny pushed me aside as he stamped out the flame and grabbed it up. At breakneck speed he dashed down the stairs and handed the stick to another soldier, who sped away. Stunned by what I had seen, I backed into the shadow on the landing, too shocked to move.

"You don't have time to stop. Move out, girl." Danny's voice sounded cold and uncaring. I supposed that's what it meant to be a soldier—to survive.

*   *   *

152

After gym class, Danny met me in the hall with some unfortunate news. "You're going to your first pep rally," he said, concern on his face.

Going to a pep rally was rather like being thrown in with the lions to see how long we could survive. A pep rally meant two thousand students in a huge room with endless opportunity to mistreat us. As I climbed the stairs, I longed to sprint to the front door and escape.

"They won't allow me to go in with you," Danny whispered. "But I'll be somewhere outside here."

I didn't respond; I was too preoccupied with finding a safe route into the rally. Nothing had frightened me more than suddenly being folded into the flow of that crowd of white students as they moved toward the auditorium. Maybe it was because they were all so excited that I got in and to my seat without much hassle. Once settled, I was delighted that Thelma was sitting only a few feet away. Nevertheless, I couldn't relax because I was crammed into that dimly lit room among my enemies, and I knew I had to keep watch every moment. I ignored the activity on stage in favor of keeping my guard up.

Over the next twenty minutes, I worked myself into a frenzy anticipating what might happen. My stomach was in knots and my shoulder muscles like concrete. I decided I had to settle myself down. I repeated the Twenty-Third Psalm. All at once, everybody was standing and singing the school song, "Hail to the Old Gold, Hail to the Black." Some students were snickering and pointing at me as they sang the word "black," but I didn't care. It was over, and I was alive and well and moving out of the auditorium.

Suddenly, I was being shoved backward, toward the corner, very hard. A strong hand knocked my books and papers to the floor as three or four football-player types squeezed me into a dark corner beneath the overhang of the auditorium balcony. One of them hurt the wound on my back as he pinned me against the wall. Someone's forearm pressed hard against my throat, choking me. I couldn't speak. I could hardly breathe.

"We're gonna make your life hell, nigger. You'all are gonna

go screaming out of here, taking those nigger-loving soldiers with you."

Just as suddenly as I had been pinned against the wall, I was released. I stood still for a moment, holding on to my throat, gasping, trying to catch a good breath. I stooped to pick up my things, careful to keep a watch around me. I stumbled back into the flow of the crowd. I couldn't stop coughing, and my throat felt as though I would never speak again. In the distance I saw Danny standing in the hallway, facing the door of the auditorium.

"What's the matter?"

"Some guy tried to choke me," I whispered in a raspy voice.

"And you did nothing?"

"What could I do?" Talking hurt my throat.

"You've gotta learn to defend yourself. You kids should have been given some training in self-defense."

"Too late, now," I said.

"It's never too late. It takes a warrior to fight a battle and survive. This here is a battle if I've ever seen one."

I thought about what Danny had said as we walked to the principal's office to prepare to leave school. I knew for certain something would have to change if I were going to stay in that school. Either the students would have to change the way they behaved, or I would have to devise a better plan to protect myself. My body was wearing out real fast.

Later that evening, after Grandma tended my back and put a warm towel on my throat, I fell into bed, exhausted. In my diary I wrote:

After three full days inside Central, I know that integration is a much bigger word than I thought.

154

15

SINCE IT WAS THE END OF MY FIRST EXHAUSTING WEEK AT CENTRAL High, I decided to claim Saturday for my very own. That's why I set my alarm clock for 4 A.M. I wanted a slice of the fresh, still morning all to myself. What I liked most was the absolute silence inside my head and heart—silence I had not enjoyed for so long. Most of all, I wanted to be alone so I could search for the part of my life that existed before integration, the Melba I was struggling to hold on to.

I had also promised myself that I wasn't going to turn on the news, read the newspaper, talk, read, or write about integration. I would listen to records, read my *Seventeen* and *Ebony* magazines, and write in my diary. I thought I'd never again be sitting on my bed, nestled between my huge white lace pillows and my stuffed animals, just like a normal girl. I was trying hard not to face the notion growing inside me that I was no longer normal, no longer like my other friends.

Nothing in my life was the same anymore. I felt so empty inside, like somebody had scooped out the warm sweet part of my spirit that made me smile and feel grateful to be alive. Integration hadn't at all worked out the way I'd planned. I didn't know it would eat up so much of my time—and so much of my life.

The changes crept over me, taking a little of my old life away each day. In the time since I'd decided to go to Central, my best friend, Marsha, had stopped the daily calls we had made to each other for so long. Each day I had meant to call her and ask why, but I was so busy thinking about integration—and even when I remembered, I didn't have time. On those now rare occasions when I called her, she spent much of the conversation telling me how her friends and family members were suffering because of me. I spent the rest of the time defending myself, explaining how in the long run it would all be worth it. We never talked about boys or movies or Johnny Mathis or new clothes anymore.

Now you see who are your real friends.

Marsha had begun treating me as though I were different. She wasn't inviting me places, she stopped calling to tell me what the old gang was doing. It felt as though she no longer wanted me as her friend. Whenever we happened to meet, she called me the "chosen one." I thought it was a strange thing to say.

Most of my other friends were behaving a little strangely as well. Some of them stared at me whenever I saw them or snubbed me or talked to me like you talk to people you don't know well. We seemed not to have things in common anymore. There was so much new information in my head, so many new worries, that I didn't have space for the ordinary things we shared before. I spent a lot of time thinking about safety and life and death and what would make the white people understand that I was equal to them.

I felt different inside, like something was stretching me, growing me, making me somebody else. So much of the past month, I had lived inside my head, pondering what would happen to me. It was as though I were forced to turn inward to get along at Central High. No one on the outside could understand what I was going through. The change frightened me because I was going somewhere, becoming someone, but I didn't know where or who. I wasn't ready to be grown up—or to not be Melba. In my diary I wrote:

I am worried about what's happening to me. I feel like someone forced me into a roller coaster that spins up and down and all around and won't stop. Nobody can make it stop but God.

Later that morning when the family sat down together for breakfast, I couldn't believe that Mama was reading the paper over the breakfast table, something we were forbidden to do.

"I see here where the head of the FBI is angry at Faubus for telling lies about the FBI holding those schoolgirls in custody." Mother showed me the *Gazette* headline and the first part of the article.

J. EDGAR HOOVER ANGERED BY FAUBUS REPORT OF FBI

September 28, 1957: FBI Director J. Edgar Hoover accused Governor Faubus of Arkansas of disseminating falsehoods by saying FBI agents held teenagers incommunicado for hours of questioning.

"He's really fired up the segregationists," Grandma said.

I shut my mind off—I couldn't listen. Their talk made me queasy. When I couldn't stand it any longer I had to speak up. "We're gonna only talk about good things," I said, gulping my last sip of milk. "No Central High talk."

"Deal," Grandma said, standing to clear the table.

By ten, we all piled into the car and started off for our big adventure. Grandma had offered to buy me a new store-bought dress—I couldn't believe my ears. Then Mama made her announcement.

"Vince telephoned. He's asked me if you could go with him to church tomorrow, then out for a bite. I said yes, provided the two of you come home to have dinner with us."

"Melba's got a boyfriend. . . ." Conrad's chant was embarrassing me.

"Shut up," I blurted out, suddenly very angry with my younger brother. Grandma looked at me disapprovingly and said, "Don't take your Central High anger out on your brother!"

She was right. I apologized and sat back in my seat, aware of my anger and wondering what to do with it. It was the same kind of anger I felt at Central when somebody was mean to me. Then I remembered Mama had said "yes" to Vince, and the happiness I felt caused my anger to fade.

Little Rock's Main Street was small and dingy by comparison to Cincinnati's enormous shopping district. We only had three fancy stores—Kempner's, Blass, and Pfeifer's. During our walk through the last store, Mama found a dress she liked and asked me to try it. I pulled the blue-and-white gabardine dress over my head. Grandma smiled, and I knew that was the dress she would buy even though the price tag said $10.99.

The day took on a comforting quality. It was as though we were just an ordinary family as we picked out a shirt for Conrad and stopped for an ice cream break. There were actually fleeting moments when I didn't think about being a Central High student. I stopped worrying about what would happen if some Central High students saw me and there were no soldiers around.

Saturday night we sat watching *Wagon Train* and *The Sid Caesar Show* on television, and all the while I couldn't stop thinking about Sunday morning with Vince, especially since we were going to his mother's church. At the same time, I wanted to keep Saturday, because it had indeed been my day. Grandma decided we wouldn't answer the phone, so she put it in the cedar chest. Only the shotgun leaning in the corner near her chair reminded me that things were different.

When Sunday actually came around, I was in a real dither over my date. I couldn't eat breakfast. Instead, I worked on new hairstyles in front of the mirror. My ponytail was absolutely childish, so I tried an upsweep, a swatch over the eye like Gloria Swanson, and a pouf like Elizabeth Taylor. Unfortunately, the ponytail looked best on me.

"Hmm, look at this," Mother Lois said, entering my bedroom holding the Sunday paper wide open. "Here's an article on Terry and his family. Talks about his parents and how they sat up late discussing whether he would go to Central—says they left the decision up to him."

I walked over to share the paper. The headline read:

NEGRO PARENTS TAKE INSULTS, PRAY FOR CHILDREN'S SAFETY

There were comments from Thelma's and Elizabeth's parents about our dilemma. They spoke about the constant harassing phone calls and the daily insults and abuse at school. There were also pictures of the violence at Central High on every day of the previous week.

But I couldn't take the time to look at the newspaper. I was frantically doing final touch-ups to my appearance. When Mother left the room, I turned slowly in front of the mirror, thinking if only I'd had another week to prepare for this date.

Not knowing how girls were supposed to behave on dates made me nervous. I kept thinking about what to do or say. I thought about the women in novels I'd read and in the true romance magazines and on the soaps. I'd try to behave like them.

When Vince arrived, I headed for the living room. Mother stopped me in the hallway and took both my hands in hers. She held me at arm's length, looking me over as if she were trying to preserve that moment in her mind. "Your first real date," she whispered. "I know you are a good girl, and I love you."

Then I was with Vince. He looked down at me, reaching out to hand me a dozen roses, my first roses, just like in the magazines and on *Stella Dallas* on the radio. Red roses.

I whispered my "thank you." I saw the clock on the wall and with a sinking heart realized that in twenty-four hours it would be Monday morning. I would be going back to school, back to Central High.

The date went better than I expected. After a while I relaxed and stopped worrying so much about what to say and do. The minister at Vince's mother's church mentioned my name and had the congregation say a special prayer for me. I could see by the look on his face that he felt proud to be with me. Even dinner with my family went well until Grandma India mentioned news of Central High. The Mothers' League was asking that the 101st be removed from inside the school or at least cut to a bare minimum.

Later, I lay in bed unable to sleep. The joy from my date with Vince was overshadowed by my uncertainty about tomorrow at Central High. I tossed and turned all night, worrying that the soldiers would be gone the next day.

When I arrived at school on that Monday morning, I had only one thought in my mind—find Danny and the 101st. He was right there, just as he had been in the days before. I kept looking back to see him because I had that nagging feeling he would be leaving all too soon. During English class I started to write in my notebook to keep calm. Later that evening I transferred what I wrote to my diary.

September 30: 9:30 A.M.
Each morning as I arrive, I look for the soldiers. I don't want to imagine what it would be like without them. Even inside the classroom where things should be safe and civilized, I am never able to be comfortable because the teachers are not in control. I can't even take pride in reciting. One boy in English class shouted "Don't let that nigger go to the blackboard."

That Monday was the day on which I came to realize the price I would pay to become a Central High student. I tried to figure out why. And then I knew it was because I was treated as though I were an outside observer, sitting and looking into a glass room that held all the white students, separate and apart from me. I was never really included in what they were doing. With that realization, a new pain seeped into my heart—a feeling I hadn't experienced before. It felt as if I were a ghost, observing life, excited about it, but excluded. I wasn't really a part of their world. I was treated as if I didn't exist. Would it be this way all year long?

Apart from that painful realization, and the whispered nasty comments and small but agitating pranks, the day was simply very, very long.

"Patience," Danny said. "In order to get through this year you will have to become a soldier. Never let your enemy know what you are feeling. You can't afford to become bored."

That evening I wrote in my diary:

A girl smiled at me today, another gave me directions, still another boy whispered the page I should turn to in our textbook. This is going to work. It will take a lot more patience and more strength from me, but it's going to work. It takes more time than I thought. But we're going to have integration in Little Rock.

16

GUARD TAKES OVER AT SCHOOL
—*Arkansas Democrat*, Tuesday, October 1, 1957

I ARRIVED AT SCHOOL TUESDAY MORNING, FULLY EXPECTING THAT I would be greeted by the 101st soldiers and escorted to the top of the stairs. Instead, we were left at the curb to fend for ourselves. As we approached the stairs, we were greeted by taunting catcalls and the kind of behavior students had not dared to exhibit in the face of the 101st.

Where were the disciplined ranks we had come to count on? I looked all around, but sure enough, there were no 101st guards in sight. Just then a boy blocked our way. What were we to do? My first thought was to retreat, to turn and go back down the stairs and detour around to the side door. But that escape route was blocked by those stalking us. A large crowd of jeering, pencil-throwing students hovered around us menacingly. We had no choice but to go forward.

"Where are your pretty little soldier boys today?" someone cried out.

"You niggers ready to die just to be in this school?" asked another.

Squeezing our way through the hostile group gathered at the front door, we were blasted by shouts of "Nigger, go home. Go back to where you belong." At every turn, we were faced with more taunts and blows. There were no 101st soldiers at their usual posts along the corridors.

And then I saw them. Slouching against the wall were members of the Arkansas National Guard, looking on like spectators at a sports event—certainly not like men sent to guard our safety.

I wanted to turn and run away, but I thought about what Danny had said: "Warriors survive." I tried to remember his stance, his attitude, and the courage of the 101st on the battlefield. Comparing my tiny challenge with what he must have faced made me feel more confident. I told myself I could handle whatever the segregationists had in store for me. But I underestimated them.

Early that morning, a boy began to taunt me as though he had been assigned that task. First he greeted me in the hall outside my shorthand class and began pelting me with bottlecap openers, the kind with the sharp claw at the end. He was also a master at walking on my heels. He hurt me until I wanted to scream for help.

By lunchtime, I was nearly hysterical and ready to call it quits, until I thought of having to face Grandma when I arrived home. During the afternoon, when I went into the principal's office several times to report being sprayed with ink, kicked in the shin, and heel-walked until the backs of my feet bled, as well as to report the name of my constant tormentor, the clerks asked why I was reporting petty stuff. With unsympathetic scowls and hostile attitudes, they accused me of making mountains out of molehills.

Not long before the end of the school day, I entered a dimly lit rest room. The three girls standing near the door seemed to ignore me. Their passive, silent, almost pleasant greeting made me uncomfortable, and the more I thought about their attitude, the more it concerned me. At least when students were treating me harshly, I knew what to expect.

Once inside the stall, I was even more alarmed at all the movement, the feet shuffling, the voices whispering. It sounded as though more people were entering the room.

"Bombs away!" someone shouted above me. I looked up to see a flaming paper wad coming right down on me. Girls were leaning over the top of the stalls on either side of me. Flaming paper floated down and landed on my hair and shoulders. I jumped up, trying to pull myself together and at the same time duck the flames and stamp them out. I brushed the singeing ashes away from my face as I frantically grabbed for the door to open it.

"Help!" I shouted. "Help!" The door wouldn't open. Someone was holding it—someone strong, perhaps more than one person. I was trapped.

"Did you think we were gonna let niggers use our toilets? We'll burn you alive, girl," a voice shouted through the door. "There won't be enough of you left to worry about."

I felt the kind of panic that stopped me from thinking clearly. My right arm was singed. The flaming wads of paper were coming at me faster and faster. I could feel my chest muscles tightening. I felt as though I would die any moment. The more I yelled for help, the more I inhaled smoke and the more I coughed.

I told myself I had to stop screaming so I wouldn't take in so much smoke. My throat hurt—I was choking. I remembered Grandmother telling me all I had to do was say the name of God and ask for help. Once more I looked up to see those grinning, jeering faces as flaming paper rained down on me. Please, God, help me, I silently implored. I had to hurry. I might not be able to swat the next one and put it out with my hands. Then what? Would my hair catch fire? I had to stop them. I picked up my books and tossed one upward as hard as I could, in a blind aim to hit my attackers.

I heard a big thud, then a voice cry out in pain and several people scuffle about. I tossed another and then another book as

164

fast and as hard as I could. One more of their number cursed at me. I had hit my target.

"Let's get out of here," someone shouted as the group hurried out the door. In a flash, I leaped out of the stall, trying to find my things. I decided I wouldn't even bother reporting my problem. I just wanted to go home. I didn't care that I smelled of smoke or that my blouse was singed. Later when my friends asked what happened, I didn't even bother to explain.

Much worse than the fear and any physical pain I had endured was the hurt deep down inside my heart, because no part of me understood why people would do those kinds of things to one another. I was so stunned by my experience that during the ride home I sat silent and listened to reports from the others. They, too, seemed to have had a bigger problem that day with hecklers and hooligans.

They really need protectors

The experiment of doing without the 101st had apparently been a fiasco. By the end of the day more than one of us had heard talk that the 101st had been brought back.

Still, despite all our complaints, there were a few students who tried to reach out to us with smiles or offers to sit at our cafeteria tables; some even accompanied us along the halls. Each of us noticed, however, that those instances of friendship were shrinking rather than growing. There was no doubt that the hard-core troublemakers were increasing their activities, and without the men of the 101st, they increased a hundredfold.

President Eisenhower says he will remove the 101st soldiers if Governor Faubus agrees to protect the nine Negro children with federalized Arkansas National Guardsmen.

I don't think the gov will protect them.

Those words from the radio announcer sent a chill down my spine as I sat doing my homework on Tuesday evening. I had hoped the rumors of the return of the 101st were true. But according to the report, the same Arkansas soldiers who had been dispatched by Governor Faubus to keep us *out* of Central High would become totally responsible for keeping us *in* school and protecting our lives.

"Sounds like the wolf guarding the henhouse to me," Grandma said. "Thank God you know who your real protector is, 'cause you certainly won't be able to count on those boys for help." She was peeking at me over the pages of the newspaper.

I didn't know how to tell her how right she was. But then I couldn't tell her I had had the kind of day that was making me think about running away where nobody could find me.

"Did you see where Judge Ronald Davies will be going back to North Dakota?" Grandma continued. "He will still retain jurisdiction over your case, though."

"That really frightens me," I said. "I feel safer with Davies being here."

"He is being replaced by Judge Harper from St. Louis, it says."

"Bad news," I replied. I didn't know bad things about Harper, but I had come to trust Davies as an honest and fair man with the courage of his convictions. St. Louis bordered the South; that Judge Harper might not be as open-minded.

"Of course, there is good news here," Grandma said, rattling the newspaper. "Seems as if some moderate white businessmen are getting together to oppose that special session of the legislature Faubus wants to call."

"The one to enact laws that would make integration illegal?" I asked.

"Yes, I hope they can do something to slow him down."

IKE REJECTS FAUBUS'S STATEMENT
AND AGREEMENT FALLS THROUGH
—*Arkansas Gazette*, Wednesday, October 2, 1957

The Wednesday morning *Gazette* reported that Governor Faubus and the President had come to the brink of an agreement to remove the federal troops from Little Rock the day before, but at the last minute the President called it off because he didn't believe the governor would act in good faith.

As we walked toward Central that day, I was looking forward to having the 101st come back to make my life inside school at least tolerable. But right away my hopes for a more peaceful day were dashed. Showers of loud insults greeted us. Straight ahead, in front of the school, I could see a group of about fifty boys waiting at the top of the stairs as they had the day before. This time, however, they descended on us like locusts.

"Get the coons! Get the coons!" The boys were brash and bold, behaving as though they feared no consequences. There were no parading 101st soldiers to stop them. Frantically, we looked around for someone in authority, but none was in sight.

Minnijean, Ernie, and I decided to retreat, but just then, vice-principal Huckaby made her presence known at the bottom of the stairs. Tiny, erect, and determined, she stood there all alone between us and our attackers, demanding they leave us alone. One by one she challenged the leaders, calling them by name, telling them to get to class or there would be hell to pay. I had to respect her for what she did. Whether or not she favored integration, she had a heck of a lot of guts.

We circled around to the Sixteenth and Park Street entrance. As I climbed the stairs, there was no sign of Danny—or the other 101st guards I knew. In fact, I didn't see any uniformed soldiers. Just inside of the front entrance, where Danny usually stood, I saw some of the same hooligans who had tried to block our entrance only moments before. They moved toward me, and I circled away from them and walked quickly down the hall. I was desperately trying to figure out why there weren't any teachers or school officials guarding the halls the way there usually were.

I panicked; I couldn't decide where to go or what to do next. I was being pounded on my arms, my back, and my legs by angry students. Their blows hurt so much that my desire to stop the pain and survive overpowered the fear that paralyzed me. I got hold of myself. No matter what, I knew I had to stand up to them even if I got kicked out of school for doing it.

"Dead niggers don't go to school," someone said, hitting me hard in the stomach. My first instinct was to double over. The pain burned my insides. But I stood still and stared at my attacker without flinching. He taunted me: "You ain't thinking of hitting me back?"

"I'm gonna cut your guts out," I said, standing my ground. There was a long pause while we stared each other down. It was a bluff, but it worked. Looking almost frightened and mumbling under his breath, he backed off.

Just then, I noticed the members of the Arkansas National Guard lounging against the walls like cats in sunlight. Gathered in small clusters with smug, grinning expressions on their faces, they had been watching my confrontation all along. I couldn't get used to the fact that our safety now depended on nonchalant, tobacco-chewing adolescents who were most likely wearing white sheets and burning crosses on the lawns of our neighbors after sundown.

I had walked only a few steps before I was knocked to the floor. I called out for help. Three men from the Guard gave further substance to my suspicions by taking their time to respond, moving toward me in slow motion. I scrambled to my feet.

How I longed to see Danny, standing on guard in his starched uniform, and hear the swift steps of the 101st. As I felt hot tears stinging my eyes, I heard Grandmother India's voice say, "You're on the battlefield for your Lord."

I was as frightened by the ineptness of the Arkansas soldiers as by the viciousness of the increased attacks on me. If the soldiers had been armed, I was certain they would either have shot me in the back or themselves in the foot. I watched as they stood in giggling clusters while a crowd of thugs attacked Jeff and Terry and kicked them to the floor in the hallway just outside the principal's office. A female teacher finally rescued the two.

Once I was seated in class, I felt I could take a deep breath. For the moment at least I was off the front line of battle in the hallway. But just as I was feeling a snippet of peace, a boy pulled a switchblade knife and pressed the point of the blade against my forearm. In a heartbeat, without even thinking about it, I leaped up and picked up my books as a shield to fend him off.

He responded to a half-hearted reprimand from the teacher but whispered that he would get me later. At the very first sound of the bell ending class, I ran for my life, only to encounter a group of students who knocked me down and hit me with their books. As I felt rage overtake me I recalled what Danny had told me: "When you're angry, you can't think. You gotta keep alert to keep alive."

It was still early in the day, and things were so bad that I decided I had no choice: I had to find somebody in authority who would listen to me. Outside the principal's office I found Minnijean looking as abused and angry as I was.

"We gotta get out of here!" she said breathlessly.

"You're right. They're gonna kill us today," I replied.

"Let's call our folks."

"Let's call Mrs. Bates. Maybe she can talk to the army or reporters or the President." I assumed calling the head of the NAACP would at least get some response. Merely reporting this kind of trouble to school officials might not get anything except more of the same denial that there was trouble, or perhaps reprimands for being "tattletales."

Since neither of us had change for a call, we reluctantly decided to go to Mrs. Huckaby, although we were afraid she would try and convince us to stick it out. Mrs. Huckaby greeted us in a matter-of-fact way until it dawned on her that we might be using the change we asked for to call for outside help.

"Wait a minute. What's going on?" she asked, trailing behind us.

"We're calling Mrs. Bates. We need help. Maybe she can talk to the reporters and get us some protection."

Just as we suspected, Mrs. Huckaby insisted we go to the principal's office to give him a chance to solve the problem. She assured us that he would be fair.

Principal Matthews began to speak in his slow plodding way, wearing his usual nervous smile. It was apparent he only wanted to stop us from making the call. I was in no mood to have him tell me I was imagining things, not with my leg aching and the steel flash of that switchblade knife fresh in my mind.

"Either you give us some protection so we can function without getting killed, or we go home." I heard the words come out of my mouth, but I could hardly believe it was me speaking. My knees were shaking. It was the first time in my life I had ever stood up to any adult—certainly to any white adult. But I was on the edge, ready to take the risk, because how could anything the adults might do to me be worse than the abuse I was already enduring?

"Wait here," the principal said, his tone of voice leaving no doubt he was annoyed with us. Shortly afterward, we saw the brass approaching: General Clinger and Colonel McDaniel of the Arkansas National Guard, and a third military man I did not recognize.

Clinger pointed to the two of us, most especially to me, and said, "You'll sit over there where I can look you in the face." Right away, I didn't like him, but I was ready to deal with him.

The rest of our group was summoned to the office. Everyone was vocal about the severity of the attacks during the morning. Each one had a story about how the physical abuse had increased significantly. We told Clinger that his men were not protecting us, that they stood by, socializing and flirting while we were being beaten within an inch of our lives. "Those guards are turning their backs to attacks on us, and we demand you do something about it," I insisted.

Clinger didn't deny the charges. He explained that his men had to live in the community.

"We just wanna keep living . . . period," I said.

"Don't talk directly to the guards. Go to the office and report incidents," we were told.

I said, "With all due respect, sir, how can we run to the office every time we want help. Somebody could be beating one of us at the far end of the hall, and we'd have to wait until they finished and let us up so we could come here to report it."

I felt something inside me change that day. I felt a new will to live rise up in me. I knew I wasn't just going to roll over and die. I could take care of myself and speak up to white folks, even if my mother and father sometimes feared doing so. I discovered I had infinitely more guts than I had started the school year with. I had no choice. It was my life I was dickering for. I knew that Clinger didn't care about our welfare—not even a tiny bit.

"Young lady," Clinger said, eyeballing me, "you are turning our words. I didn't say—"

But I cut him off. "My friends and I will leave school if we don't get adequate protection. It's as simple as that," I told him. The others were obviously as angry as I was as they chimed in with their complaints. They voiced their agreement that something had to be done immediately.

"You'll have bodyguards." Clinger spoke with a definite edge to his voice. He summoned another soldier and told him to select eighteen men while we waited there. Those Arkansas guardsmen were the biggest, dumbest, most disheveled hayseeds I'd ever seen. They looked as if they had slept in their rumpled uniforms. We stood there not believing our eyes, dumbfounded by the sight of them.

"These clods will trip over their own shoelaces," I whispered to Minnijean.

"Or worse yet, get us in some dark corner and beat the living daylights out of us," she replied.

After about fifteen minutes we "moved out," or in their case, shuffled out. It was a sight to behold. There we were, followed by an absurd wall of not so mighty military green trailing us like a ridiculous wagging tail.

We found ourselves laughing aloud, and the white students were laughing with us. For just one moment we all realized the ridiculous situation we were caught up in.

Four of us went to our usual table in the cafeteria; the guards took up their posts, leaning against a nearby wall. When I got up to get in line for a sandwich, they fell over each other trying to see where I was going and which of them would follow me. Two stood in line with me, arms folded, tummies out, and shoulders rounded. Each time one of us rose to get anything, two of those clowns stumbled up to follow. It was a comedy of errors.

As we moved through the halls in our oddball group, I saw, just a few feet away, the boy who had pulled the knife on me earlier. The momentary terror I felt reminded me our situation wasn't funny after all.

I missed Danny. That was another feeling taking me over. Rumor had it that the 101st waited at Camp Robinson, just outside Little Rock. But I knew that even if he came back again and again, there would come the day when he would be gone for good.

Still, I was overjoyed when on Thursday we once again had our 101st bodyguards. Maybe they were forced to come back because the morning *Gazette* had reported the story of Terry and Jeff being kicked while Arkansas National Guardsmen looked on.

As we arrived at school that morning, I noticed right away that there was a different kind of tension, as though everyone was waiting for something awful to happen, only we didn't know what. We had heard rumors of a planned student protest. I could see groups of students standing in the halls instead of in class where they would normally have been.

Just before first period, more students began walking out of classes. Rumors about a big event reverberated throughout the school. I could see and feel a new level of restlessness and a deepening sense of hostility. I was on edge, waiting for disaster any moment, like dynamite or a group attack or I didn't know what. "They're hangin' a nigger, just like we're gonna hang you," someone muttered. That's when I learned that some of those who walked out had assembled at the vacant lot at Sixteenth and Park across from the school, where they hanged and burned a straw figure.

That demonstration set the tone of the day. Belligerent student protests were firing up the already hostile attitude inside the school. Danny broke the rules by coming closer and talking to me—warning that we had to stay alert, no matter what.

Near the end of the day I was walking down a dimly lit hallway, with Danny following, when I spotted a boy coming directly toward me on a collision course. I tried to move aside, but he moved with me. I didn't even have time to call for help.

The boy flashed a shiny black object in my face. The sudden pain in my eyes was so intense, so sharp, I thought I'd die. It was like nothing I'd ever felt before. I couldn't hear or see or feel anything except that throbbing, searing fire centered in my eyes. I heard myself cry out as I let go of everything to clutch at my face.

Someone grabbed me by my ponytail and pulled me along very fast, so fast I didn't have time to resist. The pain of being dragged along by my hair was almost as intense as that in my eyes. Hands grabbed my wrists and pried my hands from my face, compelling me to bend over. Then cold, cold liquid was splashed in my eyes. The water felt so good. My God, thank you! The pain was subsiding.

"Easy, girl, easy. You're gonna be fine." It was Danny's voice, *why would* his hands holding my head and dousing my eyes with water.

"I can't see," I whispered. "I can't see." *Danny Drag Helba but the*

"Hold on. You will."

Over and over again, the cold water flooded my face. Some *pony* of it went into my nose and down the front of my blouse. Bit *ale* by bit I could see the sleeve of Danny's uniform, see the water, *and* see the floor beneath us. The awful pain in my eyes had turned *not* into a bearable sting. My eyes felt dry, as though there were a *by her* film drawn tight over them. *hand*

or some-

"What was that?" *thing else.*

"I don't know," Danny said, "maybe some kind of alkaline *—* or acid. The few drops that got on your blouse faded the color immediately. Hey, let's get you to the office so we can report this. You gotta get to a doctor." *• Even if they went to the office they won't do any-*

"No. No," I protested.

"Why not?" *thing.*

"School's almost over, I wanna go home, right now. Please, *—* please don't make me. . . ." I felt tears. I knew he hated me to cry, but the thought of going to the office made me crazy. I

173

couldn't handle having some hostile clerk telling me I was making mountains out of molehills.

"Calm down. You can do what you want but—"

"No, home right now," I said, cutting Danny off.

A short time later, an optometrist examined my eyes and studied the spots on my blouse. He put some kind of soothing substance into my eyes and covered them with eye patches. As I sat there in the dark, I heard him say, "Whoever kept that water going in her eyes saved the quality of her sight, if not her sight itself. She'll have to wear the patch overnight. She'll have to be medicated for a while. She'll need to wear glasses for all close work. I'd really like to see her wear them all the time. I'll need to see her once a week until we're certain she's all right."

Glasses, all the time, I thought. No boy wants to date a girl with glasses.

Despite the doctor's instructions to wear an eye patch for twenty-four hours, I had to take it off. I couldn't let the reporters see me with the patch because they would ask questions and make a big deal of it.

By the time we got home it was seven o'clock, and I wasn't very talkative for the waiting reporters. Once inside I fell into bed, too exhausted to eat dinner. "Thank you, God," I whispered, "thank you for saving my eyes. God bless Danny, always."

THE HANGING, STABBING, AND BURNING
OF A NEGRO EFFIGY NEAR CENTRAL HIGH
—*Arkansas Gazette*, Friday, October 4, 1957

The newspaper story contained several vivid pictures of Central High students gathered the day before, hanging the effigy, then burning it. They were smiling gleefully as though they were attending a festive party.

"You made it. It's Friday," Danny said, greeting me at the front of Central once more. "Your peepers okay?"

My eyes still felt very dry and tight. There were floating spots before them, but I could see. They only stung when I went too long without putting the drops in.

Later that afternoon there was a movie star—someone I'd never heard of—speaking before a pep rally: Julie Adams, a former student. She was there to boost spirits because, she said, Central High School's reputation was being tainted.

Over the weekend of October 5th, a great thing happened that took the Little Rock school integration from the front pages of the national news. The Russians launched their 184-pound satellite, Sputnik.

But as the next week began, local radio, television, and newspapers claimed that 101st guards were following us females to the lavatory and harassing white girls. GI'S IN GIRLS' DRESS-ING ROOMS, FAUBUS SAYS ran as a banner headline in the *Gazette* for Monday, October 7. Of course it wasn't true. However, it made the military tighten up rules about where soldiers could or could not go with us and prompted them to launch a massive internal investigation.

I could see a steady erosion in the quality of security in response to charges of interference by the soldiers. It was evident as the early days of October passed that whenever the 101st troops relaxed their guard or were not clearly visible, we were in great danger.

[handwritten margin notes:] How would Faubus know that GI's were in the dressing room if he wasn't even there to witness it.

17

FAUBUS WANTS SCHOOL RESPITE:
STILL SAYS NEGROES MUST BE WITHDRAWN
—*Arkansas Gazette*, Thursday, October 10, 1957

THE GOVERNOR CONTINUED TO CONDUCT A PUBLIC CAMPAIGN, complaining loud and long in a nonstop series of newspaper, radio, and television interviews that integration must be halted. Inspired by his attitude, those who did not want us at Central High were digging in their heels and becoming much better organized in their efforts to get rid of us.

Each day we arrived to find we were facing a different set of circumstances. Officials experimented with ways of protecting our safety that would at the same time please politicians who wanted the troops gone from school and gone from Little Rock. Increasing physical violence brought back the 101st guards on some occasions. We found ourselves spending our days with one personal bodyguard from the 101st, or with varying numbers and kinds of bodyguards, or totally alone.

For example, when one of us had a major problem, they brought in a three-hundred pound 101st guard nicknamed Goggles. With nightsticks and other equipment strapped at his side, he made the kind of shield that fended off even the most hard-core segregationists. We grew to love him because being with Goggles meant a safe day no matter where you went. God bless Goggles and keep him in good health forever, was my prayer.

The beginning of the second week of October brought with it the realization that I would have to settle into some kind of routine that would allow me to cope with day-to-day harassment. Beyond the noise and hoopla of integrating school, beyond the glitter of news conferences, beyond anything else going on in my life, I had to figure out how to make it through seven hours with Central High segregationists each day.

My diary entry for Tuesday, October 8, read:

The ride to school today seemed livelier than ever. The driver of the jeep was friendlier. He finds all this confusion quite amusing.

I like what I wore—my orange blouse and quilted skirt. On my way to the third-period class, someone squirted ink on my blouse. I went to class feeling hurt and angry because I knew it would never come out. In English class, a boy was called on to recite. When he failed to answer the question, I raised my hand to recite. When I gave the right answer, he said, "Are you going to believe me or that nigger?"

Two days later, on Thursday, October 10, I wrote:

This morning I was given two new guards. This made me feel quite uncomfortable. I left home without eating breakfast and gee was I hungry. But I couldn't go to lunch in the cafeteria because that room is becoming the main place for them to get me.

On some days I found myself thinking every waking moment about nothing else but my safety—consumed with learning skills that would keep me alive. When would someone get the best of me, and how could I head them off? By October 11, I had made myself ill with what appeared to be flu but was probably greatly compounded by a real case of fear and exhaustion. On that Friday, I stayed home from Central and snuggled down into my bed where it was safe.

I was well aware that my illness was more sadness and exhaustion than flu. I knew I had to get myself together because the next day I was supposed to meet with some of the eight others and some hard-core segregationist student leaders for a discussion that might lead to an understanding. To insure my speedy recovery, Grandma came after me with castor oil. I protested, but I knew it was no use.

I had tried to explain to her that I was just weary of hostile white students, hurtful deeds, soldiers and army jeeps back and forth to school, and news reporters with their endless questions. "Weary" had always been an older person's complaint. But I knew for certain I was weary. Grandma was having none of it.

"The orange juice will cut the taste—here, drink," she said, leaning in so close that I had no prayer of escape. "Don't make me bend over this way, my back hurts." Her spectacles slid to the end of her nose. I looked into her huge determined eyes, and I knew I was trapped. I gulped it down. The warm oily liquid was oozing across my tongue, down my throat when she popped a peppermint drop into my mouth.

And it wasn't only the castor oil I had to endure with my claim of flu. That was just the beginning of a whole official ceremony that included Grandma's garlic and herb poultice on my chest, which I figured was guaranteed to asphyxiate the germs. If that didn't do it, the inch-thick Vicks salve she smeared over every centimeter of my body would surely send the flu bugs running. Yet as awful as some of her healing treatment was to endure, it felt better to be there at home with her than at Central High.

"It's too bad you have to miss a day of school." Mother Lois fluffed my pillows and tightened the sheet at the bottom of my bed. Dressed in her tan gabardine teaching suit with black blouse, she was off to school. "Hope you'll be able to attend the meeting tomorrow." She leaned over to kiss my forehead and to fetch her briefcase from the chair where she had left it. "Meeting with those Central High kids could be a first step to some kind of peacemaking."

I knew very well I would have to force myself to attend. It would be the first time ever that segregationist student leaders would be coming to talk to us integrating students in a reasonably safe place where we all could speak our minds. It was sponsored by a Norwegian reporter, Mrs. Jorumn Rickets, who had set it up with Ernie, Minnijean, and me, and the group spotlighted as staunch troublemakers: Sammy Dean Parker, Kaye Bacon, and their crowd. Sammy Dean Parker had been seen in the newspaper embracing Governor Faubus as she thanked him for keeping us out of school.

People referred to the meeting as a possible turning point, a time of coming together. I had thought about nothing else for several days. I even dreamed that we would go to the meeting, and afterward things would calm down considerably at school. After a real heart-to-heart, the white students would see the light, and that would be the beginning of a smooth year.

It was that hope that made me drag myself out of bed on Saturday morning and head for the Parish Hall of St. Andrew's Cathedral. Upon arrival I learned the meeting would be recorded by the National Broadcasting Company for future use on a network radio show. I hoped that wouldn't change our being able to speak our minds.

The meeting room was a stark white setting, with mahogany straight-back chairs. It was the kind of place that could well inspire a deep, honest talk that might help us get along with each other. Mrs. Rickets, a woman of medium stature with blond hair pulled to the nape of her neck, began asking questions.

Joseph Fox, labeled a Central moderate because he didn't violently oppose our presence, said, "I lay the whole blame for this thing in Governor Faubus's lap. We wouldn't have had nearly so much trouble if he hadn't called out the National Guard."

"That's not so. I think our governor is trying to protect all of us," said Sammy Dean Parker, an avowed segregationist seen embracing the governor on the front page of the newspaper.

"He's trying to prepare us. He said we'd have to integrate, but he has to prepare us."

Ernie said, "All we want is an education and to be able to go to school and back home safely."

When Mrs. Rickets asked why some of the white children objected to going to school with us, Sammy Dean replied: "Well, it's racial, marrying each other."

"School isn't a marriage bureau," Ernie said.

"We don't have to socialize," I said.

Kaye Bacon said she had heard rumors that we wanted to "rule" over them.

"I don't think you know much about our people. I don't think you ever tried to find out," Minnijean said.

Kaye admitted she hadn't tried to understand much about us until that meeting.

"We're scared to death five hundred of you'all are gonna be coming into school," Sammy Dean said.

The white students also expressed their feelings about the troops. Several times they spoke of their outrage at having soldiers in their school. "How do you think we like being escorted in and out of school?" I said. "How do you think we like not knowing who will hit us and when or where we'll be attacked?"

Later in *The New York Times*, Sammy Dean Parker and Kaye Bacon said that as a result of the meeting they now had a new attitude. One headline in the *Gazette* read: TWO PUPILS TELL OF CHANGE IN ATTITUDE ON SEGREGATION.

Sammy Dean Parker was quoted as saying, "The Negro students don't want to go to school with us any more than we want to go with them. If you really talk with them, you see their side of it. I think the NAACP is paying them to go."

When I read her statement, I realized Sammy hadn't understood at all our reason for attending Central High. I wondered where on earth she thought there was enough money to pay for such brutal days as I was enduring. I wouldn't know how much money to charge for all the good days I wasn't having in my old high school with friends who liked me. What price could anyone set for the joy and laughter and peace of mind I had given up?

I stayed in bed all day Sunday, telling myself I was ill, but the truth was I was partially suffering from downhearted blues. That meeting hadn't helped the integration at all. Those white students didn't understand. Even when Vince called for our regular Sunday date, I didn't give up my claim of illness. Snuggling down into the safety of my bed made me feel as though I were a carefree little girl who hadn't been to Central High and hadn't yet discovered that miracles don't happen exactly when and how you want them to.

In my diary, I wrote:

October 14, Monday

Flu, absent—Governor Faubus is still speaking out and causing turmoil. Quotes in daily papers make me know he will not let us rest.

Today Mother Lois brought home a new hi-fi. I guess she thought it would cheer up my sadness.

October 15, Tuesday

Flu—absent

With my head under the covers so Grandmother could not hear or see me, I cried myself to sleep. I know I am fighting for a good cause—and I know if I trust God I shouldn't cry. I will keep going, but will it really make a difference?

I feel like something inside me has gone away. I am like a rag doll with no stuffing. I am growing up too fast. I'm not ready to go back to Central and be a warrior just yet. I don't have any more strength. I want to stay right here, listening to Nat King Cole.

On Tuesday, October 15, my friends entered Central with only one soldier from the 101st as an escort. Once inside the school, only twenty-one National Guardsmen and nine 101st Airborne soldiers guarded them in the hallways.

A story in the Wednesday *Arkansas Gazette* was headlined: TWO NEGROES ILL. I thought it was funny to read about myself and Terry Roberts being out of Central High with the flu. By the time the paper printed the story, I was already back in class. According to that same article, Terry had said that things had been so bad for him the week before that he had almost decided to quit Central and go back to Horace Mann.

By the time I returned to school on Wednesday, things had deteriorated. The headlines that day read:

101ST DIVISION CUT BACK FORCE TODAY;
½ GOING BACK TO KENTUCKY

Until that time, when soldiers were taken away it was only to Camp Robinson—a stone's throw away. The announcement of their departure to Kentucky gave segregationists reason to celebrate, and it was evident in the students who bragged about their renewed hope of getting rid of us.

As I stepped into the hallway, just for an instant the thought of fewer troops terrified me. But the warrior growing inside me squared my shoulders and put my mind on alert to do whatever was necessary to survive. I tried hard to remember everything Danny had taught me. I discovered I wasn't frightened in the old way anymore. Instead, I felt my body muscles turn steely and my mind strain to focus. I had to take care of myself. I could really depend only on myself for protection.

A new voice in my head spoke to me with military-like discipline: Discover ink sprayed on the contents of your locker—don't fret about it, deal with it. Get another locker assigned, find new books, get going—don't waste time brooding or taking the hurt so deep inside. Kicked in the shin, tripped on the marble floor— assess the damage and do whatever is necessary to remain mobile. Move out! Warriors keep moving. They don't stop to lick their wounds or cry.

*   *   *

182

During early morning classes that day several students heck-
led me about Minnijean, saying that if she tried to take part in
their school activities there would be a big retaliation. Word had
gotten around school and to the Central High Mothers' League
that Minnijean would be participating in a student talent show.
Segregationists demanded that we not be allowed to participate
in any extracurricular activities.

"That nigger ain't gonna sing on our stage. My daddy says
he'll see her dead first." The boy shouting this ran past me,
knocking my books out of my arms. When I bent over to pick
them up, someone kicked me from behind and pushed me over.
I landed hard on my wrist. It felt broken.

"Okay. Get yourself up, and I'll get the books." It was a voice
I didn't recognize, speaking to me while students rushed past,
laughing and pointing as I lay in pain. An Arkansas National
Guard soldier was standing beside me, gathering my books and
speaking in a gentle tone.

"Can you get up? Try to get up on your feet as fast as you
can."

I tried to get to my feet, but my head was pounding and my
body ached.

"What the hell, gal, take my hand. You're gonna get us both
killed if you don't move. We ain't got no help." He took my
hand and boosted me upright. It hurt to stand on my ankle.
"Let's move outta here, right now!" He was pushing me faster
than my body wanted to go, but I knew he was right, I had
to move.

When we finally got to a safe spot, I thanked him, blinking
back hot tears. That soldier, whoever he was, stayed within full
sight of me for the rest of the day. He didn't say anything, but
whenever I looked for him, he was there. As I was leaving
school, he was standing in the hallway, slouching against the
wall like his buddies. But he had been kind to me, and I would
remember that not all members of the Arkansas National Guard
were of the same character.

That evening, during the meeting at Mrs. Bates's house, we
were told that within a few days we would no longer have the

jeep and station wagon to take us back and forth to school. We would have to set up car pools. I tossed and turned all night, wondering whether or not we could survive without our 101st guards and the station wagon escort.

By mid-October, there were fewer and fewer 101st guards and fewer Arkansas National Guardsmen. We quickly learned that the presence of the 101st had lulled us into a false sense of security. The segregationist students were just biding their time until they could make their move. As the guards were reduced in number, our attackers revved up a full campaign against us. The less visible the 101st, the more we suffered physical and verbal abuse.

JUDGE DAVIES DISMISSES SUIT FOR REMOVAL OF U.S. TROOPS;
STATE MAY FILE, FAUBUS SAYS
—*Arkansas Gazette*, Friday, October 18, 1957

That lawsuit had been filed by Margaret Jackson and the Central High Mothers' League. Segregationists continued to apply whatever pressure they could to get the troops reduced. Governor Faubus continued to bargain with President Eisenhower for our withdrawal from school and for an extension to begin integration sometime in the far distant future. Faubus's declarations provided a glimmer of hope that made segregationists feel their oats. We were suffering increased harassment inside the hallways and classrooms, and still the troops were dwindling day by day.

Although I saw some 101st soldiers around the school, Danny didn't seem to be there any longer. At first I looked for him in every corner, but finally I was so busy defending myself that looking for him was no longer the first thing on my mind.

In the days that followed, I neither understood nor controlled the warrior growing inside me. I couldn't even talk to Grandma India about the way I was feeling. It was a secret. As Samson had been weakened by a haircut, I thought I might lose my power if I spoke of it. I stopped complaining as much to my eight friends about the awful things segregationists were doing to me. I stopped trying to figure out what might happen the next moment, the next hour, the next day and focused intensely on right now.

I thought a lot about how to appear as strong as I could as I walked the halls: how not to wince or frown when somebody hit me or kicked me in the shin. I practiced quieting fear as quickly as I could. When a passerby called me nigger, or lashed out at me using nasty words, I worked at not letting my heart feel sad because they didn't like me. I began to see that to allow their words to pierce my soul was to do exactly what they wanted.

My conversations with my eight friends began to change, too. We joked less with each other, and there was considerably less talk about our hopes that the students might immediately begin to accept us. Instead, we exchanged information about how to cope: "Don't go down this hallway to get to the cafeteria, that's where the hit-and-run trippers wait for you." "Stay out of the third-floor doorway; boys with knives hang out there." "Don't exit that set of stairs; that's where the boys with the dynamite sticks always wait."

It was the kind of information warriors exchange to wage the battles they must win, or die. My energies were devoted to one goal—planning for my own safety and shielding myself from hurt. Even though I wasn't totally satisfied with the grades on my report card of October 17, I decided I had to make staying alive my priority.

October 20's newspaper carried an article saying that Clarence Laws, Southwest Regional Field Secretary for the NAACP, denied rumors that we nine were being paid to go to Central, or had been imported from the North to integrate Little Rock schools, or that our parents were planning to take us out of school.

On October 23, we left school without a guard and walked to the station wagon alone. On the morning of October 24, we walked to the front door once more without an escort. The evening headlines read:

Melba Pattillo Beals

NEGRO STUDENTS ENTER SCHOOL WITHOUT ESCORT
REDUCED TO SIX 101 AIRBORNE

My brother, Conrad, complained that I wouldn't play games with him—not even our favorite Monopoly. I realized he was right. Lately I had no time for play. Vince was complaining as well because I wasn't available to speak on the phone or to go out with him. My after-school time was filled with meetings and news people and sometimes just sitting silent in my room to ponder what would become of me. Central High integration was slowly destroying my life.

During one late October after-school meeting, we discussed the fact that President Eisenhower would not stop withdrawing 101st troops even though our parents and Mrs. Bates had sent a telegram informing him that opposition against us was more violent with each passing day. We discussed trying yet another approach to change the attitudes of school officials so they would take control of the hooligans.

The next day was a living hell. In addition to increased heckling in the hallways, it was the beginning of a series of experiences in my gym class I would not soon forget. It all started with a verbal barrage I tried to ignore.

"You're already black meat, and what is black meat? It's burned meat," said the lanky brunette, with a devilish gleam in her eyes, as she stood outside my shower space. I stood stark naked, my privacy invaded, while others joined her, leering and spouting insults. I was racking my brain, wondering what she was talking about, and then it came, the scalding water. I felt myself cry aloud as the sheet of steaming water spread pain across my shoulders and back. I was stunned, paralyzed by the cruelty of their act. Two other girls appeared just at that moment to shove me directly beneath the spray and hold me there.

I suddenly felt surging inside of me a strength that matched my determination. I grabbed my attackers' arms and pulled them in with me as close as I could. I let them feel my anger with my elbows, my feet, and with words that would take me to brimstone and hellfire later, but at least I'd have time to prepare. I was using some of the same language they used on me.

As the girls backed away, I emerged to find they had removed my clothing and books. There I was, scrambling about wearing only a towel and a bad attitude. When finally I found my outer clothing, it was stuffed in a corner, but my underwear was on the floor of another shower, soaking wet. I would freeze all day. I could look forward to damp spots seeping through to my outer garments. As I got dressed, my clothes irritated my scalded skin. It hurt to move.

Later in the day I encountered the "heel-walking committee." Groups of students would walk close up behind me and step on my heels, generating the most excruciating pain. I would walk faster, but they would catch up and continue doing it. After a while my heels were bleeding through my socks. When I went to the office for Band-Aids, the woman on duty turned up her nose and sneered. "If you can't stand an occasional tap on the heel, why don't you leave."

By the end of the day, I was exhausted from defending myself and trying to figure out what would come next. And I was beginning to have an uncontrollable urge to fight back.

On Monday, October 28, Mrs. Huckaby notified us in writing that we were to contact our parents to come to a meeting in School Superintendent Blossom's office, downtown, at 4:45 P.M. That last-minute request meant Mother Lois had to rush over from her teaching job in North Little Rock. But it was necessary, because we all hoped that meeting would signal the beginning of the school officials' willingness to do something about the incredible increase in attacks against us. I couldn't imagine what else they'd want to discuss.

18

AS WE CLIMBED THE STAIRS WITH OUR PARENTS TO THE MEETING in Superintendent Blossom's office, it was clear that we all had one thing on our minds—that school officials provide a concrete plan to stop the abuse by Central High's hard-core segregationist students.

"I'm angry enough to hunt bear without my shotgun," said one of the fathers. "These folks had best do something really big to show me they wanna make this integration work."

"I'm tired of them counting on us to make all the sacrifices," said another parent. "We need to know what they're willing to sacrifice."

Thirty minutes into that meeting, neither Blossom nor any of his people had addressed the issue we had told him we were anxious to discuss. Instead, all the school officials present were giving us the same song and dance about our not responding to our attackers in order to maintain peace. They were lecturing us on "the proper attitude" and the responsibility of our parents. There were no words from them about how they were going to take any responsibility for keeping students from abusing us.

"Excuse me," Mother Lois said, suddenly rising to her feet, interrupting Superintendent Blossom midsentence. I was fright-

188

ened to see her standing there so tiny, wringing her hands nervously. "What I want to know is whether or not you have any specific plans for protecting our children."

"That's none of your business," Blossom replied in a rude tone.

"Oh, I'd say it's very much my business." Mother's words came rapid-fire. Still he ignored her, continuing his rhetoric as before. Silence fell over the room. She interrupted him once more. "As parents we have a right to know how you will protect our children." He gave her neither an answer nor any acknowledgment that she had a right to ask such a question.

Instead, he continued his meaningless comments, ignoring her as she stood there for several minutes expecting him to answer her. Finally she took her seat. Her face was red with anger and embarrassment. I felt that by disrespecting Mother that way, the superintendent was disrespecting all of us seated in that room. I was very angry with the others, especially the fathers, who did not stand up and defend my mother. The humiliation and fear I felt so upset me that I couldn't consider anything that was said during the remainder of the meeting. Nevertheless, it was clear by the time we left for home that nothing had been resolved.

———

NINE NEGRO STUDENTS ENTER CENTRAL AT DIFFERENT DOOR
—*Arkansas Gazette*, Thursday, October 31, 1957

On Wednesday, with no sign of our military escorts, we decided to avoid the hecklers who were starting to greet us each morning. We arrived early and entered the Fourteenth and Park Street entrance, a block to the right of the front entry. We had determined that going in the front door presented more risks than it was worth.

The repeated recitation by Governor Faubus that our voluntary withdrawal and the departure of all troops was the only way to bring peace was reflected by a change in the students' attitudes. It was as though they counted on our getting kicked out at any moment. Those few who had earlier tried to reach out had obviously been pressured to turn away. One girl who happened to meet me alone in a rest room said that she and the other moderate white students were being harassed with telephoned threats and were being ostracized. It was evident that school officials and teachers were under more and more pressure from segregationists to help them get rid of us.

For me the most frightening events at school were the increased number of pep rallies and assemblies that came with the football season and the beginning of the holidays. At those times, I was surrounded by a sea of hostile faces and a chorus of hurtful words. There weren't enough teachers or guards on earth to corral the out-of-control students. We came to refer to the auditorium as the torture chamber.

I had grown to expect being elbowed, poked, and kicked, to have my hair pulled, to be punched in the back or trampled as I was entering or leaving the auditorium. But having glue doused on the back of my neck and in my ponytail was more unpleasant.

I was at first paralyzed by the terror I felt when during one assembly a boy thrust a knife at me. As I sat in a shadowy corner beneath the balcony overhang, he placed the blade against the right side of my face and whispered obscene threats. I surprised myself by biting down hard on his wrist, and then springing up out of my seat to find a teacher. But she wouldn't listen to my complaint.

"Both of you sit down right now. You're disturbing the others," she hissed, directing me back to my seat and returning her attention to the stage.

No sooner had she turned to leave when out of the corner of my eye I saw the flash of the steel blade as the boy thrust it at me once again. Only this time he gripped me even tighter. I felt the sharp blade shave the side of my cheek. No matter how I struggled, I couldn't break his hold. Once again, I bit down as hard as I could into his forearm, drawing blood. He quickly pulled back his arm, muffling his outcry. "A rabies shot, I'll need a rabies shot now," he growled at me.

The teacher listened impatiently to my second report and then said, "These children have tolerated a lot of upheaval." Even though she ignored me, I felt better because at least I wasn't a whining wimp anymore.

———

ALDERMAN ORDERS ARREST OF NAACP OFFICIALS
—*Arkansas Gazette*, Friday, November 1, 1957

The adults we counted on were showing ever more stress. Mrs. Bates's newspaper was being strangled economically. At the same time she and other NAACP officials across the state were under increased pressure from State Attorney General Bruce Bennett to turn over all records, including names, addresses, and phone numbers of members and contributors to the organization.

Bennett had, a few months before in August, filed a civil suit against the NAACP saying the organization had been doing business in Arkansas for seven years although it had only recently registered as a foreign corporation. He had early on begun to badger Mrs. Bates for information about all the members and contributors of the state's twenty-seven branches. It frightened us to see our allies being abused.

In my diary I wrote:

What will become of us if the NAACP is not strong. It feels as though segregationists are attacking from all sides. They know very well we count on Mrs. Bates and the local NAACP people as well as Mr. Marshall. If they're busy defending themselves, who will see after us?

During those first days of November, we found ourselves coping with yet another crisis brought on by insensitive Central High School officials. The tiger was their school mascot, and the Tiger Directory was a list of all the students' names, addresses, and telephone numbers. Despite our requests that our names and numbers not be listed and despite the fact that school officials had overwhelming evidence that our lives were in jeopardy, our information was nevertheless included. Yes, newspapers had printed the information before, but they had stopped. This new release summoned into action passive students who might up until then have thought twice about calling us. So of course we got more and more phone calls. Whether they were threats and vicious language or mere hang-ups, those calls took our time and energy.

I continued to yearn for the return of the 101st full-time. We were told that a couple of hundred soldiers remained at nearby Camp Robinson. Somehow, I figured that maybe, since things were so bad, they would come back to be with us every day—guarding us up close as they had in the beginning, but it wasn't happening. The next time I saw Danny, he said he didn't think they would return on a regular basis because the powers that be wanted us to stand alone. Those times when we were lucky enough to get our 101st guards were wonderful. We treasured their presence, as infrequent as it had become.

Sometimes we were guarded by the Arkansas National slobs, as we called the federalized soldiers, who, by then, had shown us in every way that they loathed the responsibility and didn't take it seriously. They had become visibly hostile toward us, sometimes whispering threats and taunting and teasing us when they got us alone. Segregationists were publicly urging them to abandon their duty stations rather than guard us.

On one of the first days of November, Minnijean arrived at my house after school to show me *Life* magazine. It had a full-page picture of my back in it. There I was, ponytail and all, saluting the flag. It wasn't the first time we'd seen ourselves in print or on television, but we giggled at the wonder of it all—Miss Minnijean and Miss Melba could now be seen on the pages of *Life, Look,* or *The New York Times*.

We did, however, begin to notice there was a price to be paid whenever we appeared in periodicals or on television; the next day the harassment inside Central would always increase.

As Minnijean and I spent time together that evening, I could tell she was beginning to be deeply affected by what was being done to her at Central High. She seemed especially vulnerable to the isolation we were all struggling to cope with. She had decided she would be accepted by white students if she could just show them how beautifully she sang. She was almost obsessed with finding an opportunity to perform her music on stage. She said she was definitely going to participate in a school program and had in fact already made inquiries about it.

Little did we know that even while we were discussing her performing in school programs, the Central High Mothers' League was preparing to make a bigger fuss than ever before to exclude her. With each passing day the furor about her wanting to participate was building. But their threats did not stop Minnijean. She was already waging yet another campaign to sing on stage. This time it was to sing "Tammy" in the talent show. It was as though these objections fueled her need to do what wasn't wanted.

I wondered whether or not she had considered that the audience would boo her off the stage. Did she figure they would be enraptured by her performance? I shuddered at the thought of what the students would say or do to her if she made it. But I could tell that her anxiety over the constant abuse we endured and sadness over being left out was clouding her view. She delighted in planning for the performance, announcing and displaying a joyful glee about the possibility of singing in front of the white kids.

When I talked to Ernie about my concerns, he brushed them aside. As usual, he was taking the situation in stride. Even when he was punched with punishing blows or was kicked to the floor, he kept a positive attitude. I liked his attitude even when I didn't agree with his view.

Like me, Thelma was very concerned about Minnijean. We talked about how we could convince her to stop pushing to participate. Each of us was hearing increasingly negative responses to her desire to do so. It was clear to us that both students and outsiders would take the opportunity to make a huge issue of her request.

Terry was philosophical about it: Let her try and she'll learn her lesson, once and for all. I could see Terry becoming more fatalistic about our predicament. His hopes that we could change people's minds were visibly reduced. He was nervous, not as cheerful, not humming his funny tunes.

Stress was beginning to tell on Gloria, too. She was clamming up, becoming solemn. I could almost see her mind working to try to set things right so she could keep going in her meticulous way.

Elizabeth had never fully regained her composure following her awful encounter with the mob. Continued harassment was also taking its toll of her. She reacted by becoming silent and withdrawn. When I discussed Minnijean's predicament with Elizabeth, she appeared alarmed and agreed that we ought not attract unnecessary attention to ourselves.

Carlotta strained to keep smiling. Although she often took a lot of heat, especially in gym class, she tried to make the best of it, as did Jeff. Like the two other boys, Jeff was taking a lot of brutal physical punishment. He was quick on his feet, but he often got trapped in gym class or in corners of the hall, where he was kicked and punched.

Whenever we compared notes, we all agreed: the students' attitudes had become polarized. We felt it would be best for Minnijean to back off, but none of us could talk her out of it. She was adamant. The more we pleaded, the more determined she seemed to become.

Only during fleeting moments did I allow myself to have fantasies of what it might be like to sing with the chorus or perform in the Thanksgiving program. My hopes of being a part of normal activities had long since faded. I refused to set myself up for disappointment. I simply wanted to make it through the year alive and uninjured. I resigned myself to devoting all my energy to that goal.

I was surprised when I was invited to speak to the students who attended chapel, a fairly safe corner of the school. It had been the one place where I had found brief moments of peace on those days when I arrived early enough to go there. I ago-

194

nized over the invitation, but finally Grandma made it easy for me. "This is your opportunity to witness."

"But what if they throw things?"

"In the house of the Lord? Surely not. These white folks aren't heathens. While you speak, they will come to understand you are all worshipping the same Lord." So I prepared my talk, but I kept my invitation to myself. I didn't want to hurt Minnijean's feelings, given the heroic effort she was making to convince school officials to allow her to sing on stage.

ARMY HAS ORDERS TO REMOVE TROOPS OF 101ST AT SCHOOL
—*Arkansas Gazette*, Tuesday, November 19, 1957

The 101st Airborne Troops were going back to Kentucky. My heart pounded as I raced through the article that told how Major General Edwin Walker, head of the Arkansas Military District, would head the force of about 225 men from the Arkansas National Guard. They would take full responsibility for enforcing the court order. In other words, we would now have to rely solely on them to keep us safe and alive. I sat paralyzed on the living room couch reading the article aloud once more as Grandma was organizing the family to prepare for our traditional Thanksgiving celebration. I consoled myself with the fact that there was no specific departure date for the 101st; maybe they meant after the first of the year. I would go on hoping that article was mistaken. Surely they couldn't really be leaving.

"Put that paper down girl, it's time." We had begun our holiday ritual. Grandma was desperately trying to wrestle Conrad's old train set away from him to give to the poor.

"Thanksgiving, son, that's time to our count blessings. We've gotta give deep this year because those benevolent white people who gave to our folks in years past are holding out on us to make us give up the integration."

White charity groups were breaking traditions by taking away their Thanksgiving gifts and threatening to take away Christmas as well. To make matters more difficult, they were taking away as many jobs from my people as they could and cutting credit at the local stores.

It was our tradition each year to sort through our toys and clothing at Thanksgiving and give away all the things we didn't need or use, as well as two things dear to us that we would especially like to keep. "Conrad, have you got that train boxed yet?"

"Not yet, Grandma."

"When, Conrad?" Mother said as she dried the dinner dishes and handed them to me to put away. She and Grandma had been trying all day to get Conrad to see things their way.

"Melba's giving away her favorite blouse," Grandma said. "And she's donating her favorite cord skirt and a pair of shoes." She glanced at Conrad to see whether or not her prodding was affecting his stingy attitude.

"Melba likes suffering and doing without; that's why she goes to Central. But why do I have to?"

"Where did you get a notion like that about your sister?"

"Clark said that's what his folks say because Sis stays in that white school being mistreated every day."

"Her staying there means she has made a promise that she intends to keep, because she told God she would and she doesn't want to let herself and God down," Mother Lois said, walking over to look Conrad in the eye. "So you must explain that to Clark the next time he inquires about your sister's motives."

"Yes, ma'am. But I'm not giving up the train. It's mine."

"Let's get down to basics, boy. If you don't ante up, you won't get any Thanksgiving dinner, and nobody will play Monopoly with you for a full week." Conrad's eyes got large and his forehead wrinkled as he let go of the train's engine and Grandma placed it in the gift box with our other contributions.

U.S. OFFICIALS DROP PLANS TO PROSECUTE AGITATORS AT SCHOOL—
WON'T PRESS ACTION AGAINST MOB LEADERS
—*Arkansas Gazette*, Thursday, November 21, 1957

Based on an assurance by local authorities that they would maintain order, the federal government announced it would back off and not even prosecute segregationist mob leaders.

The segregationists' leaders were celebrating their victories, and the students at school were letting us know about their triumph. At the same time, Governor Faubus was saying in print and on the air that "the withdrawal of federal troops is distasteful because the Arkansas Guard will be left with the distasteful task of enforcing the integration."

He said he "would not take any state police forces or National Guardsmen to transport anybody to school or guard them while they were there. For Arkansas Guardsmen to do what the federal government ordered would be unfair because they didn't enlist to enforce integration but to defend their country in a time of need."

At school that day, Minnijean and I talked about how frightened we were because, even though the harassment was getting worse, we were seeing fewer and fewer uniformed guards of any description. There were always rumors about FBI men being all over the place. Sure enough, we would occasionally see men who fit our fantasies of what FBI men should look like, but they never stopped to help us.

To add to our distress, on that same day two state courts demanded that the NAACP's records be made public, and six men who were arrested for rioting during our first days at Central High School were cleared of all charges. On November 23, an article described how Judge Harry Robinson suspended fines of two men found guilty of rioting.

And even as our problems with segregationists multiplied yet again, Minnijean focused on her audition for the glee club and Christmas show. She had worked herself up into a real dither. Time and time again, Thelma and I had tried to talk her out of participating, but she wouldn't listen. Moments before the tryouts got underway, I stood in the doorway of the auditorium nervously wringing my hands as Minnijean tried to register.

Mrs. Huckaby wore a pleasant smile as she explained to Minnijean that the day to register for the tryouts had long since passed, and they couldn't violate the rules for her. We knew at once that she had been tricked. Had school officials been sincere about offering Minnijean the opportunity, they would have been clear about the terms for participating. Blinking back tears, Minnijean turned to us, then walked away. Thelma and I trailed behind trying our best to console her.

TEACHERS, STUDENTS SAY CENTRAL HIGH SEETHES
WITH UNDERCURRENTS
—*Arkansas Gazette*, Sunday, November 24, 1957

Six reporters had been dispatched to talk to anyone connected with the school. What they found was what we already knew: as the reporter said, it was a time of tension and testing. There was widespread talk of gangs dedicated to making trouble for us when the troops left.

Those interviewed said they already made as much trouble for us as they could. However, we were described as students who studied and moved about most of the time in almost total isolation from our two thousand white classmates, because the whites who once tried to befriend us had been intimidated either by social ostracism or by threats.

Reading the article made me shudder, but it also helped me know we weren't imagining things. It was indeed getting more and more difficult to survive inside Central. We now had it confirmed from the most reliable source—hard-core segregationists themselves. And as far as I could tell, there was absolutely nothing we could do about it.

On Monday, November 25, I prepared myself to speak to 250 students gathered for Central High's early morning chapel service. As I walked toward the front of the room and faced those white students, all staring at me, my knees felt weak and the back of my neck was tight. I stood at a podium in a room filled with people who didn't relish my speaking to them.

Taking a deep breath, I began the talk I had practiced in front of the mirror and in front of Grandma and Mama. The light from the window at the back of the room was my focus. Mother Lois had said never to look any single member of the audience in the eye when you're speaking. At first, I garbled some of the words, and then, as I remembered Grandma India's advice, I calmed down. She had said, "God's speaking. You're merely the instrument he chooses at this time. God is a wonderful speaker, so you have absolutely nothing to be nervous about." I didn't speak about integration or say things about us or them— I just talked about God and how he cares for each of us.

At first I could tell by the students' expressions that they didn't like what I was saying. Some frowned while others contorted their faces to show their contempt. Many had perfectly blank looks, but a few listened intently and nodded their heads in agreement. Afterward, two people came up to congratulate me and ask why I had a Northern accent and used such correct English.

"Northern accent, did they really ask you about that?" Mother Lois grinned as I described my speaking. "You tell them your mama's an English teacher, and in this house we speak only the King's English."

We were discussing my day, sitting in our robes at the dining room table, after dinner and baths, playing Monopoly. The house was festive, and we were surrounded by the aroma of mincemeat and sweet potato pies cooking in the oven.

"Any flying objects?"

"Actually, some of them were very nice. You were right, Grandma." She didn't look up. She was preoccupied with examining her next move on the board. We were already resigned to the fact that she would skunk us all once again.

"Right, how so?" she mumbled, not taking her attention off the game for even one instant.

"Well, for just that moment, I felt we had something in common, our love of the Lord. I think they felt it, too, because some of them smiled and spoke to me."

"Someday they'll have the courage to be nice to you outside that room of worship."

"I don't think so, Grandma, because they would have to take so much criticism from their friends and families."

"This year is different, it won't always be this way." She rolled the dice, bought the last available property, and once again we'd all been trounced by our sweet Grandma, the Monopoly Champ.

When Mrs. Bates telephoned to say the nine of us would be gathering for an "official" Thanksgiving dinner to be held at her house Tuesday evening, before the holiday, she mentioned that there would be a news conference.

I cringed at the thought. Whenever there was special press coverage on us, the abuse we later suffered at Central was in direct proportion to the size and quality of the story printed or aired.

When Mother and I arrived at Mrs. Bates's home for the Thanksgiving dinner, I knew even more people than usual were there, because we couldn't find a place to park. When I entered the spacious living room, there was standing room only. I had never seen so many people, most of them reporters, squeezed into that space under hot glaring lights.

At the center of the room, some of the other nine students, dressed in Sunday best, were sitting at a table set with the same care Grandma used on holidays: linen and lace and silver and a beautifully prepared bird. Mrs. Bates directed me to a seat, and I squeezed past Jeff and Gloria to get to my place.

Even more reporters with more cameras and equipment packed into the room as we tried to give the impression of having a normal meal. Some of the others were reviewing speeches they had prepared. I hadn't prepared anything, because by now the art of giving an interview was second nature, or at least that's what I thought. Once the cameras were rolling and the microphones recording, the questions began to fly.

When Mrs. Bates asked, "Do you kids want white meat or dark meat?" I spoke without thinking: "This is an integrated turkey." The annoyed expression on her face matched the one on Mother's, letting me know that maybe I should have prepared a speech. The reporters began snickering as they posed a series of questions on turkeys and integration, calling on me by name to answer. My palms began sweating, and my mouth turned dry. I hadn't meant to put my foot in my mouth. I didn't want the others to think I was trying to steal the spotlight, but once I had spoken out of turn, "integrated turkey" became the theme.

"You'll live to regret that statement, Melba," Mother said as we were driving home. I knew she was agonizing over the consequences of my frivolity. She was right. I would suffer.

There came a day just before Thanksgiving break, when Danny broke the rules again and came close up to talk to me. He wouldn't say whether or not he was leaving for good, but he behaved in a strange way—saying over and over again, "Take care of yourself, you hear me. Don't bend over to pick up any books or walk in dark corners." He winked and smiled as he backed away, giving me a military salute. I stood frozen in my tracks, holding back the tears.

Over and over again, I asked him if he were going away for good, but he wouldn't tell me. "Just mind your p's and q's." He turned on his heels. I couldn't admit to myself it was really true. I turned away and ran in the opposite direction, never looking back—never turning to let him see the tears in my eyes.

From that moment on, whenever I thought about Danny and the 101st being gone for good, I pushed the idea out of my mind because I couldn't bear to deal with it. I just had to pretend it wasn't so, even though some part of me kept saying I truly had to fend for myself now.

My real Thanksgiving at home was a special day of peace and joy. It was wonderful being with all my relatives, and I was able to convince them not to talk about Central High. For just that day, I felt normal, and I hoped that my life could be that way soon. I came face to face with reality later that evening as I read the *Gazette* headlines: LAST OF 225 GI'S LEAVE SCHOOL;

ARKANSAS NATIONAL GUARD IN CHARGE. The article said the 101st troops had left the day before.

Thanksgiving night I wrote in my diary:

> Danny and the others have truly gone. He didn't even say good-bye. I will always remember this man. How could I forget his name? I will never know if he only behaved that kindly because he was a great soldier or a good person or both.
>
> It doesn't matter. He was wonderful.
>
> I want to remember the names of the other nice 101st soldiers as well—Jody, Marty, Mex, and Goggles.
>
> I wish Danny had told me he was leaving forever. Although I don't know how I could have thanked him in words. I might have cried, and he wouldn't have liked that. I never thought I would have tears in my eyes over some white man. I don't think I'll ever see him again. Thank you, Danny.

On Friday, November 29, the *Gazette* headline brought more bad news, especially for Minnijean:

MOTHERS' LEAGUE HEAD PROTESTS NEGRO'S PART IN CHS TALENT PROGRAM

The Mothers' League of Central High School has issued a protest on behalf of their organization against a Negro girl's participation in a talent program sponsored by Central High School.

The article went on to name Minnijean Brown specifically and to say that we should not be allowed to participate in any extra-curricular activities. That night, Grandmother added to my worry list. "President Eisenhower's had a slight stroke," she said. "We gotta pray for him quick."

I knew the President was important in my life. If things got rough inside Central, I needed him to be alive and well so he could send the troops back. Mother said we should send him a telegram of hope and prayer, and so we did.

I spent much of the day agonizing over how much worse things could get on Monday, what with the paper's printing my "integrated turkey" line and announcing the final departure of the 101st.

19

WE WONDERED HOW THE *GAZETTE* EDITORS HAD COME TO THAT CON-
clusion since they didn't have anyone inside the school to see
us being kicked or inked or spat upon or scalded in the showers.
They were like so many of the adults around us, content to
pretend for the moment that all was well as we began classes
at Central High on December 2. But we knew better. Our day-
to-day experience showed us that the situation was worsening.

On that day, Minnijean, Thelma, and I rode in a car pool to
school. Once again, Minnijean talked enthusiastically about her
hopes of appearing on stage in yet another Central High program. Sometimes her enthusiasm even sparked a flickering hope
in me that we could be included in the holiday festivities springing up all around us.

We heard only bits and pieces of what was going on, but still
it all seemed to be so much bigger and more exciting than anything we'd seen at our old school. At Central there was money
for costumed plays and lavish stage productions and parties in

fancy hotels. They were doing all the things I'd seen in magazines or on television.

When on a rare occasion someone ventured to explain to us what was going on, students nearby would draw them aside and chastise them. I felt like a child peeking in the window of the candy store. I hungered for more details of the activities I was excluded from. I put together snippets of conversation as one does a puzzle, anxious to see the final picture. I would forever have an empty spot in my heart when I thought about Christmas of my junior year.

We nine had been very active in our former school—choral groups, honor society activities, Scouts, sports, and especially Christmas pageants. I felt the loss of that participation deeply, and I could tell the others did as well. And now we weren't even invited to holiday parties with our old school friends. Some of them feared for their safety when we were around—others didn't agree with what we were doing and refused to have anything to do with us. Still others didn't mean us any harm; it was a case of "out of sight, out of mind."

I consoled myself by believing it was probably for the best that I was so preoccupied with staying alive at Central. That meant I didn't have as much time to think about how lonely I was.

When I heard Minnijean talking about joining in, I wished her well, but underneath it all I knew she had gotten her hopes up too high. She was being targeted because of her persistence. And thanks to my Thanksgiving comment, so was I.

"Do all niggers eat integrated turkeys?" one boy shouted, putting his foot out to trip me in the hallway on the way to my first class.

"Ooooops," I said as I stepped on his foot, hard. "Oh, excuse me." I grinned. His face reddened. The subject of the turkey was brought up many more times by the end of the day and not in a friendly fashion. The only thing that kept me going was counting the days until Christmas vacation.

I could see that surviving was wearing all of us down. Thelma, who had always managed her heart defect, was forced to rest much more often, squatting down close to the floor, her head bowed to catch her breath. Ernie wasn't smiling quite as much. He was getting a wrinkle line in his forehead. I teased him about being our senior member and showing his age.

Carlotta had slowed down. All along, the 101st had called her "the roadrunner" or "speedy," and her agility had sometimes protected her from would-be attackers. Now she was a bit jumpy and no longer spoke of wanting to join the athletic events at Central. Minnijean was visibly agitated and jittery, heartbroken that she would not be included in any performances and feeling more and more trapped by the edict that no matter what was said or done to us, we could not retaliate.

Terry seemed jaded and speculated about whether or not we would last the year. Gloria and Elizabeth were quiet and pensive like Jeff. Each one of us talked of how much we looked forward to the upcoming two weeks of Christmas vacation when we could stay home and recharge our batteries. And in our weakest moments when we stood with physical wounds or bruises to our spirits, there was even talk that the Christmas break might be an opportunity to let go of our dream and choose another school.

As I entered Central a few days before my December 7 birthday, I suspected that the glaring headlines in the *Arkansas Democrat* the previous evening would be flaunted in our faces. The report said the troops that guarded us had cost taxpayers $3.4 million. Needless to say, we had that figure pushed in our faces over and over before the day was done.

But the *Gazette* headlines told the story that gave real cause for alarm that day:

JUDGE RESETS TRIAL ON NAACP LEADER

The vice-president of the North Little Rock chapter of the NAACP was being charged with not making records available.

MRS. BATES FINED $100 BY ROBINSON

The state president of the NAACP was fined $100 yesterday in Little Rock Municipal Court for failure to supply informa-

206

tion on the NAACP requested by the city under a new ordinance.

BENNETT NOTICES SERVED ON NAACP

Three more officers of the NAACP have been served notices to supply information to the city under the Bennett Ordinance.

City officials continued to harass the NAACP leaders just as the students were harassing us at school. My days inside Central were now graded by the severity of the pain I endured. Two huge boys with flattops and sideburns had begun a full-time mission of making my days miserable. Each morning they stood in front of my homeroom door to greet me first thing. "Good morning, nigger—aren't you'all gonna talk some of that coon jab you speak?"

I mustered the coldest glare I could manage, determined not to show how much they really frightened me. They followed me from class to class, walking up close, stomping my heels, and littering my trail with flying objects, punches, and degrading catcalls. By the fifth day, I was getting rattled. But I knew I had to endure with grace, because nothing could make them go away except a fair-minded teacher who witnessed their antics and took action on my behalf. I had little hope of that happening.

By the tenth day, their nonstop torture made me feel as if I were losing my mind. I had to keep telling myself what Grandma said: I couldn't ever lose my mind because God is my mind. Still, I imagined I had one of those machine guns television gangsters use. I would fire round after round over their heads to frighten the living daylights out of them. I shook my head to clear my thoughts. I would have to do more prayer for them and for me. I knew guns were forbidden even in my thoughts.

At the same time I dreaded my English teacher's choice for a book report assignment—*The Adventures of Huckleberry Finn*. She had assigned one of the most radical segregationists to present his report in front of the class. In an annoyingly loud voice he repeated the words "Nigger Jim" at least seventeen times. After each time, he paused to eyeball me with a devilish grin and wait for the reaction of other snickering students. At the end of his report, he curtsied to applause.

I was overcome with the thought of my hands around his throat, squeezing tight. To stave off the anger bubbling inside me, I wrote the Twenty-Third Psalm as fast as I could. Just as I was asking God to forgive me for so despising any of his children, one of the boys passed my seat and kicked my ankle. I had to bite my lip to keep from crying aloud at the pain. My ankle was swelling fast. I waited until everyone left the classroom before I tried to walk. Limping as best I could, I struggled to get up the stairs to my next class. I couldn't be late for fear of getting a tardy slip.

We were well aware that school officials were waiting for any excuse to kick us out. That point was hammered home to us during meetings with the NAACP. Repeatedly we were told, "Don't give anyone the slightest opportunity to accuse you of being out of line. Don't be late, don't talk back, watch your decorum, watch your grades. Complain only when something is injurious to your health, or life-threatening."

All the while, a deep yearning for human contact was growing inside me. I had nobody to talk to from 8:20 each morning when I said good-bye to my friends until the bell rang for lunch. I longed for all my old school friends, for the laughter and conversations we had had about the latest fashions, songs on the hit parade, or newspaper headlines. I imagined how it would feel to say hello to the white students and to have them answer with kind words. I longed to say, "Hello, how are you? I like your blouse. What's going on with you?" I longed for someone to acknowledge that I was alive by saying something pleasant to me, and allowing me to say something back.

It was frustrating to have people so close, have them chatting to each other while saying absolutely nothing to me, and never even looking me in the eye. Occasionally students stood or sat close enough to touch, talking over and around me as though I didn't exist. It was a very painful insult I didn't know how to combat. They were treating me as if I were invisible. Sometimes when a classmate said something funny, I would smile and even laugh out loud, forgetful for just one instant of my predicament.

"We weren't talking to you, nigger," they would say. Jolted back to reality by their cruelty, I would catch myself, neutralize my expression to hide my feelings, and stare straight ahead.

"Nigger," I would whisper to remind myself. That's all I am to them. They don't see me as a real person. There even came a moment when I pinched myself to see if I was really there. So many times I wanted to shout, "I'm Melba, don't you see me? I play the piano, I can make blouses, I can write poems . . . and I sing." When I felt I couldn't hold it in anymore, I talked to Grandma India.

"So you say you feel neglected because the white folks are ignoring you."

"Yes, ma'am, I really do." I took a seat at the kitchen table.

"Let me heat up that milk for you; it's a mite chilly in here." Grandma smiled and stroked my hand as she took the cup and walked over to the stove. She remained silent as though she were rearranging her words just for me while she turned to put jelly-bean eyes onto the faces of the freshly baked gingerbread men in the pan resting on top of the counter. And then she turned to look me in the eye as she said, "Did you count on those Central people for your spiritual food before you went there?"

"Well, . . . uh . . . no, ma'am, but . . ."

"Have you been waiting on them to treat you good and tell you you're all right so you'll know you're all right?"

"Uh, well, uh . . ." She had me. When she explained it, it didn't sound the same as when I felt it.

"Does God know your value?"

"Yes, ma'am, He does. But I'm lonely for humans."

"You can never in this lifetime count on another human being to keep you from being lonely. Nobody can provide your spiritual food . . . not your mama, not your grandma, not your brother, not your 101st guards, not your boyfriend, and certainly not your husband."

"It's so hard sometimes. I don't know if I can make it."

"Patience is a virtue, my child."

I felt my teeth grind and my jaw tighten as anger welled up inside me. Grandma read my thoughts as she always had. "Anger brings defeat," she told me. "If you fight back, you have a battle, and you will be the loser."

Grandma walked over to take the second pan of gingerbread men from the oven. I thought about how anxious I had been over the past few days, anxious to get the whole thing over with, anxious for revenge against the two boys who had been harassing me. I had even imagined threatening them with a gun. Grandma's answer had not quelled my anger. "Fighting back is never the solution," she continued.

"But I'm so angry I'm afraid it's gonna swell up and explode."

"Not likely." She turned to give me her full attention. "I want you to read about Gandhi," she said, walking closer to me and touching my cheek with her hand. "You read slow and take it all in. You think about all he accomplished without violence or anger."

"Gandhi, yes, ma'am." I knew about Gandhi, about his courage even in the face of people beating up on him and calling him ugly names. I didn't think I was that strong and pure.

"Those segregationists are counting on you to fail. Go ahead, hit back, make them happy."

"Your grandmother is right," Mother Lois said as she entered the kitchen and threw her jacket over the chair. "You hit back every day you get through. You kick them every week you get through. And if you make it through the year, you've hit them with the biggest blow of all."

20

"SWEET SIXTEEN?" HOW COULD I BE TURNING SWEET SIX-
teen in just a few days and be a student at Central High, I
thought as I entered the side door of the school. Looking
around, I wanted to take care that no one would bang me on
my head or trip me up. I had relished so many dreams of
how sweet my sixteenth year would be, and now it had arrived, but I was here in this place.

As I walked deeper into the dim passageway, I thought about
how I had always hoped that my sixteenth birthday would be
second only to my wedding day as the most perfect moment of
my life. I had planned every detail of the celebration, beginning
at school with my friends, a party at home with a new dress,
red and white balloons all over the house, and "Sixteen Can-
dles" playing on the hi-fi. All my friends would arrive, and I
would have my first real date and my first kiss.

Sixteen had always seemed the magic age that signaled the
beginning of freedom, when Mama and Grandma might let
loose their hold and let me go out with my friends on pre-dates.
But with the integration, I was nowhere near being free. And
in the midst of everything else, I'd almost forgotten my own
birthday. I hadn't even begun preparations.

Sixteen was also going to be my debut year—I had planned

to launch my campaign to become a popular girl about school. I would run for student council president maybe. I would perform on stage—sing the songs of Dinah Washington in school talent shows. Maybe they'd like my singing so much that I'd get a recording contract and be able to help Mama and Grandma so they wouldn't have to work so hard. None of that was going to happen now—nobody would let me even say "good morning" at Central, let alone sing on stage.

"Hey, nigger, . . . you here again?" A boy's voice pulled me from my thoughts. A strong hand grabbed my wrist and doubled my arm up behind my back, like a policeman arresting a criminal. Frantically I looked for a teacher or guard. There was none.

"Hey, we got us a nigger to play with." He was shouting to his friends. Soon I'd have several of them on me. I struggled against him, but it was no use. Then I remembered I'd always been told, "If a fellow's got so little manhood he'd hit a woman, it's up to that woman to relieve him of what few morsels of his masculinity remain." I bent my knee and jammed my foot backward, up his crotch.

"Damn you, bitch," he shouted. "You'll be a dead nigger before this day is over."

Grabbing my purse, I raced down the hall, leaving my textbooks behind. I felt the power of having defended myself. I walked up the stairs to homeroom, only to be greeted by the same two boys who had been taunting me every day. I squared my shoulders and glared at them as I whispered, "I will be here tomorrow and the next day and the next."

THE NINE WHO DARED
New York Post, Thursday, December 5, 1957

Newspapers across the country started carrying a series of articles and profiles on the nine of us. Central High segregationists used the details to taunt us. The articles gave specific information on what our homes were like, our backgrounds, our

212

hobbies, our aspirations—all there was to know about us. I began to regret that exposure. Students didn't let up for one minute chirping on about my folks, my mother's teaching, and things I considered personal and sacred.

When the nine of us got together to compare notes, we discovered we were all facing an increasing barrage of injurious activities. What was noticeably different was the frequency and the organized pattern of harassment. Teams of students appeared to be assigned specific kinds of torture. One team concentrated on slamming us into lockers, while another focused on tripping us up or shoving us down staircases; still another concentrated on attacks with weapons. Another group must have been told to practice insidious harassment inside the classrooms. Still others worked at entrapment, luring the boys into dark corners or the girls into tight spots in isolated passageways. Some continued to use the showers as a means of abuse.

At the same time I was feeling alarmed about rumors of segregationist training programs to sharpen the skills of hooligans inside school. I was also increasingly worried about Minnijean. She was waging yet another battle with school officials to get permission to appear with the choral group in the Christmas program. No matter how much Thelma and I tried to convince her to let go of the idea, she wouldn't give up the notion that if she could perform, somehow the white students would see she was talented and therefore accept her.

Perhaps because of that determination, Minnijean was receiving more than her share of daily name-calling, kicking, and hitting, but she was suffering in yet another way. She somehow had more faith than we did in school officials. She continued to count on them to respond with compassion to her reports of being mistreated. It was as though she couldn't believe what she was seeing, so she had to test them to be certain they were really as inhuman as they seemed. The pressure she felt was sapping all her energy.

She had also allowed herself to be sucked into the game I called "herky, jerky, or now I speak to you, now I don't." Occasionally, really vicious students would make overtures to us;

they would smile or say "hello" for a few days in a row, pretending they had had a change of heart and were now our dearest friends. Just as we were growing to trust them, anxious for the connection, they would ignore us or make us the object of ridicule amid a group of their friends. Sometimes their overtures were intended to make us trust them so they could lead us into traps where we'd be physically abused. But most often it was for the sheer pleasure of watching the pain we endured when they harshly rejected us.

When one girl pretended to befriend Minnijean, only to betray her a short time later, Minnijean was crushed. She cried in front of school officials. That's when I knew she must be on the edge, because it wasn't like her to show her vulnerability in front of white people. With each passing day I watched as she grew more fragile.

I fretted about Minnijean as I plunged into my birthday party plans, but the more I tried to console her, the less she listened. She was the only one of my eight Central friends I had invited to my party, because I wanted to escape all thoughts of being an integration person. I made her promise not to talk about Central in front of our Horace Mann friends.

Not inviting the others made me feel guilty; but had the eight come, I knew I would have been separate—one of the Little Rock Nine and not just plain Melba—a member of my old group. I counted on reconnecting to my friends from my former school. I wanted them to accept me, to take me back into their fold. I had personally called or left messages with the parents of all the people on my guest list.

On the morning of my birthday, Saturday, I felt relieved when Minnijean called to say she couldn't come after all because she had a family event that day. Maybe with only me there, I could fade into the group and just this once be one of them.

Vince was the first to arrive, looking a little ill at ease. "Good evening, birthday girl," he said, handing me a small box with a bow. I hadn't seen him in a while. I'd almost forgotten how light-skinned he was. With his dark shiny hair piled high and his sideburns, he resembled those sideburners at Central.

"Thanks, I'm glad you came," I said, as my mind worked hard to separate the way he looked from the images of the boys who treated me so badly at Central. Vince is one of my people, no matter how white he looks, I told myself. I tried to think about the first date we had and to focus on how much I had liked being with him.

"Long time no see," Vince said as I led him into the living room. "You never return my calls."

He was right. Somehow the whole integration thing had even dulled my desire for daydreams about him. He had become lost in the shuffle—an afterthought, but I couldn't tell him that. "I think about you," I told him, "especially when Grandma goes to the wrestling matches. I wanted to call." He nodded his head, but he didn't look like he believed me.

As we continued polite but strained talk I kept my eyes on the clock. I unwrapped his gift, squealing with delight at the tiny gold hoop earrings. Mama and Grandma made several trips to bring food in, then take it out for warming, then bring it back. After an hour, when no other guests had arrived, Conrad insisted we begin eating.

The explanation came when my old friend Marsha phoned to say she wouldn't be coming, but she'd drop off my birthday present the next day. I had counted on Marsha's coming, she was kind of the leader of the group. If she didn't come, I worried that nobody else would either. Then she confirmed my worst fears. She explained that another friend, Ann, was giving her annual Christmas party, and most of the people I invited would be going there. But I knew that wouldn't begin before eight. When I asked why they couldn't stop by beforehand, there was a long silence, and then she said, "Melba, the truth is we're all afraid to come to your house."

"Afraid," I mumbled nervously.

"Sure, some of us get those same calls you get from those crazy white people saying they're gonna bomb your house. One of you'all already got bombed; what's her name, Carlotta, had a bomb under her porch. And that Mrs. Bates, she's had several. What's to keep them from bombing your house tonight while we're all there?"

"Why didn't you say so earlier, when I called?"

"I didn't wanna hurt your feelings. You gotta get used to the fact that you'all are just not one of us anymore. You stuck your necks out, but we're not willing to die with you."

"Marsha, I thought you were my friend." I heard my voice get loud as anger rose in me. "At least you could have told me there was another party going on," I shouted into the receiver, slamming it down.

My feelings were doubly hurt. No one bothered to tell me to move my party to another date, and worse yet, they were having the biggest Christmas party of the season without inviting me.

Even though I felt so embarrassed I could die, I kept smiling, trying to pretend to Vince that I wasn't brokenhearted about the empty room we sat in with all those balloons on the ceiling and all that food getting cold on the dining room table.

"Let's turn on the TV now, since nobody's coming. That just means more food for us." Conrad's voice sounded like he was speaking through a booming microphone as he burst into the room. I felt myself cringe as I watched Vince's face turn red.

"Shush your mouth, boy, and get back into that kitchen." Grandma was trying her best not to look disappointed. But I could see she felt sad for me. I moved toward the dining room and started taking things to the kitchen. I caught Grandma unaware. I could see there was moisture in her eyes.

"Don't worry about the party, Grandma. It doesn't matter," I said, touching her shoulder.

"You just sit yourself down and entertain that young man."

"He doesn't want to be entertained. He wants to go to Ann's Christmas party where everybody is. He's asked me to go with him." I was hoping that since it was my birthday they would make an exception and allow me to go with Vince.

"How can we allow you to go out that way, in public? Don't you see those two white devils parked in their car across the street? Mutt and Jeff are just waiting for us to make a mistake so's they can hang you. We couldn't rest easy with you out at night that way."

"Even on my birthday?"

"Especially on your birthday. This day reminds us of how important you are to us. Now, you invite Vince to sit a while. We'll have a nice evening playing games and all."

But Vince clearly wanted to move on to Ann's party. He had promised he would go, and he wanted to be with our friends— only they weren't our friends anymore. They were his. I saw him to the door and stood in the doorway looking at Mutt and Jeff's car parked beneath the streetlight. Grandma was right. It wasn't safe. The integration had stolen my sixteenth birthday.

Later that night before I sobbed into my pillow, I wrote:

> *Please, God, let me learn how to stop being a warrior. Sometimes I just need to be a girl.*

STEP UP IN RUMORS, INCIDENTS, COMPLAINTS NOTED AT SCHOOL
—*Arkansas Gazette*, Saturday, December 14, 1957

ARMY TO CUT GUARD FORCE AT CENTRAL HIGH SCHOOL BY 432 MEN
—*Arkansas Gazette*, Saturday, December 14, 1957

With four days to go before the Christmas holidays, we were very aware of a last-minute drive to get us out of school before the new year. Flyers and cards appeared saying "Two, four, six, eight, we ain't gonna integrate—no, not in '58." There was lots of talk about how we wouldn't come back when the new semester started.

Meanwhile, Minnijean continued to bang her head against that stone wall trying to get permission to participate in the Christmas activities. She could not explain why, but it was as though she were driven. When Principal Matthews once again turned down her request to sing with the glee club in the Christmas show, she balked.

Her mother requested a meeting with assistant principals Powell and Huckaby along with Principal Matthews and Mrs. Bates. Even after that confrontation, they turned her down, but she refused to take "no" for an answer. Students used all the flack over Minnijean's persistence as another reason to taunt us and to escalate their campaign against her. She had shown herself vulnerable by displaying her temper and her pain, and by letting them know how badly she wanted to participate. That was all they needed. They worked hard at getting her to blow her fuse.

By that time, we were all suffering from extreme fatigue as we marked our calendars and counted down the moments before the blissful two weeks of Christmas vacation. Most of all I looked forward to feeling safe, to having fun with maybe a party or two, and lots of lounging in front of the television—that was my plan.

Grandma had already begun shopping, hiding gifts, and testing the Christmas lights so she could replace burnt-out bulbs. She had also begun making dough for Christmas cookies and placing it in the freezer. Mother Lois was eyeballing trees so we'd choose the perfectly shaped one.

On Tuesday, December 17, when we had one more day to go before vacation, five of us entered the cafeteria. Lunchtime was always a hazard, and recently even more so. I had been avoiding the cafeteria, eating my sandwich alone in any safe place I could find. The cafeteria was such a huge place, with so many of our attackers gathered at one time. There were no official-looking adults or uniformed Arkansas National Guardsmen inside the cafeteria. Without fail, we knew we could expect some form of harassment.

As always on Tuesday the hot lunch was chili, which Minnijean loved. So while I took my seat with the others, she went to get in line to buy her chili. Ernie emerged from the line ahead of her and sat down at our table. As Minnijean made her way back toward us, her tray loaded down with a big bowl of chili, we saw her hesitate. She had to inch her way through a tight spot where mostly boys sat at tables on either side of her path. She had stopped dead in her tracks. We all froze, realizing she must be in real trouble. We could see two boys near her—one directly in her path. Something awful was happening, but there was no way any of us could do anything to rescue her. We had been instructed that in such instances we were never to move toward the person in danger for fear of starting a riot.

I was panic-stricken. Minnijean was being hassled by those boys. Snickering among themselves and taunting her, they had pushed a chair directly in front of her. For a long moment, she stood there patiently, holding her tray high above their heads.

It was all I could do to hold on to my chair and not go to help her. Like a broken record, the words played over and over in my head—intervening on her behalf would blur the lines between who was the victim and who was the person at fault. If other white students joined the melee to rescue the other side, we'd have a brawl. They outnumbered us at least two hundred to one. Still, I wanted to go to her, move the chair, take her tray, tell her to back up and go another way, do something, anything.

As more and more people realized something was brewing, the chatter in the cafeteria quieted down. I could tell Minnijean was trapped and desperate, and very fast running out of patience. She was talking back to the boys in a loud voice, and there was jostling all around her.

Frantically I looked around to see if there were any adults nearby who could be trusted to help. We had come to believe that the vice-principal for girls, Mrs. Huckaby, made some efforts to be fair during these situations, but she was nowhere in sight. I beckoned to Minnijean to go around her hasslers, but she was standing perfectly still. It was as though she were in a trance, fighting within herself.

Later, she would explain that the boys had been taunting her, sticking their feet in the aisle to trip her, kicking her, and calling her names. But we were not close enough to see details of the dilemma she faced. All we saw was her wavering as though she were trying to balance herself—and then her tray went flying, spilling chili all over two of the boys.

Everyone was stunned, silent for a long moment. Her attackers sat with astonished looks on their faces as greasy chili dripped down over their heads. All at once, our people who were serving food behind the counter began to applaud. This was greeted by an ominous silence, and then loud voices, all chattering at once, as the chili-covered boys stood up. I wondered whether we'd ever get out of there alive. Suddenly, a school official showed up, and Minnijean was whisked away, while we were hustled out of the cafeteria.

Word got around school immediately. I could tell there was an undercurrent of unrest among the student body. More clusters of people gathered along the hallway chanting, "Two, four, six, eight, we ain't gonna integrate." Some were applauding and laughing. I wondered why some students were jubilant, almost celebrating. I especially noticed that some of the segregationist leaders seemed very pleased with themselves.

As I went to my afternoon classes, I couldn't help being very anxious about what was happening to Minnijean that caused such a jovial uproar.

"Looking for your little nigger friend?" one of the students said as I walked down the stairs to study hall. "She's done got herself suspended. She can only get back in if the superintendent lets her, and you know what that means."

"One nigger down and eight to go," was the cry we heard as we left Central High for Christmas vacation. I could hear those declarations shouted even above the festive Christmas carols being played: "One nigger down and eight to go."

220

21

NEGRO GIRL IS SUSPENDED FROM SCHOOL AFTER INCIDENT
—*Arkansas Gazette*, Wednesday, December 18, 1957

MY HOPES FOR A BLISSFUL TWO-WEEK RESPITE FROM CENTRAL High over Christmas vacation had been dashed by the dilemma we all faced because of Minnijean's suspension. By dumping the chili over the white boys' heads, whether accidentally or not, she had opened a door through which segregationist leaders announced they would eject all of us. It was the beginning of the end of Little Rock school integration, they said. Immediately, cards and flyers appeared all over town reading: "One nigger down, eight to go."

Her suspension notice stated Minnijean could not begin the process to apply for readmission until six school days had passed. Classes would resume on January 3 of the new year. Our greatest fear was that Superintendent Blossom would use this opportunity to get segregationists off the school board members' backs by refusing her reentry. Segregationists had long been threatening a recall of the school board. If the board denied

Minnijean readmission, they might stave off that recall and save their jobs.

So instead of the peaceful, happy, safe Christmas vacation I had dreamed of for months, I was embroiled in integration meetings and worry. It was that nagging kind of problem that stays at the back of your mind, no matter what else is going on. Will they or won't they let Minnijean back in school, and if they don't, what will it mean to the rest of us?

Local and national NAACP officials were alarmed because they saw the incident as the first sign of significant progress in the segregationists' campaign to get us out of school. It jeopardized the progress they had worked for so many years to realize. The outcome of her case could affect not only the Little Rock case, but all integration efforts across the South. If expulsion were a way to stop integration, segregationists would make it their weapon.

As I entered the living room early one evening, Grandma was setting up the manger scene, gingerly placing each of the crudely carved wooden figures that had been handed down from her mother. She wouldn't allow any of us to help for fear we'd drop a piece. What with all her baking and decorating and gift making, this was her favorite time of the year, next to spring planting.

"Did you see that nasty letter on the front page of the *Gazette* telling businesses to stop advertising in that paper?" Grandma asked.

"I sure hope nobody listens."

"It's a sign the segregationists have begun their campaign on a whole new level," she said. "They're gonna dig in folks' pockets now."

"I guess they're pretty hopping mad at the *Gazette,*" Mother Lois said, breezing into the room. "They're accusing that paper of breaking down segregation laws with its attitude." She made a funny face as she continued. "I don't know how they figure that."

"Well, anyhow, that great lambasting in the paper ought to

prepare you for what they just might plan for Minnijean. You've got to get ready for it," Grandma said.

I wondered what awful thing they could possibly have in store for us. "You've been a bit down-spirited lately," she went on. "When did worry ever make anything happen your way? Minnijean either is or is not going to stay in school. Worry won't fix it."

I took a deep breath and sank into the couch, waiting for Mother Lois to get dressed for a party we were to attend to honor the Little Rock Nine.

"Where are you going?" Conrad asked.

"Mama and I are going to a grown-up Christmas party," I answered. I didn't want to make too much of it because I figured he was beginning to feel left out, what with all the fuss being made over me in newspapers and magazines and now a party planned in our honor. The National Organization of Delta Sigma Theta, a professional women's sorority, had decided to give us a Christmas party at the Dunbar Community Center. It was the first time some of my own people were saying a public thanks to us. It lightened some of the pain I felt for all those who were critical of our going to Central.

As I entered the Community Center, sorority women, showing off their high fashion and high spirits, greeted us as though we were very important. They had made us their secret project, with members of the nationwide organization mailing gifts and loving notes from across the country to be presented to us that evening.

I was bursting with pride as people said nice things about my courage and about what we nine were doing for future generations who would be able to attend integrated schools. It wasn't the kind of party where you have teenage fun, but it was wonderful just the same, especially because I had so few opportunities to socialize.

Minnijean's suspension was only mentioned in passing. Despite that worry, we nine enjoyed each other as friends, once outside the pressure we shared at Central High. We compared our gifts, of course. My favorite was a carved mahogany jewelry box. I'll keep this forever and give it to my grandchildren, I thought to myself as I carefully placed it on the nightstand beside my bed later that evening. In my diary I wrote:

Tonight I feel love from my own people. Everybody tried to make us happy. There is the tiniest flicker of hope and joy inside me. Maybe things will work out. Please, God, won't you allow Minnijean to come back to school just this once. I promise I'll help her be stronger.

———

"I see where Mr. Bennett is applying pressure to that interracial human rights group, bugging them to give up their membership records again," Grandma said over breakfast the next morning, as she folded the newspaper. "You know he and that law he got passed are becoming more than just a nuisance. He's doing some real damage."

As Grandma read snippets of information from the paper and discussed it with Mother, we noted alarming and increasing examples of segregationists applying pressure to our people in new and different ways. They were systematically attacking on all sides anyone who might support us in any fashion.

However, I wasn't going to let it bother me today. This was one of my favorite times of all—the family's annual last-minute Christmas shopping spree in downtown Little Rock. We had avoided going there for a long time, afraid I might be attacked. But I wasn't about to let the integration steal my Christmas shopping trip. I argued with all my might. I could wear a disguise, stores couldn't afford to invite trouble that might interfere with sales—on and on I went.

Thank God I'd won, I whispered, as we all piled out of the car. Looking around, I was absolutely awestruck by the holiday decorations and music that surrounded us. Inside, the stores were filled with Christmas magic and all the delightful things I had seen in magazines that I so desperately wanted but seldom could afford. On this one very special day of the year, as a

Christmas treat, Mother Lois gave us each twenty-five dollars to shop. She asked that we remain within shouting distance of her and Grandma while we browsed.

As always, the white clerks gave me dirty looks whenever I touched the merchandise. They had only recently allowed my people to try on clothes in a few of their stores. They behaved as though they begrudged our being there, even though we were going to hand our money over to them. Having all that shopping fun enabled me to ignore their disapproval.

"Hey, a nigger without a soldier guard." It was the boy who had threatened to kill me ever since I kicked him in the crotch. My first thoughts were to shout for help, to run away, but I couldn't let him think I was a coward.

"We've only got eight niggers in our school now." He spoke very loud to the boy standing beside him. "We're getting rid of the others, too. But this one here, she's not gonna live to go anywhere."

"Yeah, Andy, if you get her out, you get that big prize money everybody's talking about."

"Ain't no money gonna make me feel as good as killing her," Andy said, glaring at me.

Frantically I searched for a way to get us all safely out of the store. Trying to behave as though I were not alarmed, I casually examined items that lay on the counter nearest me. When I had moved a short distance away from Andy, I quickened my pace. Just then Conrad approached me. Grabbing him by the collar, I tried to signal him that something was wrong, but he didn't understand.

"Hey, Melba, let's put our money together and buy this new game. Look, it's got . . ." The thud of my heart racing in my ears drowned out his words. I hoped his excited voice would attract Mother and Grandma, but it was Andy who responded to him.

"Two niggers . . . I wonder what I'll get for both of them." Andy moved toward us.

"Don't you call my sister a nigger," Conrad was yelling back at him. I hoped their voices wouldn't cause a storewide fracas.

"This way," Grandmother India said, shoving us ahead.

"Hurry!" Mother said.

Conrad protested in a loud voice as we quickly hustled to I didn't know where.

"This isn't the way to the front door," I protested.

"Move it, girl." Grandma whispered.

All at once I realized where she was going—the rest room. Great, I thought, we'll be temporarily safe there, but then they'll call the police and we'll be trapped.

Once inside, I had to catch my breath and bring up a polite smile to greet three ladies from our church, who stood preening themselves in front of the mirror.

"Gracious, Lois, that boy is old enough to do his business with the men," said Sister Floyd, annoyance on her face.

"My baby is just a little ill. I'll have to tend him."

Grandma shoved Conrad into a stall, beckoning Mother to come closer as she whispered to her. I imagined a big ugly scene where policemen arrested us as Andy and a crowd of hecklers cheered.

Mother didn't seem as frightened as she ambled up to Mrs. Floyd and started a conversation about the Christmas social. As the ladies headed for the door, Grandma ushered Conrad and me to follow close on their heels.

Sure enough, Andy and his friend stood just outside the door looking like angry lions waiting to devour prey. Grandma glared at them as she said, "Why, my goodness, I guess you two gentleman are forced to make a pathway so's the seven of us can squeeze past."

The scowls on their faces melted into sour frustration as they eyeballed the church ladies and slowly backed off. Sister Floyd weighed at least 250 pounds. Sister Lanie probably weighed a tad more, and Sister Bell was no slouch, what with her sleek, athletic six-foot body. After we had traveled some distance, I looked back to see Andy and his friend following us but not up close.

"Well, young lady, from now on, you can just give me your list, and I'll take care of it. I don't know what we would have done without the sisters," Mama said as we piled into the car and looked all around us, taking deep breaths.

"It was the Christmas spirit that lulled us into letting our guard down," Grandma grumbled on the way home.

Going downtown, seeing all the people shopping and the decorations, had always been one of the best parts of my holiday celebration. The segregationists had stolen yet another important piece of my life—they had taken away my Christmas shopping fun.

The day before Christmas the *Gazette* carried two major local stories: "WHITE CHRISTMAS" BANNED AT CHS? and 13 LAWSUITS PENDING OVER INTEGRATION. I was reading the articles as Conrad and Mother Lois prepared to go shopping without me. The first story about "White Christmas" embarrassed me. How could they assume we didn't know the difference between white snow and white folks.

The second article said the federal courts were deluged by new filings and a backlog of cases on the racial integration issue. They would all be settled in the next months before the start of the new school year. Some of the issues to be ruled on applied to our case. If the judge ruled against integration, our surviving all the brutal punishment at Central would be in vain because they would use those rulings to kick us out of their school.

When Mother Lois and Conrad left for downtown, I told myself being left behind didn't matter anymore. At least I was grateful that I didn't have to go to Central that day. Besides, nothing could make me sad with Christmas so close and Grandma rattling paper and hiding gifts while I felt safe and snuggled warm, watching television as I dusted the living room.

Christmas Eve was delightful as we sat sipping hot chocolate and wrapping gifts to place under the tree. Each of us traded a personal gift. If during the year one of us coveted something that belonged to another, we might get the temporary loan of that item for January of the new year. We especially looked forward to those gift notes in our stockings. For example, I was thinking about granting Conrad the privilege of using my stereo twice a day for one month, but I wasn't certain I could be that generous so I wrote "maybe" on my note to him.

Vince called to say he would come by on Christmas, with Mother's permission. The thought of our being together near the tree on that special day, listening to carols, really sparked romantic daydreams. But as always my daydreams were so much better than the reality of being with him because we now had very little in common. He still spent most of his time questioning me about Central and teasing me about being a celebrity.

Of course, like lots of young people and adults, he teased me about Minnijean's chili incident. It made me feel uneasy about continuing to like him so much. If he really understood what I was going through, he should realize that the chili incident was a big crisis in my life, one that worried me every moment of every day. I began to wonder whether I was better off just being with Vince in my daydreams.

Each day of vacation, Minnijean and I spent time on the phone or on visits, talking at length about what might happen to her. The more we talked, the more we realized it was something we could do little about. The final word rested with Superintendent Blossom.

Later that evening, Papa Will came by to bring his presents. I hadn't seen much of my father since the integration began, but this time he was in a good mood. He didn't bother to say "I told you so," even though his awful predictions about integration causing trouble had for the most part come true. He was pleasant and genuinely concerned. The best part was the surprise he had hidden on the front porch, a brand-new television set with a big screen. He had chosen a special small gift for each of us. The fact that he put lots of time and thought into the gift selection made me feel that despite the way he had behaved, maybe he really did love me.

He and Mama looked at each other fondly for just an instant, and it felt as though we were a family again. I sometimes prayed they would get back together. At first Conrad and I had hoped against hope. As the years passed, we watched them grow apart in odd ways that made us sad. Rumors around church were

I can't imagine my parents Divorced.

228

that Papa even had a girlfriend now. But just for an instant, Conrad and I eyed each other, both thinking how nice it would be if he stayed. Maybe they would go with us to the family dinner and announce they were getting back together. But then Papa looked at his watch, cleared his throat, and off he went as though he had an important thing or person to get back to.

As Mother walked him to the door, I heard her invite him to our family Christmas dinner the next day at Aunt Mae Dell's house, but he said he didn't feel comfortable there.

Dear Diary,

It's Christmas Eve and Papa's not coming home to stay. For nine Christmases now I've prayed he would be with us. Maybe it's not gonna happen. Could I please have a nice, new stepfather. Thy will be done. By next Christmas either I want things to be a lot better at Central or I want to be somewhere else, please God. Merry Christmas.

Christmas dinner with the family was the biggest occasion of the year, a time when we spent the day catching up on family love and bloodline gossip, as Grandma called it. We were twenty-seven laughing, chatting people. I had waited all year to see all the relatives who weren't at Thanksgiving.

Even though all of them had definite opinions about my adventures at Central High, I had vowed not to talk about it. No matter what it took, I wanted to pretend life was normal again. I wanted the feeling of Christmas before integration. By late evening, as we sat in front of the fire singing Christmas carols, I realized maybe I had my wish. I hadn't felt that content since the summer before in Cincinnati.

———

LITTLE ROCK STORY SECOND ON AP'S BEST LIST
—*Arkansas Gazette*, Sunday, December 29, 1957

The stories ranged from number one, the launching of Sputnik, to Nikita Khrushchev emerging at the top of the Kremlin, the Teamsters Union hearings, Hurricane Audrey, President Eisenhower's stroke, Asian flu, and the passage of the Civil Rights bill.

How strange, I thought, to be involved in something that the whole nation considers among its ten most important stories. If it's that important, you'd think somebody would be able to do something to make the Central High students behave themselves. Is it that nobody cares, or nobody knows what to do?

By New Year's Eve, I only thought about Central High perhaps every other hour. Vince had invited me to a party, but of course Grandma and Mama said no. Besides, our famous shadows, Mutt and Jeff, were parked across the street, faithful as hound dogs in their vigilance. Although we discussed reporting them to the police, we knew full well that might bring on more trouble. So we simply lived with their being there, watching us. Mother didn't like my coming and going at night even when the party was in my neighborhood. Only on rare occasions did any of us go out after dark. Once dusk came, we locked all the doors and windows and closed the curtains.

So on New Year's Eve, I sat home completing my list of New Year's resolutions:

1. To do my best to stay alive until May 29.
2. To pray daily for the strength not to fight back.
3. To keep faith and understand more of how Gandhi behaved when his life was really hard.
4. To behave in a way that pleases Mother and Grandma.
5. To maintain the best attitude I can at school.
6. To help Grandma India with her work.
7. To help Minnijean remain in school—to be a better friend to her.

22

THOSE FIRST SCHOOL DAYS OF THE NEW YEAR WERE FRIGHTENING without Minnijean because it made us realize any one or all of us could be next. Posters and cards reading "One nigger down and eight to go" were everywhere. Segregationists left no doubt that they were seizing Minnijean's suspension as an opportunity to fire up their campaign.

Governor Faubus was adding to our insecurity and revving up segregationists' hopes by publicly announcing that the school board should file a petition asking the courts to delay integration. He cited a recent order to that effect in Dallas, Texas, as evidence that Little Rock could do the same. He also constantly threatened to call a special session of the legislature to enact segregation laws unless the feds would immediately take us out of school and halt integration.

Once we got back into our daily routine, it was evident that segregationists must have spent their holidays thinking up ways to make us miserable. I could feel their electrifying hope of victory all around me: they walked differently, talked differently, and didn't hesitate to shower us with angry words and deeds, letting us know we were short-timers.

I had by then withdrawn from French class because I wasn't able to concentrate with the combined pressure of the extremely hostile students and coping with everything else. I was also concerned that I couldn't do my best in my English, shorthand, and typing classes, all of which would have been a breeze under any other circumstances.

Even before lunch on our first day back, we had all begun to experience a hell we could not have imagined. The rumor was that the White Citizens Council would pay reward money to the person who could incite us to misbehave and get ourselves expelled. It was apparent that many students were going for that reward.

Boys on motorcycles threw an iron pipe at the car in which Gloria and Carlotta rode to school. Inside school, the group of students whose talent was walking on my heels until they bled met me after each and every class to escort me to the next. I would speed up, they would speed up. I couldn't escape no matter what I did. Ernie and Jeff were bombarded with wet towels, and boys overheated their showers. Gloria and Elizabeth were shoved and kicked. Carlotta was tripped in the hall, and I was knocked face forward onto the floor. Thelma was spared some of the physical abuse during that period because of her petite stature and fragility, but even she was jostled.

One of the ever-present and most annoying pastimes was spraying ink or some foul-smelling, staining yellow substance on our clothes, on our books, in our lockers, on our seats, or on whatever of ours they could get their hands on. We complained long and hard to the NAACP.

TOUGHS AT CHS DRAW NAACP FIRE
—*Arkansas Gazette*, Friday, January 10, 1958

Thurgood Marshall, Chief Counsel for the NAACP, said Little Rock officials should get tough with the forty or fifty hard-core white students causing trouble at Central. "The toughs are still pushing our kids around, spitting on them and cursing them," he said.

On Monday, January 6, Minnijean and her parents met with Superintendent Blossom. She was allowed to return to school

Monday, January 13, with the proviso that she not respond to
her attackers in any way.

I drew a deep sigh of relief as we discussed the good news
by telephone that evening. "Fine," I said to her. "You can do
it." I tried to explain to her what Grandma India had said about
freedom being a state of mind. I tried to impress upon her that
our being able to make it through the year was the biggest talk-
back and fight-back we could give them.

A short time after Minnijean's return, a boy doused her with
what appeared to be a bucket of soup. She froze in her tracks
and did not respond, even as the greasy liquid trickled down
her chest and horror painted her face. Afterward, a group of
perhaps fifty students gathered outside the principal's office to
shout cheers for the douser, saying he had paid her back. He
was suspended, but we were frightened that he had set in motion an all-out soup war that could lead to the drenching of each
one of us and guarantee a real brawl if we tried to fight back.

On January 11 a white girl was also suspended for pushing
Elizabeth Eckford down a flight of stairs before a genuine adult
witness—a teacher. She was punished, but the others who
pushed us down stairs were not. Headlines in the newspapers
told of some of the other perils we faced over the next few days:

January 15: GUARD PLATOON SENT TO SCHOOL AFTER THREATS
OF BOMBING

January 17: ANOTHER RACIAL CLASH REPORTED AT CENTRAL HIGH

January 21: DYNAMITE FOUND AT CHS—BLOSSOM SEES CAMPAIGN
TO TRY AND CLOSE SCHOOL

January 22: ANOTHER BOMB SCARE DISRUPTS CHS ROUTINE—BLOS-
SOM APPEALS FOR THE END OF THREATENING CALLS

January 23: CHS PLAGUED BY MORE BOMB SCARES

January 24: NEW BOMB SCARE AT CENTRAL HIGH PROVES FALSE

January 27: ANOTHER BOMB TOSSED AT LC BATES HOUSE

The segregationists were becoming even more vocal, urging the students to harass us at every opportunity. The Central High Mothers' League announced a nighttime rally with the Reverend Westley Pruden, president of the Citizens' Council, speaking on "What Race Mixers Are Planning for Us." They issued a special invitation to Central High students. We heard that almost two hundred hard-core segregationist students protested our presence by being absent from school on the day of that rally.

In addition to all the other indignities and physical pain we endured, we were now taunted by large groups of students who picked certain days simply to stare at us. They came to be known as "stare days." Large, boisterous groups of hecklers stared intensely and harassed the living daylights out of us. On several occasions, seventy or so students showed up at school wearing all black to protest our presence. Those were known as "black days."

The segregationists organized a systematic process for phoning our homes at all hours of the night to harass us. They also phoned our parents at their places of work and any other relatives or friends they could annoy. One day, Terrence's mother rushed into the principal's office, having been called and told her son was seriously injured, only to find the call had been a hoax. Repeated bomb threats were telephoned to our homes.

Somebody was also calling in reports to the news media that Minnijean had done outrageous things like running nude in the school's hallway. Time after time, she was devastated by reporters' inquiries about some bizarre thing she was said to have done in school and gotten away with. Those stories, when printed, only served to agitate students who had already made it their life's work to get her out of school permanently.

Late one afternoon, Minnijean was waiting outside school for her ride home when she was kicked so hard she couldn't sit down for two days. That incident was embarrassingly painful to her in many ways. Her bottom was discussed in the news-

paper and by people as though it were an object without attach-
ment to her body, and that hurt her feelings. That incident made
her the victim of ridicule. Whenever we spent time together, I
could tell she was growing more and more weary. I feared she
couldn't take much more of the constant mental and physical
pounding. And yet school officials seemed unwilling or unable
to stop the war being waged against her.

I remember a moment near the end of January when I was
struck by the fact that all the school officials were increasingly
nervous and behaving as though things had gotten out of control. Even the soldiers of the Arkansas National Guard seemed
fearful of what could happen in the hallways of Central. Their
presence had always only added to our problems; now we saw
mirrored in their faces a reflection of the danger that surrounded us.

I could also see the fear in Mrs. Huckaby's eyes. Somehow in
the course of time, she had become our liaison to the other
school officials. Even though she was the vice-principal of girls,
she was the one person we all, both male and female, reported
our problems to. Not that she could do anything about them,
but she would usually listen. We had also come to trust her at
least to be as fair as she could under the circumstances. I
thought that she, too, must be under a lot of pressure. During
those late January days, we had kept the door to her office
swinging. We would meet each other coming in and going out
with our complaints, sometimes teary-eyed, sometimes smolder-
ing with anger.

On January 27, I wrote in my diary:

> *The National Veterans Organization has awarded us the Ameri-*
> *canism Award. They think we are heroines and heroes. Why are*
> *we only Niggers to beat up on to the students at Central High. I*
> *don't know if I can make it now. It's really really hard. Why*
> *should life be so hard, when will it ever be fun to live again?*

We had real evidence that school officials weren't certain of
their ability to protect us, when, on the day of a pep rally, Mrs.

Huckaby suggested that Thelma, Minnijean, Elizabeth, and I sit in her office rather than be exposed to the hostility and physical abuse that certainly awaited us.

We were having more frequent meetings with Mrs. Bates and other NAACP officials about our problems. Despite our conversations and all the public declarations that school officials could protect us, the truth was, things were getting worse by the moment. When it came to Minnijean's suspension, segregationists were like sharks who tasted a drop of blood in the water. Their determination to have their kill—to see her gone—brought us to an impasse. If some resolution were not found, it seemed certain all of us would be forced to leave school within the week.

MRS. BATES SAYS 9 NEGROES WON'T QUIT DESPITE TROUBLE
—*Arkansas Gazette*, Wednesday, January 29, 1958

As determined as everyone else was to have me remain at Central, with each passing day I began to doubt that I was strong enough to tough it out. Even as I watched the others weaken, I could feel myself growing weary and nervous. When I had a long period of time alone on a Saturday, I leafed through the pages of my diary. I had not been fully aware of how deeply the turmoil at school was affecting me. I was stunned to see what I had written.

"I wish I were dead." That was the entry for several days running, in late January. "God, please let me be dead until the end of the year." I was willing to bargain and plead with God. I revised my request; I just wanted to become invisible for a month or two. I clutched the diary to my chest and wept for a long time. "No," I whispered aloud, "I do wish I were dead." Then all the pain and hurt would be over. I fell to my knees and prayed about it. That's when I knew I should go and talk to Grandma India. I told her about my wish to be dead.

"Good idea," she said. She didn't even look up at me as though she were alarmed after I whimpered out my confession. Instead, she continued dusting the dining room table. My feelings were hurt. And then she looked me in the eye and said it again. "Good idea! How did you plan going about it?"

"Ma'am?" I wasn't certain I'd heard her. "I said I wish I were dead—did you hear me?"

"And I said, good idea." Her voice was louder as she peered at me with a mischievous expression. "The sooner you get started, the sooner you'll make the segregationists real happy. They'll love broadcasting the headlines across the world." She braced the palm of one hand on the table to balance herself as she paused for a long moment to think. "I've got it. The headlines will read, 'Little Rock heroine gives in to segregationists— kills herself.' "

"What do you mean?" I gasped. I felt really angry that she talked as though she didn't care. She kept on creating new headlines about my death.

"Or maybe they could write: 'Melba Pattillo died by her own hand because she was afraid of facing God's assignment for her.' "

"Oh, no, ma'am." I slumped down into a chair.

She wouldn't let up. "Then, of course, there would be the celebration all the segregationists would plan. Let's see now, I'll bet they would rent the Robinson Auditorium for their party. It would be kinda like the wrestling matches, you know, loud, with all the cheering, singing, and dancing." She looked back down at the scratches on the table and continued dusting. "So do as you please, but I'd also think about that moment at which you'd have to face the Lord and explain your decision to him." She ignored me, humming her hymn, "I'm on the Battlefield for My Lord." I stood there for a moment watching her.

That did it. I realized dying wasn't a good idea. I was almost certain God wouldn't allow people to die for only a short while and come back. After that, Grandma arranged for a daily time when I had to come to her room, get down on my knees, and pray with her. Then she and I would talk about what was troubling me and what I would like. We would play Yahtzee or read pages from some fun novel I would choose. Sometimes we'd read through the newspaper together, but only the good things like the launching of an American satellite into orbit that circled the earth in 116 minutes.

During those days I felt so close to her, and I knew I had been silly for wanting to give up. Several times she looked at me and said, "Don't you know, child, how much I love you, how much your mama loves you? Whenever you think about going away from this earth, think about how you'd break my heart and your brother's heart. You might as well take your mother with you because she'd be beside herself."

She made me get a project I really liked and encouraged me to keep on top of it. I chose the blast-off of the Explorer, the satellite that put our country into the space race. I had always been interested in rockets and space. Once I had run away to the Strategic Air Command Base in a nearby town to see if they would allow me to become a pilot. Grandma studied up on the topic, and we talked for hours while she taught me how to do the quilting for Mother's birthday present.

Meanwhile, Mother Lois urged me to give Vince a standing invitation to Sunday supper. I couldn't understand why she was being so nice. I think Grandma talked to her about our conversation, and she was trying to cheer me up. Sometimes Vince came even when I didn't want him to. There were times when I just wanted to stay in my room and think, because I had no energy or desire to do anything else. Everything in me was devoted to being a full-time warrior. When I wasn't actually on the battlefield, surviving, I was thinking about how to do it or worried that I wouldn't be able to make it.

Every day, Grandma and I prayed hard for Minnijean to have strength and peace of mind and for all of us to be able to feel God's love for us, even in the face of those who spewed so much hatred our way.

For the second time, on Thursday, February 6, Minnijean was attacked by the boy who dumped soup on her. During the ruckus that followed, there was a great deal of confusion. The identity of who attacked and who fought back was not clear.

Her attackers accused her of retaliation. "White trash" were the words they reported her to have said. In addition, they accused her of throwing a purse at a girl.

When she was sent home without receiving a suspension notice, I breathed a sigh of relief. But at the end of the day, Mrs. Huckaby gave Carlotta a sealed envelope to be delivered to Minnijean.

If the paper in the envelope was a suspension note, well she shouldn't get suspended. she was defending herself.

23

"THEY BOTHER YOU ALL THE TIME,"
OUSTED NEGRO STUDENT CONTENDS
—*Arkansas Democrat*, Thursday, February 13, 1958

IN THE ARTICLE THAT FOLLOWED, MINNIJEAN EXPLAINED THE PRES-
sure she had been under at school. She said she had only had
half a white friend at Central, a two-faced girl who ran hot and
cold. Of the other students she said: "They throw rocks, they
spill ink on your clothes, and they call you 'nigger'—they bother
you every minute."

I cried for an hour when word came that the envelope sent
to Minnijean was a suspension notice. I was devastated when
Superintendent Blossom said he would recommend her expulsion. But when the NAACP and her parents announced they
would push to have a hearing, I kept a glimmer of hope.

Back at school, I didn't have very much time to be sad. We
were under siege, at the mercy of those who saw Minnijean's
expulsion as their victory and evidence they could immediately
get rid of all of us. I was warned that since I had been Minni-

240

jean's good friend and, like her, I was tall and not at all shy, I would become the next target for expulsion.

"One Nigger Down, Eight to Go" cards and signs flooded the school. We couldn't turn around without somebody pushing a card in our faces or chanting awful verses at us like: "She was black but her name was brown, and now she ain't around." Attacks on us by hostile students increased.

I read in the paper that Thurgood Marshall said he didn't know how much more unpleasant treatment we could take at Central High. That night I wrote in my diary:

I sometimes wish I could change myself into a psychiatrist to determine what makes me such a hated member of this school. Can they really be treating me this way simply because I am brown, that's all. • Answer: yes

"Ooooooo, no, no," I heard myself shout as I was walking up the Fourteenth Street stairwell one morning. It wasn't yet 8:40, and I was already the victim of a dousing with raw eggs from someone standing on the stairs above my head. The odor bothered me, but even more, it was the feel of that slimy substance oozing very slowly through my hair and onto my face, while at the same time raw egg slithered over the sweater Aunt Mae Dell had given me for Christmas. I stood still, wondering what to do and where to go. I felt so humiliated, I prayed that a huge dark hole would appear in the floor and swallow me up.

"The nigger's come to have breakfast. I can tell, she's wearing eggs," one boy called. I never said a word back to the group hovering with their ugly catcalls. I knew they were just hoping I'd do or say something that would result in my expulsion. I backed down the stairs and out the door to go home.

"Well, this egg is wonderful for putting moisture in the hair," Grandma said. "Some people use it for that, you know. Maybe we ought to start it on a regular basis." She was trying to wipe out as much as she could; then I would have to bathe and wash my hair. "Hold still," she continued. "After a nice long bath, you can hurry back to school, and this will have been just a refreshing break in your morning."

"I've never been so embarrassed."

"Oh, I'll bet there've been other times and there'll be more. Embarrassment is not a life-threatening problem. It can be washed away with a prayer and a smile, just like this egg is washed away with a little water."

"I know, but it's the same way I feel when they spit on me. I feel like they've taken away my dignity."

"Dignity is a state of mind, just like freedom. These are both precious gifts from God that no one can take away unless you allow them to." As Grandma spoke, she motioned me to turn my head to the other side.

"You could take charge of these mind games, you know."

"How do you mean?"

"Take, for example, this egg in your hair. Suppose you'd have told the boys who did this, 'Thank you,' with a smile. Then you've changed the rules of the game. What they want is for you to be unhappy. That's how they get pleasure."

"Yeah, but that would be letting them win."

"Not exactly. Maybe it would defeat their purpose. They win when you respond the way they expect you to. Change the rules of the game, girl, and they might not like it so much."

"They'd think I was crazy."

"They'd think you were no longer their victim."

For the rest of the morning as I walked the halls, amid my hecklers, I couldn't stop thinking about what it would be like to feel as though I were in charge of myself. I always believed Grandma India had the right answer, so I decided to take her advice.

As I tried to open a classroom door, two boys pushed it closed. At first I tried to pull it open, but then I remembered changing the rules of the game. I stood up straight, smiled politely, and said in a friendly voice, "Thank you. I've been needing exercise. You've done wonders for my arm muscles." I chatted on and on as if they were my friends. They looked at me as though I were totally nuts, then they let go of the door.

I felt great power surging up my spine like electricity. I left them standing there looking at each other.

During lunch, I learned Ernie and Terry had been the victims of yet another devilish deed. While Terry participated in gym class, someone took his school clothes and dumped them in the shower. Ernie had so much trouble with students stealing his gym clothes that he bought his own, which he carried with him in a briefcase until someone wrested it away and stuffed his clothes into the toilet in the girls' rest room.

On February 14, Valentine's Day, it snowed. That afternoon, as we stood in the snow waiting for our ride, we were attacked with snowballs filled with rocks. Mr. Eckford, Elizabeth's father, bolted from the car to rescue us, but he, too, was bombarded. Little Rock's finest police officers and members of the federalized National Guard stood by watching with their arms folded as we were hit time after time. Even when we pleaded for their assistance, they did nothing.

When I arrived home, Grandma handed me a large oddly shaped envelope. "I suspect it's a special greeting from that young man you ignore most of the time. After all, it is a special day."

I took the envelope to my room to open it. It was a card from Vince. As I read the beautiful words, I was sad that I couldn't talk to him on the phone or see more of him, but for the life of me I couldn't fit him into my schedule. Even my daydreams about him were beginning to fade because integration was taking up all the space in my mind.

———

THREE CHS PUPILS SUSPENDED; MINNIJEAN BROWN EXPELLED
—*Arkansas Gazette*, Tuesday, February 18, 1958

Minnijean was expelled after a forty-minute hearing. The official announcement of her expulsion coming after all that had been done to stop it was a devastating defeat for us. The fact that the school board at the same time suspended three white pupils, two for wearing "One down, eight to go" cards and one for pushing Gloria down a flight of stairs, didn't lessen the blow. The NAACP had counted on getting Minnijean's expulsion reversed, but Blossom and the school board were adamant in sticking to their conclusion, despite all the pressure on them.

National NAACP officials arranged for Minnijean to have a scholarship to a famous private New York high school called New Lincoln. She would live with the family of a renowned psychologist, Dr. Kenneth Clark. I had read that it was his research that had supported Thurgood Marshall and the NAACP's legal suit that resulted in the 1954 Supreme Court decision to integrate the schools.

It was a fabulous opportunity for her, but all I could think about was how far New York would be from Little Rock. We would no longer be able to get together to have our usual talks. At the same time, I tried not to be jealous that Minnijean would be escaping the hell that was my daily life. Still, I found myself daydreaming about what it would be like to get on that airplane with her and go to a place where there was no Central High School, no segregationists, and no pain stinging my heart every time someone called me a nigger.

I imagined that she'd have normal dates with nice boys, a real junior prom, and friends who smiled at her and talked with her every single day. She wouldn't be lonely anymore. But most of all, she wouldn't have to be frightened all day long that somebody was going to hit her, say nasty things, or even try to kill her.

Late one afternoon, a few days before Minnijean was to leave, I sat on the side of her bed, watching her pack. The two of us were talking and giggling. Again I was overwhelmed with those mixed feelings. I desperately wanted her to stay, and at the same time I would have given anything to go with her. She was showing me her wardrobe, gifts from friends to help her adjust to her new life. They were the most beautiful clothes I had ever seen: angora sweaters in deep autumn shades of rust and green, with matching corduroy skirts, a few of those wonderful fuzzy collars everyone was wearing, a velvet blazer, and even a beautiful trench coat.

I was so sad I could barely speak, but I was pretending everything was all right and that I was happy for her. What I really wanted to say was I miss you already, I love you like a sister . . . I don't know what I'll do without you. But that would sound too mushy, so I kept my thoughts to myself.

Suddenly she slumped down onto the bed amid all those beautiful clothes and her new luggage and started to cry uncontrollably. "I'm really sorry all this is happening. It's going to make it hard for the rest of you."

I tried to console her. "It's not your fault, Minnijean."

"I'll miss you." She embraced me. "I'll miss riding home with you and playing records with you and . . ."

"Yeah, but look at where you're going. New Lincoln High School is a famous place. Those are rich people you're staying with. I'll bet you get your own phone and maybe even a car. You'll meet important people."

"Do you forgive me?"

"There's nothing to forgive. But for the grace of God it might have been any one of us." To distract myself from the tears welling up inside my heart, I began folding things to put in her suitcase. "If you don't pack, I get to keep all these gorgeous things and go away and you'll have to stay here in my place," I teased.

It is very sad to loose a close friend.

With the announcement that Minnijean was definitely out, the segregationists went wild. The signs on the walls said: "All niggers go north." An article in the newspaper announced hall patrols by federalized National Guardsmen would be eliminated, although they would remain in the building and make periodic checks. That announcement granted segregationists more permission to have a field day with us. The school days that followed were noted in my diary in terms of the particular indignities I suffered. Putting every detail down on paper would give God a chance to see for himself what was going on, I thought.

February 18, 1958.

A red-haired, freckle-faced girl, the one who taunts me in home-room, keeps trailing me in the hallway between classes. Today she spit on me, then slapped me. Later in the day as I came around a corner, she tripped me so that I fell down a flight of stairs. I picked myself up to face a group of boys who then chased me up the stairs. When I told a school official about it, he said she was from a good family and would never do such a thing and I needed a teacher to witness these incidents if he were going to take any action. He asked me what did I expect when I came to a place where I knew I wasn't welcome. He warned me to keep Minni-jean's expulsion in mind.

February 19

Andy again. He's really beginning to frighten me. As I emerged from the cafeteria today, he walked right up, face to face, stepping on my toes so I couldn't move for a long moment. He shoved me backward and then held a wrench up to my face. He waved it around and shouted all sorts of threats that he could do a lot of awful things to my face with it. My knees were shaking and I didn't know what to do. I said, "Thank you." His eyes grew huge. Quicker than the speed of light, I jumped away from him and ran. "Just think all night about what I'm gonna do to you tomorrow," he shouted after me.

February 20

I got hit across the back with a tennis racquet. I managed to smile and say, "Thank you." Andy said, "What did you say, nigger?" I repeated, "Thank you very much." I spit up blood in the rest room. I felt as though someone had stuck a hot poker through my back, into my insides. I saw him several times during the after-noon, but I never let him see me cry, and I didn't report it to anybody.

I think only the warrior exists in me now. Melba went away to hide. She was too frightened to stay here.

SCHOOL BOARD CITES INABILITY TO ENFORCE COMPLIANCE,
ASKS U.S. COURT TO HALT INTEGRATION
—*Arkansas Democrat*, Friday, February 21, 1958

U.S. WON'T GET INTO CENTRAL HIGH SCHOOL CASE
—*Arkansas Democrat*, Friday, February 21, 1958

On Saturday, February 22, a day after the school board asked the court to halt integration, Minnijean left for New York. Even her departure was marred by a bomb threat that delayed her American Airlines flight. Waving Minnijean off at the airport was difficult for all of us. There were lots of reporters and photographers taking pictures for the newspapers. We had become somewhat accustomed to their presence after all those months, and we were quite friendly with the ones from the North. We called them by their first names and frequently had off-the-record conversations with them. But just this one time we were weary of their presence. It was a moment when we wanted to be alone with our pain. At first we simply ignored them, behaving as though they were invisible. Still, even on this very sad day, we couldn't have them taking pictures of our tears—that would only be fodder for the segregationists. So we tried to pretend all was well.

That night I wrote in my diary:

> *My dearest friend, Minnijean, left today. I couldn't stop crying. People at the airport said we all looked very old and tired, for the battle must be getting harder.*
>
> *I pray Minnijean will be happy. She deserves it . . . don't we all?*

The Little Rock School Board had now petitioned the federal courts to consider again the whole question of school integration, in light of its negative experience since September 3.

By the beginning of March, I had sunk into the state of mind you get into when you know you have to take castor oil and there's no way out. I just did what had to be done, without discussing it or thinking about it. I would get up, polish my saddle shoes, bathe, get dressed, dump my bowl of oatmeal into the toilet so Grandma India would think I'd eaten it—but my nervous stomach wouldn't have to eject it—and go to the war inside that school. I listened to shouts, to ugly names, while I smiled and said "Thank you." I waited for a ride, came home, did homework, got to bed, and started over again the next day. I felt kind of numb, as though nothing mattered anymore.

I thought my routine must be like a soldier's fighting in wartime. Only I was lucky enough to have weekends in another world. One day I was doing just that, thinking about my other world and about the headline I had seen that read, "IT'S LOVELY, SAYS MINNIJEAN OF HER NEW YORK SCHOOL." What would it be like to have just one lovely day of school amid pleasant people who smiled when you looked them in the eye?

As I stood alone, outside the Sixteenth Street entrance of Central High, I was shivering against the cold, waiting for my ride home that Friday afternoon. I was immersed in fantasies about my quiet, safe weekend. My body was there, but my mind was somewhere else.

My 101st guard Danny had said, "When you let yourself lose your focus, you make big mistakes." I suddenly realized that I had done just that, made a foolish mistake. The Sixteenth Street entrance was one of the most dangerous areas of Central High's grounds. It was a place I would never have chosen to wait alone, had I been conscious of my action. It was an isolated spot with no teachers, principals, or guards keeping watch, but I was too weary to walk the two blocks to the other side where it was safer and where my driver expected to pick me up. I decided I'd be wiser to stand still and hope that the car-pool driver would figure out I wasn't waiting in the appropriate place and would come around to this side of the building looking for me. So I said a little prayer and allowed myself to lapse deep into my thoughts once more.

Suddenly there was a voice in the distance, calling my name, jolting me from my thoughts. "It's nigger Melba." It was Andy's voice shouting at me. My heart started beating fast. Where the heck was he? I looked to see how far off he was. He was more than a block away, coming up from the playing field with a group of his friends. They were walking fast, almost galloping. Even if I started running, I couldn't out-distance all of them. I looked around frantically, searching for help.

"Hey, Melba, you gotta get out of here." The second voice was much closer. I wasn't alone. There was a sleek, muscular boy, about six feet tall, wearing a varsity jacket and a cap, with a bushy shock of blond curls peeking from beneath it. He was leaning against the passenger side of a 1949 Chevy parked at the curb, only a few feet to my left. Was he one of Andy's friends, who'd come to corner me and hold me there? His face looked familiar to me. He resembled one of those big tough boys who got their kicks taunting me. But why wasn't he coming toward me, shouting ugly words at me like the others?

My mouth went dry. My feet seemed bolted to the ground. My knees were shaking so badly that I doubted whether I could run. Where would I go? Andy and his friends were dancing about each other in a circle, huddling to decide how they would have their fun with me. One boy started to run back in the direction from which they had come. Another boy joined them. What were they going back to get, I wondered. A rope?

"Nigger, nigger on the wall, who's the deadest of them all," Andy shouted as he hesitated, waiting for his friends. Now, they were only about a quarter of a block away. "Stand still, don't run, 'cause if you do, it'll be worse for you," Andy shouted.

What now? My mind scrambled to figure out what I should do.

"Melba," the blond boy whispered my name, "listen to me. I'm gonna call you nigger—loud. I'm gonna curse at you, but I'm gonna put my keys on the trunk of this car. Get out of here, now. My name is Link, I'll call you later."

"But I can't do that."

"Get the hell out of here. . . . Andy's gonna kill you."

"But I can't. . . . I . . . uh . . ." I stood there gasping for words. He's up to something, I thought. Now I'm surrounded. Why doesn't the car-pool driver come after me now . . . right now, please, God.

"You don't have any choice," he whispered. "Go!" I turned to see that Andy and his friends were only a short distance away. I wasn't even sure I could make it to the car.

"If you don't get out of here, you're gonna get us both killed," the blond boy urged.

"Hey, Andy, we're gonna have us some nigger tonight." I heard Link shout as he walked away from the car, toward them. I grabbed the keys and ran around quickly to open the door on the driver's side. I hopped in and locked all the doors. By the time I turned the key in the engine, Andy was clawing at the lock, while the other boys popped off the windshield wipers, and tried to get into the passenger's side. Link stood glaring at me with an anxious look on his face, spewing hate words just like them. I pressed down the clutch, shifted into first gear, and the car jumped forward. Andy was still running alongside, holding on to the door handle, but as I sped up, he had to let go. Even if that boy Link got me later for stealing his car, I was alive and on my way for now.

After a couple of blocks, when I could breathe a little easier, I craned to look around. I couldn't see anybody following me. "Thank you, God," I whispered, as I headed for home. "Thank you for saving me one more time."

24

I GUNNED THE ENGINE OF LINK'S CAR AND BEGAN MOVING AS FAST as I could without attracting too much attention. By the time I rounded the corner at Twelfth and Cross and headed for the backyard, I felt myself going out of control. The car careened into our yard. I was moving so fast that I knocked down the fence my uncle Charlie had begun to build around Grandma India's flower garden.

Bolting from the car, I raced up to the back door; my heart was ticking like a time bomb. I looked around as I banged hard on the door. Maybe the police were sneaking up behind me, waiting to pounce. I thought of dumping the car someplace else . . . but where? Anywhere I parked, it would be noticed. In our closely knit neighborhood, everybody knew everybody else and especially who owned which car.

"Have you lost your mind, girl?" Grandma said, wiping her hands on her apron as she held the screen door open and peered into the backyard.

"What's going on? Whose car is that?" She was stretching to see past me.

"Uh, it belongs to a school friend. Let me in."

I motioned her to back away and then carefully latched the screen and locked the door behind me. Pulling the curtain back from the glass peephole in the door, I took one last look to see whether or not someone might be following me. I started to tell Grandma what happened.

"You mean to tell me that car belongs to some Central High white boy?" She was horrified. I tried to calm her as I explained, but the expression on her face turned from astonishment to fear. Suddenly she hurried to the linen closet and started frantically searching for something. She pulled out several torn and faded sheets and a whole bunch of safety pins. Dragging me with her, she rushed out the back door. We squared off the first sheet, holding its corners like we did to make the big bed in Mama's room, and then pulled it across the hood of the car. "Maybe you'll live to see tomorrow if we can hide this car from the police." She motioned me to help her stretch the second sheet across the roof of the car.

"I s'pose you were stuck twixt the devil and the deep blue sea, child. You done your best, but we got us some real trouble now." We rushed into the house and locked the door behind us.

When Mother Lois came home from teaching, she was just as upset as Grandma. After lots of questions and lots of pacing, she calmed down a bit.

"Well, maybe this isn't so bad after all," she said. "It's been a while and nobody's come to inquire about the car yet."

Grandma put her hands on Mother's shoulders and said, "Perhaps the boy was telling the truth. Who's to say that he can't be one of God's good white people?"

"I suppose," Mother said as her frown eased a bit. "Let's assume for a moment that this boy wasn't trying to trap you. How are you gonna get the car back to him without other people finding out about it?"

"Link said he'd call," I replied, as I began to search for ways of returning the car if he didn't. I surely couldn't drive it back to school the next day. He couldn't be seen in my neighborhood, and I dared not travel in his, especially not at night. Well . . . we would have to figure out a secret way. When the phone rang, I raced to pick up the receiver.

"Hi. It's Link."

"How do I know it's you?"

"My key chain has a little gold football on it."

"Okay. Thank you, Link, thank you very much."

"Andy swears he's gonna get you next time."

"Yeah, he frightens me."

"Look, we better hurry and get this car thing over with. Andy is suspicious that you drove away in my car. I told him no—it's a coincidence that it looked like mine. But I need to make sure he sees me driving my car."

"Whatever you say." I whispered a prayer that Andy hadn't called the police.

"Why don't you drop it off in front of Double Deck Ice Cream. Nobody would give it a second thought if we were there at the same time."

"May I ask you a question?

"Shoot."

"Why did you do it?" My curiosity was killing me. I had to ask.

"Because he was real serious about killing you. Don't take his threats lightly! He means it! Hey, gotta go—be there in a half an hour."

We couldn't risk asking a neighbor's help, so even though I didn't have a license, I had to drive Link's car downtown. I wondered what he must be like. The inside of the car was what Conrad called "cherry"—clean and polished as if he'd washed it twice a week. The record albums on the backseat were the same ones I might have chosen . . . Johnny Mathis, Sam Cooke, Elvis, and Pat Boone. Who was Link, anyhow? Suddenly I felt frightened. Maybe he was a member of the Klan—maybe they were waiting with him for me to bring this car back, and they were gonna grab me. I concentrated on my driving to get rid of those thoughts.

I pulled up in front of Double Deck Ice Cream. Mama was right behind me. I looked all around to make certain there were no Central students who might recognize me. I parked Link's car at the curb, a little ways down from the front entryway. Leaving the keys beneath the floor mat on the driver's side, I walked back to our car. I couldn't resist taking a quick look around to see if I could spot Link. If he was there I couldn't see him. I climbed into the passenger's side of our car, and we were safely on our way home.

The next day when I saw Andy, he was walking past Mrs. Huckaby's office. There were two other teachers standing nearby, so although he growled at me, threatening that he would get me before the day was over, he kept walking.

Each time I passed Link in the hallway, he winked at me. It was the one kind gesture in a morning filled with hellish activity. In the days that followed, every time I saw Link, he acknowledged me in some way. His wink or pleasant expression sometimes came just at the moment I needed to know I was alive and valuable. Otherwise, my days seemed to end with awful diary entries.

March 11

Today we had a film in gym.
Shorthand class got very rough because my favorite teacher was gone. A boy entered the classroom to deliver a package. He began making a speech: "You'all mean you're gonna let that there nigger sit there peaceful like that."

March 14

Typing class is horrible. One girl tells me every day in a loud voice, "I don't believe in race mixin', especially with niggers."

March 15

Maybe the weeks following in which we have a little free time will help me feel better. I must have time to figure out why life is like this for me.

March 18

Today, Tuesday, was my worst day in a long time. Ernie and I always leave the cafeteria together. Today he wasn't there so I had to go alone. The crowds on the stairs called names—"Nigger— spick—Indian." My knees shook so bad I thought I'd fall over. I had no choice but to walk up the stairs and through the thick of them.

March 22

Went with Mom to the cleaners again today. The clerks are beginning to be very mean to us. We must stop going there immediately. They stare and talk too loud to us and attempt to make us appear silly. It's enough that I go through that at Central, why should I have to endure it at the cleaners.

March 23

The AME churches gave the eight of us white Bibles with our names engraved on them during afternoon services. It made me feel like my people are supporting me.

An article in the *Gazette* said that in a letter to Army Secretary Brucker, Roy Wilkins, Executive Secretary of the NAACP, said there had been forty-two reported incidents of harassment of us from October to February. Of course, we knew that the number of incidents reported paled in comparison to what we really experienced as we walked the halls of Central High. These days hostility was more often than not expressed through physical rather than verbal punishment. I had begun wondering once again whether or not we would make it through the year. Urgent calls to the President were not bringing about any change.

Then one night as I sat studying, Link called. Mother handed me the receiver with a questioning look.

"Don't sit in your regular assigned seat for your first class tomorrow," he told me. "Take the seat nearest the window. I know you like to sit in the back of the third row so you can protect your back. But do as I say, just this one time."

"How do you know where I usually sit?"

"Never mind, just do what I tell you."

"Why?"

• Like melba said why? why should she listen? she might get into trouble.

"Because the segregationists have got real plans for you. You're definitely their new target because you're tall, you're pretty, you're uppity, not meek—the way they think your people should be—besides, you hung around with Minnijean."

"What do you mean, uppity?"

"You know what I mean."

"Why are you warning me? What do you care?"

"I don't know. I gotta go—my dad's coming," he whispered. "Don't forget what I said." He slammed down the phone abruptly. I sat for a moment thinking about our conversation. I wondered why a white boy would take such risks.

The next day as I entered the classroom, I noticed something was different. The boys and girls who had earlier set my books afire, thrown spitballs, dumped water on my head, and called me names were all sitting in the usually empty seats surrounding my assigned seat. I paused for a moment, and then my instincts told me to do as Link had said. I crossed the room to the opposite side and took a seat in the front row.

"Put the nigger back in her cage . . . make her take her regular seat," one boy shouted.

The teacher looked up at me for a moment, then looked back at the boy voicing the complaint. All along, she had shown she was not someone I could count on for any protection. She remained passive when students threw things at me or dumped water on my head.

"Melba, take your regular seat," she demanded.

"Yes, ma'am." I stood obediently and walked toward my seat. What else could I do? To defy her order directly would be to risk expulsion. I got past the hurdles of feet stuck in the aisle to trip me. As I approached my seat, I could see there was something on it. Peanut butter . . . a two-inch-thick layer of peanut butter with shiny objects that looked like broken glass laced through it. How could Link have known about this plan ahead of time? He must be a part of their group.

I moved back toward the seat I'd originally chosen. "There's something on my seat," I told the teacher.

"Take it off," she replied.

"Oh, I think I'll let somebody else do that," I said, as the group surrounding the peanut butter seat snickered. I slid back into my new seat by the window even before she could respond.

"Why's the nigger special . . . why doesn't she have to obey orders?"

I raised my hand. The teacher acknowledged it. "Why are they special?" I asked. "Why are they allowed to be out of their seats today? It's musical chairs." I looked her in the eye with an expression that telegraphed a message I hoped she'd understand. I wasn't about to move again.

As class ended, members of the hecklers' group sitting around the peanut butter seat were all whispering to each other. I was curious about how they planned to clean up the mess before the next class. When the bell rang, I stood, collected my books, and calmly walked out of the room. Chalk one up to Link, I thought to myself.

En route to lunch, as I approached my locker, I noticed the door was open; someone had hammered the lock and dumped out my books. I had to go to Mrs. Huckaby's office to report the incident. I would need new books for afternoon class, and I would miss being with my friends for the full lunch period.

I walked into the cafeteria, after reporting my loss to Mrs. Huckaby and getting new books, to find that my friends had already left. I wondered why they had left early. Could it be that they had gone to look for me? As I settled down in my seat and began to unwrap the sandwich Grandma had made for me, I noticed a group of boys moving in close to me, much closer than usual. There had always been a wide path of empty chairs immediately surrounding our eating area because other students shunned us during the lunch period.

Maybe they felt free to harass me so openly because this was one of those days when school officials were experimenting— seeing whether or not we could survive without uniformed federalized troops or school officials posted where everyone could see them. There were no guards in the halls when we changed classes, no guards just outside the cafeteria doors, within shouting distance, as they often were. There were no officials pacing the floor or hugging the walls observing what was going on

I began to get nervous. I could tell it was no accident that I was being surrounded by the group of sideburners who appeared to have mischievous plans for me. Were they gathering to block my way, to taunt me in front of all the others? In order to get out of the cafeteria I would have to trudge through whatever barriers they erected: I would be in the same position Minnijean had been in.

My palms were perspiring, my heart racing. Was there no way out? Just before the bell rang to end the period, a second group of about five of the same sort of boys entered the cafeteria and moved directly to a spot I was eyeing as a possible escape route. Now I was completely surrounded. The hostile gang glared and hissed at me. It was beginning.

As I looked around, suddenly I saw him. There was Link, seated among my attackers, laughing, joking with them, behaving as though he were a regular member of the group.

I studied him, waiting for his eyes to catch mine, and when they did, he looked down quickly. It both frightened and saddened me to see Link among those hoodlums. I stared at him in disbelief and anger. Had he pretended to be a nice person when he was just one of them? I struggled to regain my composure. As usual, I was seated near the main entryway, with my back as near to the wall as I could get so that my rear would be protected; but with those boys becoming more vocally hostile every moment, and the guards absent, my safe seat seemed to be a trap. I looked off into the distance, where some of my people were serving food from behind the counter. There was no way any of them could help me.

There must have been a thousand or so students in that huge room. It was near the beginning of the second lunch period, a time when the cafeteria was most crowded. Even above the ear-shattering levels of conversation that blended into a hodgepodge of unsettling noise, I could hear my attackers' comments shouted at me.

Over and over again they were saying how they were going

to come and get me, and what they would do with me. I was trying to ignore them, concentrating instead on a plan for my escape, when a milk carton came flying at me, hitting me on the forehead. It was followed by something that pierced my cheek. It took a moment to realize one of the boys had a bean shooter. I flinched, but braced myself so I would not show a reaction, even though the prick was painful.

I had to look straight at the group in order to keep tabs on them. I looked directly at Link sitting there as big as you please, a part of their group. Lending me his car must have been part of a master plan, I decided.

I ducked down quickly to avoid a hard white object that came whizzing through the air. I narrowly averted the missile, and when I reached to examine it, I found a golf ball wrapped in paper. Remembering my discussion with Grandma about playing mind games, I examined it as if it were a precious treasure. I smiled and gushed, loud enough for those sitting closest to me to hear. "It's just beautiful, thank you. It's just what I need."

My hecklers began mumbling among themselves. They were far enough away that I couldn't hear exactly what they were saying, but I watched the puzzled expressions on their faces. They looked at me as if I had lost my mind. I glanced at Link to see his reaction. It was hard to read. I had to stop wondering about Link and figure out what to do. "Don't do anything," the voice in my head kept repeating.

I reached into my satchel and pulled out the book on Gandhi that Grandma had given me, along with some blank sheets of notebook paper, and pretended I was studying. I decided I would make my attackers believe I was settling in for a long study session. After all, my next class was study hall, and if I cut it, I wouldn't be missing anything important.

Recently school officials had issued a warning about students who initiated attacks. The penalty was suspension. I suspected that as long as I remained in my seat, no one was going to walk over and dump soup on my head or attack me. With all those other students seated close enough to watch what was going on, my attackers would want it to appear that I made the first move, forcing them to retaliate.

When the bell rang, the room became even more noisy with people shoving chairs, finding their books, and rushing toward the exit. I desperately wanted to get out of there, but I knew full well I couldn't move or the group would start a fight and set me up for expulsion, for sure. Word was they had psychological experts training them in ways of forcing us to respond.

I was willing to sit in that spot until the end of time rather than risk a fight. I was already wearing Band-Aids on my heels from the heel-walkers the day before, and I was sore up and down the backs of my legs from being kicked. I felt I couldn't take anymore. I knew I couldn't help but fight back against the next person who attacked me.

I pretended to become intensely involved in my book. I was reading about Mr. Gandhi's prison experience and how he quieted his fears and directed his thoughts so that his enemies were never really in charge of him.

All at once I was aware that one of my hecklers was coming toward me.

"Niggers are stupid, they gotta study real hard, don't they?" he said in a loud voice.

"Thanks for the compliment," I said, looking at him with the pleasantest expression I could muster so he would believe I wasn't annoyed.

"Study hard now, nigger bitch, but you gotta leave this place sometime, and then we got you."

"Thank you," I said again, a mask of fake cheer on my face. He seemed astonished as he slowly started to back away.

I felt myself smiling inside. As Grandma India said, turning the other cheek could be difficult, but for me, it was also beginning to be a lot of fun. Somehow I had won a round in a bizarre mental contest.

My heart slowed its rapid beating, and my hands stopped shaking. I felt safer, even comfortable, as something inside me settled to its center. I had a powerful feeling of being in charge. I was no longer allowing hecklers' behavior to frighten me into acting a certain way. For that moment, I was the one making decisions about how I would behave. A little choir of voices in my head was singing, "Hallelujah, hallelujah, hallelujah!"

The second bell rang for the beginning of the next period; by that time students were expected to be settled into their seats. I saw Link beckon the hecklers into a huddle. From the expressions on their faces, I could tell there was serious conversation about what to do next. All at once, the group, led by Link, made their way to the door.

"Hey, I'm not gonna stay in detention hall every morning for a week just for a little nigger-beating pleasure," I heard Link say as he passed close by me. I heard them arguing with each other, heard some of them agree that it would be worth it if they could get me once and for all. But I heard Link's voice as he said it was better to leave now and he'd help them get me later for sure.

25

"I DID IT," I SHOUTED WITH EXCITEMENT AS I RACED IN THE FRONT door where Grandma was standing in her usual place to welcome me home after school.

"Did what?" she asked.

"I tried to do some of the things Gandhi talks about—you know, keeping calm in your own mind no matter what's going on outside."

"Phone's for you, Melba," Conrad yelled from the hallway. I hoped it would be someone I could share my victory with, maybe Vince, but it was Link. I slammed the receiver down. Right away the phone started to ring again. I picked up and said, "Don't bother to call again!" I slammed the receiver down once more. Again it rang and rang. Grandma walked into the hallway and eyed me suspiciously. I picked up the receiver for fear of having to explain to her.

"Five minutes, that's all I ask!" Link said. "I saved your skin. At least you owe me a chance to explain."

"Absolutely not—" I said, but he cut me off before I could finish.

"I didn't want to be there, but I heard they were gonna do something big to you in the cafeteria. So I thought if I was there I could do something to help you."

"How did you know they were planning something?"

"My dad makes me go to those meetings—where they plan what to do to get you'all kicked out of school."

"Why are you telling me this?"

"Because I want to help you."

"I can't trust you after today."

"Hey, if I hadn't convinced those guys to leave, they were gonna get you. And if you don't believe I'm on your side, here's proof, listen up. Stay off the far end of the second floor tomorrow. And don't go to your locker after lunch."

"I gotta go, Grandma wants me." She was standing over me, looking as though she were upset with me.

I rushed to the kitchen with her following on my heels. I had to tell them what had happened, and it was only a matter of minutes before Mother and Grandma tore into me. Mother Lois was first to speak. "We have to wonder about Link's motives."

Then Grandma said, "Perhaps he's trying to set you up for the Klan—he's gonna lure you into a trap, and then where will you be?"

Although I, too, was undecided about trusting Link, I continued to defend Link as both of them came up with dozens of reasons why I shouldn't trust this white boy. Still, there was something inside me that said he had taken a big risk giving me his car that day.

I didn't want to defy Mother and Grandma, but Link was inside Central. He understood what I was going through. They could not help me inside that school. I had no choice but to take any help that would enable me to survive. I had to take the risk of trusting Link a little bit, at least for now.

Sure enough, the next day, I heeded Link's warnings, taking a different route to class. Later I heard there was trouble on the route I usually took. By not going to my locker in the afternoon, I avoided meeting someone who must have been very angry, as he or she broke the lock and shredded the contents of the locker. The day had gone exactly as Link had said it would, but even so, I found myself wondering if he were only building my trust in order to lay a bigger trap for me.

NAACP ASKS STERNER ACTION BY CENTRAL HIGH SCHOOL TROOPS
—*Arkansas Gazette*, Tuesday, April 1, 1957

The NAACP renewed today its demand for more militant action by troops at Central High School. Otherwise we are confronted with the incredible spectacle of the government of the United States placing the burden of enforcing the order of its courts upon the slender shoulders and young hearts of eight teenage Negro students.

Link warned me that with the beginning of April, segregationists would feel compelled to speed up their efforts, in order to get us out of Central before we could complete a full school year. Some of their tactics became desperate, and their desperation made it easier for me to avoid the more obvious traps they set. Still, on the pages of my diary, there was no real life anymore. It was as if my days consisted of only one thing—enduring pain in my mind and on my body.

April 2

Today we had a fire drill, I was very much afraid. There was pushing on the stairs and name calling. I almost lost my balance. Had I fallen down those thirty or so stone steps, I would have hurt myself or even been killed. They tried hard enough . . . that's for sure.

April 4

Excitement over the Mikado makes me very sad. I hear they will spend much money on costumes and makeup to have a real grown-up production. Oh, how I wish I could participate. Also the class play will be soon. All this drama would be wonderful for me since that is the field I might go into. I spend equal amounts of time daydreaming about becoming a news reporter and an actress. I wonder why I'm so close and yet the distance of a million miles away from this opportunity.

April 8

The boys are throwing lighted paper at me in study hall again. Oh well, not too much longer.

It made me very unhappy to read today's headline in the Gazette. *A man named Thomas is proposing that all of us withdraw from Central and everybody support his voluntary plan for desegregation. He's some businessman, president of First Pyramid Life Insurance Company. The long and the short of it is that he wants to set up all kinds of biracial boards and committees and eventually, somewhere, eons from now, maybe we'd have integrated schools. Pooo! Everybody important that suggests we withdraw just makes it harder for us.*

April 9

It feels so scary because the adults here don't know what to do. I believe the rational ones who would keep the violence in check are being controlled by those who want us out at any cost. Therefore, nobody is steering the ship—nobody's in charge—not really. I can see that it's possible we could have a riot within this school.

April 10

Today was very very hard. I had to get up and walk out of study hall. A boy stood over me shouting insults while the teacher and entire study hall looked on. He threatened to kill me right there.

April 11

I don't think I could have lasted another minute. I hope somebody performs a miracle over this weekend. Do you hear me, God?

In the days that followed, Link continued to phone me every night. Grandma India would hand me the receiver with a scowl on her face, but neither she nor Mother Lois forbade my talking with him. Sometimes Grandma even stood by, listening to the entire conversation, with arms folded and a huffy attitude. It was the first time I had ever continued to do something I knew very well they didn't want me to do. But still they put up with it. I think Mother finally realized that Link was doing something for me they could not do—feeding me vital information that could help me survive.

Whenever they confronted me with questions about our conversations, I told them the truth. Link and I mostly talked of which rest rooms to avoid, routes I might take to avoid special plans to terrorize me, how to get inside a classroom safely, and where to sit. He also explained some of the traditions and activities at Central High to me that I could not know otherwise. He described some of the regular school activities, as well as segregationist plans, moods, and behavior. I learned there were many secrets among school officials, many significant things taking place without our even being told about them, let alone being asked to participate.

Link swore me to secrecy, so other than Mother and Grandmother, none of the other seven students knew he existed. Occasionally, during a general conversation about do's and don't's, I would share some information that I thought would be helpful to them, but otherwise I kept my mouth shut. I figured I owed Link that.

After a while, having him as my friend got to be fun for both of us. We played a cloak-and-dagger game, passing notes in books and such. But we never spoke to each other in school, or walked near each other, or acknowledged each other except with our eyes for fear he would get caught. He continued hanging around with Andy and his friends and attending the segregationists' strategy meetings. He said the worst part of it for him was that he felt himself a traitor. He was torn between his loyalty to his family and friends, and his sense of guilt and responsibility for what was happening to the eight of us. Sometimes he justified what he was doing by saying if he protected me and prevented a major catastrophe from befalling any of the eight of us, he could insure some of his normal graduation activities, and besides, people wouldn't think Central such an awful place.

Meanwhile, we did indeed notice some stronger efforts by a few teachers to discipline students. The Little Rock School Board now demanded belligerent students be brought under control. At first we saw no difference, but we began to notice a slight bit of peace in the hallways, and we were heartened to hear that another girl had been expelled for handing out the cards saying "One Down, Eight to Go."

Easter. What a wonderful word, I thought to myself as I walked to Grandma's room. If Easter Sunday was coming soon, it meant the end of school was only weeks away. The 29th of May. What would that last day of school at Central High be like?

"Tonight's the night," Grandma said, making the announcement from her perch in her favorite chair. "We're going into the trunks tonight. It's time to make your selections." She smiled with her all-knowing expression, because she was fully aware of how much it delighted us to view and touch her trunk treasures. There were gifts, heirlooms, and mementos we got to touch or see only at Christmas or Easter.

There they were in the center of the room, the old trunks given to Grandma India as a young girl. One was a deep brown, with scrapes and scratches visible beneath the glossy veneer she kept up with biannual waxing. The second one was a deep garnet color and looked newer.

"Have you given much thought to what you'll be wearing to church this Easter, Melba?" Grandma India asked, as she lifted the lid of the first trunk.

I had thought long and hard about wanting to dress grown-up. The strength growing inside me to face the hostile students at Central had leaked into my home life. Now it bubbled up in me, allowing me to speak my mind. "I'd like to wear nylon stockings and little heels with whatever I wear. I am sixteen now, sixteen and a half, actually." It was a daring suggestion, considering Grandma's opinions on the subject.

"Nylon stockings—heels. Have you been reading those trashy fashion magazines again? Let's not move too fast, young lady. You've got all your life to wear stockings, but you'll only be young once." Grandma seemed adamant about my remaining a two-year-old, I thought to myself. It was the only thing she and Papa Will agreed on. He thought wearing nylon stockings and dating should begin at age twenty, but since he didn't live with us, I knew what he thought wouldn't have to be the rule for what happened in my life. But Grandma was right there, keeping me from growing up. Nevertheless, as she fussed and fumed about my wicked desires, I kept my expression pleasant, the same as I did in the halls of Central High in order to avoid expulsion.

"Let's take some time to think about the stockings," Mother Lois said, smiling and moving toward the trunk to peek inside. "Tonight we'll pick our special cloth from the trunks and get going on a design for all of our dresses and for Conrad's shirt."

"Lois, maybe something two-piece would be nice for Melba this year," Grandma said. As Mother nodded her head yes, and knelt beside the trunks, the silky waves of her hair fell down to her waist.

Meanwhile I was taking time to corral my thoughts. I wanted them to ask me what I wanted to wear. As the discussion about my outfit continued without me, I felt the same as I did at Central when people talked over and around me. I felt power surging up in me once again, so I had to speak up for myself. "I want a grown-up outfit. A suit kind of thing that will be okay for school and church and look nice over my crinoline."

Grandma seemed taken aback by my forwardness. My Easter dress had been a decision she and Mother had made up until then. I could see her pondering whether to send me off to my room or to humor me. Then she said, "Well, young lady, seems you have strong opinions. But I guess you have a right. You've grown up a lot. Why don't you tell us exactly what you want." Then her eyes lit up as she withdrew fabric from the trunk. Her enthusiasm always peaked during discussions about fashion. She adored designing and making new clothes.

Mama and Grandma could draw a picture, then sit in the

middle of the floor and cut a pattern out of newspaper, and make a dress come to life in the fabric.

For the next hour, we rummaged through Grandma's trunks filled with fabrics she had collected over the years. There were remnants of dresses and suits I had seen her wear all my life. There were brand-new pieces and full bolts she had gotten from her mother before she died or from her sisters as trades for other things. Easter was always a time when we each were allowed to choose the cloth we wanted.

Celebrating the Easter holiday was a big event in our family. Attending church on Easter was a grand ceremony when everybody dressed up in the very best they could afford. There was always an Easter-egg hunt on the church grounds, and a parade of people in special hats. A few weeks back we had officially begun the sacred holiday with the pledge of our sacrifices for Lent. It was a family tradition that Mama and Grandma would review our Lenten commitment as we shopped the trunks.

"Have you two considered adding more items to your sacrifice list this year?" Grandma asked as she began to sketch the design for my dress.

"Uh, Grapette colas. That's what I'm doing without. I haven't slipped yet," I declared, thinking how many times I'd thought about slipping.

"That's all?" Grandma's tone let me know she wasn't pleased with either the number or quality of sacrifices on my list. One year I had chosen to give up the radio, and another, candy bars. I knew for sure I would never promise to give up either of those things again.

"Well, what about giving up television to spend more time reading your Bible?" Grandma said.

"Ohhhh, Mother, Grandma, please, since I'm giving up so much in Central, can't you let me slide by this year?" I pleaded with them as I sat caressing the thick folded piece of purple velvet I had pulled from the trunk to covet. The scent of cedar balls was beginning to fill the room.

"There's lots of hard work to be done on repenting for sins. Have you listed your sins?" As Grandma spoke, she rocked back and forth a little faster, and turned her attention away from her sketching to look at me.

"I've lumped together into one big sin all the hundreds of times I thought evil of people at Central," I said. "There were also several times I thought about sassing adults back, mostly teachers and principals at school. And I didn't trust God on two occasions."

"And how about not answering all your fan mail?" Mother Lois added. "Don't you think it a sin to ignore all those people who take their valuable time to write to you? You were so good about it at first."

I realized she was right. At the beginning, I had faithfully answered those letters each weekend. They came from France, Germany, England, Africa, and Australia, from people all around the world, mostly congratulating me for going to Central High. Grandma would sift out the mean ones, which were few and far between. I got several marriage proposals from cute boys, some of them white, who sent their pictures. Grandma forbade me to send them more than a polite thank-you. I wanted at least to learn more about them and file them in an "if you need a husband when you're a grown-up file." But Grandma said that would be a personal sin.

Meanwhile, back at school, I feared my grades would suffer horribly because I couldn't concentrate. Every moment of every day was filled with awful surprises that began early each morning. I hoped and prayed I wouldn't get ejected before the end of school. I took heart because I could see signs of the kind of student activities that only come near the end of the school year.

Late one evening, Link telephoned. He was furious about the announcement of the cancellation of many of his senior class activities. He spoke of all his hard work to maintain good grades, his athletic awards, and his student leadership, and now his hopes for a wonderful senior year were dashed. The traditional senior events had been canceled because of the possibility of trouble as a result of integration. School officials also cited the presence of the Arkansas National Guard as another reason.

Now hes going to want her to stop integration or something.

Link was inconsolable. "I don't know what I can do about it," I said even as I wondered whether his disappointment and anger would make him turn against me.

"You can do a news interview saying we're not such bad people and that everything is getting better at school. That way everybody in the world won't think we're all villains."

"Link, you don't want me to lie, do you? Everything is getting worse . . . not better."

On and on he went, telling me how Central High's students were suffering and sacrificing the reputation of their nationally acclaimed school because we had come there. He was more angry than I'd ever heard him. "This was a good school, ranked high on the national scale, and now our halls are filled with soldiers and people are treating us like criminals!"

I could only think to tell him to have faith that God would make things okay. I couldn't do what he asked, I couldn't change things. That's when he really got sarcastic, saying, "Don't give me that God stuff. That's what Nana Healey always says. I don't believe in God. If He's there, why is He letting all this happen?"

"Who's Nana Healey?"

"My nanny. She's colored—like you." He had often spoken of her, but this was the first time he had told me she was not white.

"The reason I'm attending Central is so I don't have to spend my life being somebody's nanny," I said in a tone to match his indignant manner.

By the end of the conversation, Link's anger had shifted from me to the situation. He was frustrated, vowing he was going to do something about the cancellation. Our conversation aroused my suspicions anew. Was he just being nice to me temporarily to get me to lie to the news people? Who was he? After all, I had no way of checking him out. I couldn't tell the others about him or talk about him to the NAACP people. I was at his mercy, having to decide on my own whether or not he was genuine. I would have to be on constant alert from now on, watching for signs of what his real motives were.

But meanwhile he warned me to watch out for any students who tried to hand me election pamphlets. School officers were to be elected on April 24. They would be nice and offer us literature, he said, but as we paused to take it they would ink our dress, grab our books, or worse. "I've been to some of those planning meetings recently, and I can tell you they're gonna pull out all stops and do everything they can to get you out of school before it ends, to make certain you're not coming back next year."

"What more could they do. They're already exhausting us."

"Yeah, but it's gonna get much worse. The thing is, lately, they've been talking about pulling off something really big that will not only hurt you but your families—something that will force you to quit."

———

JUDGE DAVIES OUT OF INTEGRATION SUIT.
AN ARKANSAS JUDGE IS PREFERABLE TO HEAR A LITTLE ROCK
SCHOOL BOARD PETITION ASKING POSTPONEMENT OF INTEGRATION
IN LITTLE ROCK SCHOOLS
—*Arkansas Gazette*, Wednesday, April 16, 1958

This more than any other story in the newspaper made me fear that the segregationists were making real progress in their constant hammering to defeat integration. Getting rid of that judge who was so important to our cause must have been an occasion for celebration among their ranks. Slowly, they were waging an effective campaign on every level, even at the federal level, to have things their way.

Back at school on Monday, just as Link had warned, people approached us as though they were including us in the election process. They would come up and offer a pamphlet with one hand while using the other hand to shower us with all manner of smelly liquids. Sometimes they would kick or even punch us, and usually whatever they did was followed by a shower of rude name-calling.

The elections at our old school, Horace Mann, weren't nearly so sophisticated. At Central, people put up signs, wore buttons, and passed out materials, just as though it were a real election. They held debates and voting parties and did all manner of campaigning. I was intrigued watching the process, delighted at the complexity of it all compared to what I had been accustomed to seeing at our old school. It made me extra sad that I wasn't allowed to participate.

Distributing campaign literature also gave renegade students an opportunity to hand out more flyers opposing us, like the "One Down, Eight to Go" cards. We figured somebody somewhere must have a full-time press going, dedicated to anti-eight campaign literature. Meanwhile, avid segregationists were fueling the battle against us by regularly appearing on television in order to enroll more people outside school to fight against us. For example, one group orchestrated a bizarre parade of cars that drove back and forth in front of the school honking their horns. That outside pressure ignited more explosions inside as the atmosphere became like a devil's carnival with us as the central attraction.

The experience of walking down that hall to my homeroom each morning got so worrisome that I doubled my repetitions of the Lord's Prayer as I walked from the front door up the stairs. Inside the homeroom class, I was entertained by a whole new series of indignities. I arrived one day to find a doll that resembled me, with a rope around her neck, hanging from the door frame. Another time, someone had provided genuine urine to spray in my seat and on my clothing.

I decided to ask the teacher whether or not she could stop people from throwing rocks at me and pushing chairs into my back. She told me I'd have to speak to Vice-Principal Huckaby because there was little she could do. The next day, I asked Mrs. Huckaby what could be done, and when she said she didn't know, my heart sank. It felt like no capable adults were in charge. Later, Link confirmed that the teachers who made a big thing of disciplining segregationists hoodlums were themselves the victims of ostracism.

More frequently now, Link was full of talk about graduation events. Under any other circumstances, this would have been an exciting time of year, filled with wonderful events. He told me about the parties for the juniors and seniors. He told me about a huge gala at the Marion Hotel, and said the junior and senior picnics at Central High were better than Christmas and New Year's combined. It made me feel more isolated, because now I had also been left out of the events at my old high school.

As our conversations grew more relaxed, Link began telling me about his parents. His father, a wealthy and very well-known businessman, had been forced to contribute money to the Citizens' Council campaign in order to do a healthy amount of business in Little Rock. "He isn't for race mixing, but he also isn't for beating up anybody's children," Link explained.

————

JUDGE LEMLEY TO HEAR SCHOOL BOARD'S PETITION
—*Arkansas Gazette*, Tuesday, April 22, 1958

As I read the article I felt despair creeping over me. Judge Harry Lemley of Hope, Arkansas, had been named to hear the Little Rock School Board petition asking for a postponement of integration for public schools. The first hearing was set for the following Monday at 9:30 A.M. He promised the final hearing would be held long before September. The article described him as a native of Upperville, Virginia, and a man who "loved the South as though it were a religion." It was evident from that description that he wouldn't be likely to violate southern tradition for my people.

I desperately needed the break that came with the Easter holiday. As usual on Easter Sunday morning, each of us twirled

274

and pranced in our family fashion show. "Spiffy do," Grandma India said as we climbed into the car. The church was filled to the rafters with people we didn't see during all the rest of the year.

And Vince was there, smiling and beckoning to me. I smiled back but continued down the aisle to sit with my family as usual. The Easter sermon was much longer and louder than on ordinary Sundays. "Old Rugged Cross" was sung with tears and organ chords that made goose bumps and chills climb up my spine. As we sang the last song and prepared to gather for a traditional Easter dinner, I even felt a moment of contentment.

Vince and I sat together at the church dinner, reminiscing about our earlier dates, and for the first time I felt as though we were good friends again. Still, he was not someone with whom I could talk about my Central High experience. I had lived through so much turmoil since we first met that my thoughts and dreams were now totally changed from a year ago. We had simply drifted apart because we had so little in common, except our past relationship. I now felt as grown-up as I had once thought him to be. Nevertheless, as we sat sipping lemonade on that sunny day, there was no doubt in my mind I was enjoying one of the special moments of my life. Still, I couldn't help thinking that I had more than a month to go until the end of the school year. Central High was never out of my mind.

In my diary I wrote:

I am happy today, but I am also frightened. The appointment of Lemley means we have to pray hard. This is not supposed to happen in America. I mean segregationists aren't supposed to be able to have their own judge.

I salute the flag every morning as I look at a picture on the home-room wall directly in front of me. I will never forget that picture as long as I live. It is a brown pasture with white sheep. As the boys behind me call names and the girls to each side sneer, I look straight ahead because those sheep are smiling at me. I think it is a smile from God. It is a promise that if I salute the flag like a good American, all these integration problems will be worked out eventually.

26

INSIDE CENTRAL, EVERYONE WHO WASN'T TALKING ABOUT GET-
ting us out of school seemed to be talking about the upcoming
production of *The Mikado*. I listened intently for every little
crumb of information I could get. I felt a vicarious delight just
being near the excitement. From what I could learn, the production was nearly professional, with many props and the kind of
fancy equipment I'd never even heard of. How I longed to be
included, or at least permitted to attend. I thought I had resigned myself to being left out, but it was haunting me again.

When some of *The Mikado* actors in full makeup appeared in
the hallway, I was naturally curious. I must have relaxed my
guard as I stared at them a bit longer than I should have.

"Hey, nigger," one of them yelled at me across the hall, "I'm
made up to be almost as black as you." That started a whole
round of taunting in the hallway. I snuffed out the spark of
delight growing inside me, donned my warrior veneer, and
walked away.

The segregationists' campaign against us seemed to get even
worse during that week. Sign-carrying, card-dispensing, tripping, kicking crusaders revved up their efforts to reduce our
number to zero. Meanwhile Mrs. Huckaby, the woman I considered to be somewhat near fair and rational about the whole

situation, had lapsed back into her attitude of trying to convince me there was nothing going on. It seemed like whenever I reported anything to her, she would work herself up into a lather: I was seeing things; was I being too sensitive, did I have specific details?

When she stopped behaving in a reasonable way, it took away the only point of reference I had. I desperately tried to understand how such an intelligent woman could be reasonable and understanding one moment, then seem so cold, distant, and dispassionate the next. I supposed that she must be under an enormous weight and doing her best. I tried to see the overall picture—to remember that over the long haul, she had been a tiny pinpoint of light in the otherwise very dark experience of dealing with Central High's administration. But once again I had to accept the fact that I shouldn't be wasting my time or energy hoping anyone would listen to my reports. I was on my own.

By the end of that week I had flashed endless smiles in response to negative deeds or words. If God was giving stars in crowns in heaven, as Grandma always promised, I'd earned two or three.

By Saturday morning, as my family rushed about the house making breakfast and doing household chores, I lay with my face down in my pillow, hoping they would be quiet. But it was not to be. I had an early morning phone call from Link.

"I need your help," he said. "I want you to come with me now."

"You're crazy. You know we can't be seen together."

"It'll be okay. I promise. I'm going where it'll be safe."

"Where?" I asked.

"You'll see. Meet me on the other side of the bridge—just inside North Little Rock."

I was confused about meeting him. I wondered whether or not this was the trap the KKK asked Link to set for me so they could get rid of me.

"Please, Melba," he pleaded. Hearing the urgency in his voice I decided to do what he wanted. I felt queasy as I explained to

Mama and Grandma that there was a big emergency with Thelma and I was going to visit her. It was the first time in my life I had ever looked them in the eye and told an untruth. They were reluctant to let me go, but I promised I would stay in our own neighborhood where it was safe. I prayed for God's forgiveness for lying as I drove away.

I spotted Link's car, just on the North Little Rock side of the bridge. In broad daylight, I parked my car and got into his. He told me we were going to Nana Healey's house. I didn't say much as we drove along. It felt awkward being with him. Although we had talked lots on the telephone, he was in some ways a stranger—a white stranger. Sitting next to him made me wonder again who he was and what he wanted with me. I tried to close my mind to Grandmother's words: "The only thing a white man ever wants with one of our women is personal favors."

The neighborhood got more and more dismal. It was a part of town where our people lived in awful, run-down chicken-shack houses, some in such bad condition that they looked as though they'd fall down any moment. Folks stood around in clusters talking. There were groups of men dressed in ragged, filthy clothing, drinking from liquor bottles as they chatted. I'd seen places like this before on those rare occasions when Grandma and I passed through as we went to visit friends or our relatives in North Little Rock. Being there made me feel so fortunate that Mother had her teaching job. Without that job, I might very well be living in a place like this.

"Hey, why so quiet?" Link touched my arm, and I turned to face him.

"I'm frightened, I guess."

"I'm not gonna let anything happen to you. You're a lot safer here than inside Central, aren't you."

We pulled into the yard of one of the shabbier places. I wanted to turn and run. Instead, Link opened the door and reached for my hand as I stepped out into a puddle of water. He teased me about being graceful and having shaky ice-cold hands as I watched him fumble with the key to the trunk.

"Well, don't just stand there, grab a bag." He was pulling bag after bag of groceries out of the trunk and stacking them on the hood of the car.

"She hasn't got any kin, so I've got to keep her fed."

"Why you? Where are her own people?" I grabbed two bags of food and followed as he led the way.

"She hasn't got any people. She worked for my family all her life. As a young girl, she worked for my grandparents. When Daddy got married, Grandmother sent her to him as a kind of gift. She's been with me all my life."

"Why isn't she with your family anymore?"

" 'Cause she got sick—real sick. My folks let her go, just like that, after all the time she'd been so good to us. She's got no money for a doctor. She won't take my money. I think she's got tuberculosis. But I don't know for sure." He knocked on the weather-beaten door.

"Nana, it's me. May I come in?" His voice was loud but ever so gentle as he called out to her. A feeble voice called back. Holding bags of groceries in his arms, he pushed open the door with his elbow.

There in a dark room sat an aged woman, her profile etched against the sun shadow in the one window of the room. Long silver-gray hair in braids framed her lined face, which was worn and weary. Wrinkled skin was stretched taut over protruding cheekbones. Her fingers were stiffened into position as though she were holding an apple, but her hands were empty.

As I moved closer I could see she was wearing a freshly starched, flowered cotton dress just like my own grandmother might have worn. Her appearance was immaculate, her posture was erect, and she tilted her chin upward, demonstrating her own dignity and pride despite her circumstances.

The tiny, bare shack was spotlessly clean. It was one room with a makeshift bathroom in plain view. In one corner there was a cracked sink, over which a slab of a broken mirror hung. Despite the rundown condition of the few pieces of furniture and the torn curtains on the window, there were touches of pride all around. A picture frame on her night table held a photo of a small boy with blond curls. It must be Link as a child, I thought.

"Nana, I want you to meet my friend Melba," Link said, raising his voice to an ear-shattering level. Then he leaned over to whisper to me, "She can't hear good, go closer. I want you to convince her to see a doc, somebody you know and trust."

"Your friend?" said Mrs. Healey.

"Yes, ma'am, she's my friend, aren't you, Melba?" He was talking loudly and grinning at me as though he wasn't certain of what I would say.

I didn't say anything, turning instead to read Mrs. Healey's reaction. Her expression was angry. She could barely move about or speak, but she gathered her strength, and after a long moment she said, "Boy, you'all are gonna get yourselves in a heap of trouble. You know better."

"Yes, Nana." He knelt beside her and took her hand. "Don't you worry about it. I'll handle it. You talk to Melba while I make a cup of tea for you." He took off his jacket, rolled up his sleeves, and began putting the groceries away. I watched as he placed staples in the splintered wood cabinet and on the sagging but meticulously lined shelves above the sink. He behaved as though he had performed those same tasks many times before.

"Mrs. Healey, you're looking very nice today." I drew near to her.

"Well, I don't feel so good. But I gets up and dresses myself. Cleanliness is next to Godliness." Suddenly her emaciated body was racked with a cough. She reached for the handkerchief tucked in her sleeve. On and on she coughed. Link turned from his chores, staring at her with a pained expression on his face. He reached for a cup from the cupboard and filled it with water. Holding it up to her mouth, he gently helped her to drink from it.

"Nana, we gotta get you to see a doc." He nudged me with his elbow. "Your turn," he whispered to me.

"Mrs. Healey, this sounds like the kinda cough that isn't going away real soon unless you get some doctoring and the right medicine."

"Oh, I'll be fine," she said, clearing her throat. "Jus' takes a while for me to get my bearings after one of these spells." Her voice was raspy, and the coughing started again. On and on she coughed, her feeble body shaking as I tried to hold on to her. Link got a cold cloth. I held it to her head, and the coughing finally stopped. I made up my mind I was going to help Link get a doctor to come and see her.

After a while, he went back to his work. He opened the door to the icebox. The wheezing old appliance, without light, looked as though the inside panels were ready to fall. It was empty until he started packing shelf after shelf.

"Wolf was about to get you, Nana," he said. "You're running kinda short." They giggled to each other as though they understood without speaking.

We spent the rest of the morning there with Mrs. Healey. She coughed continuously as we went about our chores. Link again urged me to convince her to take money for a doctor. He said I could tell her it was a loan from the church. I agreed. Watching him tend to Mrs. Healey, I would never again have reason to question his motives.

There was silence between us for a long time as we drove away. And then I couldn't help asking, "And why didn't your folks make some provision for her?"

"Whenever I ask my folks, my father turns me off by saying I'm weak—that I'm a you-know-what lover. He says colored folks are used to doing without, and I ought not spoil them."

I found a doctor in our community who did not know Mother Lois or Grandma India and asked him to go to Mrs. Healey's. When I spoke with the doctor later, he said there was not a lot he could do for Nana Healey except make her comfortable. What she really needed was long-term care in a hospital. I asked if she was dying, and he told me yes. One of the hardest things I ever had to do was tell Link. There were tears in his voice as he spoke through a rush of anger.

"Damn my folks. They didn't even pay social security for her. She's got nothing. I share my allowance with her, and some of the folks in her church give her a few pennies. But they've got nothing like what it will take for a hospital. I've gotta go now, I'll take care of it."

I decided that I had to tell Grandma India about Nana Healey. It took time, but Grandma got over her anger at my disobedience, and sure enough, she promised to visit Mrs. Healey on her weekly trips to North Little Rock. So in the end Link and Grandma formed something of a friendship as they discussed all the tasks surrounding Nana Healey's care which compelled them to get to know each other.

COURT ACTION SET FOR TODAY IN CHS CASE
—*Arkansas Gazette*, Monday, April 28, 1958

The lengthy and bitter Little Rock Central High School integration case will be reopened at 9:30 A.M. today in Federal District Court under an Arkansas judge. Judge Harry S. Lemley of Hope will take over from Judge Ronald N. Davies of Fargo, N.D.

At issue is a Little Rock School Board petition asking for a postponement of integration at the school. The National Association for the Advancement of Colored People has asked that the petition be denied.

Reopening that case meant my year of suffering was in vain. If the school board was not committed to integration, how could Central's students be expected to accept it. Even if the NAACP was successful in getting the petition denied, it set a tone segregationists would seize as a weapon against us. Downhearted couldn't even describe how low I felt.

To cheer myself up, I decided to wear my Easter dress to school, the one Mother and Grandmother had made for me. Lately, the ink spraying had slowed down a bit in favor of more exotic torture. Even as I entered school that morning, I could tell the prospect of the hearing had already put wind into the sails of segregationists. "Won't be long now," one boy hissed as I entered the door. "Don't phone or drop us a card 'cause we ain't gonna miss you, nigger."

I had survived the whole day and was walking through the hall to the Fourteenth Street side of the school to go home. A boy approached me, behaving normally, so I paid him no mind. As he got closer, suddenly I felt the warm liquid spray across my chest. Ink. The front of my new dress was soaked with ink spots. Before I could get away, he danced around to my right side and showered me once more.

[handwritten marginalia: · I would do some- thing to the person that put ink on my new outfit.]

I ran toward the exit as I held back the tears brimming my eyes. Suddenly Link was there a bit ahead of me on the walkway.

"What happened?" He stopped dead in his tracks. I tried not to let him see how upset I was. I wiped away my tears.

"Shhhhhhhhh, don't talk to me." I kept walking, but he followed.

"Melba . . . stop. Are you all right?"

"Get outta here," I shouted at him. Just at that moment a group of boys approached us. Link paused, but I kept moving toward them as though nothing could stop me. I was determined to make it to the car, which waited at the curb to take me home. Suddenly, one of the boys moved closer to me and drew back his fist.

"Hey!" Link shouted. "You like the way I redecorated the nigger's dress. Looks better than it did before, don't you think?" The boy turned to answer Link and then started snickering. I darted around him and into the car. As I looked back, Link stood with them, laughing and chatting. I couldn't stop my tears.

In the days that followed, we were repeatedly warned that nothing mattered more than avoiding any activity that would get us expelled. Now the hoodlums were mounting a last-ditch effort to get us out of school before May 29th. They wanted no possibility that we could register for the next school term.

Meanwhile Link seemed nervous, asking me each day what had happened. He kept harping on the fact that he was hearing that segregationists were going to do something to somebody's family. "Something big that will be certain to get one or more of you guys to voluntarily leave school," he said.

But as the days passed, I was less concerned about Link's warning and more worried about the boy who now came into study hall each day threatening to toss me out of the window, and the girls who encircled me at least once a day, saying every negative thing they could about the parts of my body. Fat thighs, ugly hair, ugly clothing, funny eyes, all shouted in a chorus. I thought sadness would force the tears in my heart to flow, but I never said a word.

At the same time I was worried about Mother Lois, who was becoming more tense with each day. At dinner, she hardly spoke. She seldom laughed and didn't offer any of her corny jokes. It was a Monday evening when Mother gathered us in the living room for a family conference. I had never seen such a grave expression on her face.

"They're not going to renew my teaching contract for next year. I don't have a job," she told us.

"But why?" we all asked. We knew very well that there was no reason to fire her. They couldn't possibly fire her for doing a bad job. She had fourteen years of teaching experience with lots of awards to her credit. There were no complaints in her record.

And then with tears brimming in her eyes, she explained. "They say they'll give me back my job only if I withdraw Melba from Central High School immediately. They do not want her to finish the year."

27

"WE HAVE NO CHOICE. WE HAVE TO TAKE THE RISK OF TALKING to newspaper people. Who is going to feed us and put a roof over our heads if I don't get my job back?" Mother Lois's face was tear-stained, but her expression reflected the determination I heard in her voice. We sat around the big, old mahogany table in the dining room, discussing a plan to save her job.

"Those segregationists will stop at nothing to get what they want." Grandma appeared angry and anxious as she spoke.

During the last few days of April, Mother Lois had humbled herself to make several trips to North Little Rock's school headquarters to plead for her job, but they had refused to reinstate her. On five different occasions, her superiors told her they were taking away her contract because she had allowed me to participate in the integration of Central.

When the man who held our second mortgage heard Mother would lose her job, he called the note. It took all the money she could scrape together to persuade him to be patient and take huge payments. The grocer became reluctant to give us credit. Money was running out. Mama didn't feel safe taking the loan she usually borrowed from the bank at the beginning of each May to support us through the summer. We made ends meet because she worked during the school year for $2,700 and then

286

borrowed money to carry us through to August. Each year when her salary started in September, she'd pay back the loan.

Already Mr. Henson had called about our late house payment on the first mortgage. The bank was calling about the car. Mother didn't want to plead for any more credit at the grocery store, so the cupboards held a sparse supply of staples. The refrigerator shelves were almost bare. Grandma India was preparing more stews and casseroles with less meat and lots of rice and potatoes. She was dividing one chicken so it stretched into three full meals by using the back and wings in her lemon-rice soup. She was baking plain white bread instead of buying it at the store.

"Sitting and wishing never made man great. The good Lord sends the fishing, but we gotta dig the bait. I say we've got to force the hand of those administrators. They're ignoring you." There was fire in Grandma's eyes as she spoke.

The loss of Mama's teaching position had upset all the members of our family. Thinking about it, talking about it, planning for it had taken us up like an Arkansas tornado that pounded and pounded us in the wind. Now my home life was completely taken over by the same tense fretting and worrying as my school life had been. It had happened without warning. Mother explained how the administrator had called her into his office and told her he had the connections to see that she got offered a job in Oklahoma.

"You know I can't leave Little Rock," Mama told him. "Melba is in Central. I'm buying a home here. All our roots are here." She felt an awful sinking feeling as she remained standing, holding on to the back of the wooden chair across the desk from her boss. Her instincts told her she should not be seated.

"You have young children and a mother to support. You need a job."

"But I have a job, here," she told him. She felt panic rise in her as she wondered why on earth he'd offer her a job out of state. How was he able to do that? She concluded there must have been a conspiracy of sorts—the Southern good old boy network getting together to remove a thorn in their side.

"Your contract here with us will not be renewed. The job in Oklahoma is your only option," he said.

"But why? I've done a good job here. There have never been any complaints from parents or from this administration."

"This is just one of those things that happens, Mrs. Pattillo. It has nothing to do with the caliber of your work. It's simply that we've been ordered to hire a different kind of teacher." He paused. "Of course, there is one way you can keep your job."

"Yes, sir?"

"If Melba were to withdraw from that school, we could talk about renewing your contract this year at quite a handsome salary increase," he said.

Mother was certain he was being pressured by his bosses, North Little Rock's all-white school administrators who were fighting integration in that city. Still, she had not expected such harsh retaliation. As she walked away from his office, she recalled what Link had said, "Something bad will happen, something involving the whole family."

As we sat mulling over our fate, I realized that the segregationists had taken away the one thing we couldn't do without—Mama's job. If there was anything that could cause me to leave school, it would be to get Mama's job back.

Grandma was soft-spoken, calm, but emphatic as she said, "Well, Lois, you've tried every polite and proper way of getting that job back. I think some sort of drastic action is called for."

"I don't know . . ." Mother pondered the idea in silence. I had watched her expression become a little more drawn with each passing day.

"We could call some of those reporters. The main goal would be to get a story in the local white papers," Grandma said.

Mother Lois paused and took a deep breath before she answered. "It could backfire. It will attract even more attention to Melba inside Central. The kids will see her name in the paper, and they'll single her out. And it could make my bosses at school even more angry. Those people at the school administration could keep me from ever teaching anywhere in Arkansas again."

"Still, we got to live. We got to eat. Ain't nobody gonna feed us—not the NAACP, not those white folks—nobody."

"I guess we've got no choice. I've thought about it and prayed about it," Mama finally said. "Tomorrow morning I'm going to write down a paragraph or two and call some of those news people."

The next day, Friday, May 2, I entered the Sixteenth Street side of Central High. While I walked the gauntlet to get to my classroom, I escaped into my daydreams about the junior prom. In the middle of all the upheaval over Mama's job loss and the turmoil at school, I was feeling sorry for myself. I desperately wanted some remnants of what my life might have been had I not come to Central. Maybe next year, I consoled myself, maybe it wouldn't be so frightening to walk to class. Perhaps I would even be able to attend Central's senior prom.

There was lots of excitement for the next few days as the yearbooks were distributed. Some of our regular adversaries complained loud and long about how the inclusion of some of our pictures had tainted their precious yearbook. But as they became preoccupied with exchanging autographs, a few of them let up on chasing and taunting us.

The halls were electric with energy and chatter while students giggled and pointed to each other's pictures and wrote in the books, creating those funny sayings and rhyming verses they would treasure thirty years later at class reunion time. I found myself standing perfectly still in a shadowy corner, lingering at the edge of a circle of joy I could not be a part of.

We continued to hear snippets of the fancy plans for Central students to have fun during the final weeks of the school year, plans that we could only speculate about. Certainly none of the eight of us received even one social invitation, nor could we have risked attending even if we had. To make matters worse, I did not receive any graduation celebration invitations from my old school. At first I had deeply resented being left out, especially since all of us were making huge sacrifices that would benefit everyone in the future. But after thinking about it, I realized that sometimes we were excluded not as an act of hostility but because they had forgotten about us since we weren't visible in their lives anymore.

Over the next few days, I was anxious to get the newspaper to see if somebody would print the story about Mama's job loss. I had watched her go through the awkward ordeal of phoning news people. Three of them listened patiently as she read her two paragraphs explaining the situation. They called back later with questions, and one man interviewed her.

On Wednesday morning, May 7, I was awakened by the slam of the front door and Mother Lois calling out to us from the living room. "It's here. The newspaper did it—they printed the article about my losing my job!"

"What on earth's all the noise about?" Grandma said as she entered the living room, sipping her morning tea.

"That Mr. Reed, the reporter, is a fine fellow. May the good Lord bless him," Mother Lois said, as she held up the paper for us to see. She was so excited she could hardly contain herself. She handed the paper over to Grandma, who began reading aloud immediately.

CHS CRISIS COST HER JOB, SAYS NORTH LITTLE ROCK NEGRO TEACHER, the headlines read. The article stated our problem precisely as Mother had told the reporter: The North Little Rock School District has refused to renew her contract to teach seventh-grade English because of her participation in the integration issue.

"Praise the Lord, we got us some power now," Grandma shouted. It was the first time in days I saw hope in everybody's eyes, hope that we could fight all those high-powered white men who were taking Mama's job away.

"I think this is a turning point. Lois did what she had to do. Let's wait and see how the Lord works this out." Grandma read the article aloud for the second time.

The phone started to ring. One after another, the calls came. We raced for the telephone, delighted with the people saying they were on our side. Only a few people said negative things, like Mother deserved to lose her job for being too uppity.

But some of those who wished us well were people calling from other cities. The wire services had teletyped the story around the country. People from everywhere promised they'd call the administrator's office and say it was an awful thing to take Mama's job away.

It had been the best morning in many days. We actually laughed over the breakfast table. That good feeling lingered as I entered the front door of Central and climbed the stairs to my third-floor homeroom.

"You better pack your rags and get on outta here, nigger. Your mama's lost her job. What you gonna do now?" The baiting went on for most of the morning. They had all read the paper, too. I wondered if it had been one of their parents who caused Mama to lose her job.

"Thank you for your concern," was my reply. I was struggling to practice the technique of not responding in kind to their mistreatment. I had begun to master it to the point that it was almost automatic. Still, I had been startled by an alarming increase in the verbal assaults and kicking and shoving incidents in hallways during the early days of May. The shoving was harder, and often people drew back their doubled-up fists to strike at me.

GAZETTE AND EDITOR WIN TWO PULITZER PRIZES
FOR RACE CRISIS STAND
—*Arkansas Gazette*, Tuesday, May 6, 1958

The Arkansas Gazette *and its executive editor, Harry Ashmore, won two Pulitzer prizes today and became the first newspaper in the 41-year history of the journalistic awards to win the Pulitzer Gold Medal and the editorial writing prize in the same year.*

As I read this article, I wondered when we would get big prizes for what we were doing. After all, this guy was just observing our troubles from afar and writing about them. Not once did I see him spend a day in hell with us. Grandma said

my attitude was sour and I had to say the Twenty-Third Psalm—
at least twenty-five times—to cleanse my thinking. She was
right, I was not in a good mood. During those last days, school
was more tedious with the kind of grinding passage of time that
made me look at the clock almost every five minutes.

Just as Link had warned, the segregationists were heating up
their campaign to prevent Ernie, who was a senior, from graduating. They were already saying they were sure we wouldn't
be coming back next year because we'd never last through the
semester. I could tell that Mrs. Huckaby also sensed real trouble,
because she summoned us one by one to discuss our problems.

Until that time, I had been observing fewer and fewer Arkansas National Guard troops inside school each day. It was said
they were mostly not on the school grounds but "on call as the
situation warranted." There had been days in late April when
there were no guards visible to us in the hallways. But lately,
as tension increased, we were aware of them in the building.
As those days of May brought more and more physical punishment, for the first time in four months I was assigned a personal
bodyguard to follow me from class to class.

However, I never really felt protected by the insolent-looking,
boyish grown-up who wore the sneer of a brooding Elvis. The
soldiers' loyalties were not to us. They made that very clear in
their words and deeds.

BOARD SEEKS 3-YEAR DELAY IN INTEGRATION
—*Arkansas Gazette*, Thursday, May 8, 1958

The Little Rock School Board has suggested its plan of
gradual integration be suspended until January 1961.

In a speech to the State Junior Chamber of Commerce on that
Friday, Faubus declared that racial integration was not the law
of the land—only Congress could make laws.

With the publication of those two bombshells we suffered yet

292

more increases in the number of attacks on us. Just when I thought I had endured the greatest insult or most painful physical attack, someone would come along and prove me wrong. They would go for the championship in meanness.

NAACP officials had written to the Department of the Army complaining about the "do-nothing troops," asking for the return of the 101st. But President Eisenhower had ignored the complaint, announcing that the Arkansas Guard would remain until the end of school on May 29.

As we faced days of grueling punishment, I was also coping with the fact that despite the newspaper article, we had heard no word from the North Little Rock school administrators about Mama's job. I was bringing sandwiches made of apple butter on bread ends to school for lunch. One of Grandmother's friends had given us a basket of apples, so there was apple strudel, apple pie, apple butter, baked apples, and apple jelly.

Well-wishers continued phoning. It was rumored that there was a groundswell of protest from all over the country in the form of letters and phone calls to the North Little Rock school administration office. Hearing about that made us feel good, but the fact was, there was no real change, and we desperately needed the money from Mama's loan. Mama's bosses hadn't budged. In fact, if anything, he had become hostile toward her, telling her that by going to the news people she had ruined everything. When more than a week had passed and there was no renewal offer, Mama was panicked.

"We haven't exhausted all our blessings. We haven't knocked on the Lord's door the right way . . ." Grandma concluded. So she and Mama decided the next step would be to go to the presiding bishops of our community's churches. One of the most powerful of our people was Bishop O. J. Sherman. He told Mother to go back to the white administrator and say one simple sentence: "Bishop Sherman asked me to tell you he would like me to have a job."

Mother did as she was told. The administrator stared down at the papers on his desk, silent, ignoring her for an uncomfortably long moment while he picked the lint off his trousers. "Oh, he did, did he?" He looked up into my mother's eyes, a slight smile creeping onto his face. "Mrs. Pattillo, you don't like the idea of working in Oklahoma, do you?"

"No, sir," she said, speaking firmly.

"I read the articles about you in the newspapers, and we've gotten a lot of calls. Now you've gone and riled up the bishops from your community."

"Yes, sir." Mama's tone let him know she meant business.

"Got anything else in mind?"

"Yes, sir. I've got to do whatever it takes to keep my job, because I've got to feed my family. I'm a woman alone. Besides, I've done nothing wrong. I've been a very good teacher all these years. I don't deserve to be treated like this."

The administrator dismissed her politely without saying another word. The next day, when Mama got to school, her boss came to her classroom and congratulated her on her fine teaching abilities. "It'll be nice having you back here next year," he said.

"I assume your accolades will be forthcoming in writing," Mama replied. The next afternoon she arrived home carrying her contract. She sat down at the kitchen table and handed it to Grandma, who was placing the dinner plates on the table. Tears streamed down Mama's cheeks as she wrung her hands together to stop their shaking.

"Let's hold hands and pray," Grandma India said. "Praise you, Lord. I knew you wouldn't forget us."

PRESIDENT ORDERS MOVING OF TROOPS
FROM CENTRAL HIGH SCHOOL
—*Arkansas Gazette*, Friday, May 9, 1958

Governor Faubus said yesterday that the National Guard troops might be needed again next fall to prevent Negroes from entering Little Rock Central High School under a federal order.

On Friday as I entered Central, I was wondering what would become of us next September. Link stood at the top of the stairs, pretending to ignore me. His being there was a signal that I should expect something out of the ordinary. It meant he had just learned that something awful was about to happen, something he didn't know about the night before when we spoke by phone.

He winked, and I gave him a thumbs-up indicating I understood. Exploding objects that looked and sounded like firecrackers but were really more dangerous were all around us that day. They went off at my feet, flew past my head, got tossed into my locker, and even once into my book bag. By noon, I had become a nervous wreck. I was shaking, thinking that maybe I should go home, give up, withdraw.

I began praying for peace and for strength to finish the day. That's when I remembered that I had a lot to be grateful for. Mama had her job back. I could hear Grandma India's voice saying over and over again, "If you have to depend on yourself for strength, you will not make it. But if you depend on God's strength, you can do anything."

So on I went, humming "On the Battlefield for My Lord." At the end of the day, Mama told us that she'd received the money from her loan. We started our celebration with a gigantic shopping spree at the grocery store. After restocking our shelves with basics, each of us got to pick one favorite item, and then it was off to church for a choir sing.

As I marked the May days off my calendar, I felt as though I was caught up in a whirlwind. Ernie was rehearsing for graduation. At the same time, there was a constant shower of threats about stopping him from graduating. Using new tactics, with more frequent attacks that involved more people, the segregationists watched and followed us constantly, looking for ways to isolate us.

One frightening development was a series of accusations that Ernie had a roving eye and was flirting with a particular white girl. That mortified us because we all knew it was an explosive lie that could get him killed and maybe us along with him. The rumor was spreading around the school and being used to fuel the protests by the Mothers' League and the Citizens' Council.

It was apparent this was a desperate plan to entrap and get rid of him only days before his graduation. However, if they had known Ernie as I did, they would have thought of another way. Cool-headed and very much in command of himself, he wasn't about to be caught in that trap. At every turn, he watched himself so that there could never be the slightest opportunity for confirming such accusations.

Even when the girl in question forced herself on him, sitting too close to him in the cafeteria and fluttering her eyelashes as she dropped her book, expecting him to retrieve it, Ernie ignored her and went about his business. I admired the way he conducted himself in the face of enormous pressure. And he did it with a casual, relaxed manner and smile, although I knew he had to be nervous about all the furor over his Central High diploma.

The barrage of flying food in the cafeteria got so bad that we could seldom eat our lunches there. One day, with people dumping water on my head, throwing nails at my back, and shouting abuse, I was forced to leave school. I saw that Gloria, Jeff, and Thelma also had to check out of school early that day to escape the harassment.

"You'all think you're gonna have a graduation, but a funeral is what you're really gonna have—no, more like eight funerals." The voice was familiar. Of course, it was my persistent attacker, the ever-present Andy, who continued his threats to get me, no matter what. He had taken to chasing me from the gymnasium through the dark walkway that connected it to the main building. He suddenly began backing up his threats by waving a bone-handled switchblade knife in the air. My Arkansas National Guard protector calmly looked on as Andy chased me, getting so close with his knife blade that the book I held up to protect me got slashed through the cover.

"Hey, boy, you could get us into real trouble if you keep that up. You've had your fun, now you gotta move on," the

Guardsman said with a twisted smile, his cold eyes looking at me as though he would much rather have let Andy have his way with me. I stood there trembling, wishing for Danny. My heart was pounding, but I consoled myself with the knowledge that pretty soon I wouldn't have to deal with Andy. Only a few days remained before school would be out. I decided to duck out of gym class, vowing I would never walk that way again.

All at once the planned events of the year were coming to life. On All Seniors Day, Central High graduates took off to go to the park. Ernie wisely chose not to participate. He was under incredible pressure as more and more graduation celebrations were taking place. Meanwhile, cards were being passed out that read: "Open Season on Coons."

NAACP LOSES IN 2 MOTIONS TO HALT SUITS
—*Arkansas Gazette*, Friday, May 16, 1958

It felt as though parts of the foundation beneath us were crumbling. At the same time, Mrs. Daisy Bates's newspaper seemed to be toppling because advertisers were boycotting it; the NAACP was being attacked on all sides.

Since the beginning of the organization's efforts to integrate Central High, Arkansas Attorney General Bennett had harassed its officials. First he demanded they submit the names and addresses of all members and contributors. When the groups failed to do so, he arrested the organization's leaders. He had also filed suit claiming that both the NAACP and the Legal Defense and Education Fund were New York corporations doing business in Arkansas illegally. Although it had seemed at first that the NAACP was winning the struggle, not being able to halt the suits was a setback.

One piece of good news was that the Thomas plan for our immediate withdrawal and gradual—in the distant future—integration was being rejected by all sides. Thomas had met with those people from our community who condescended to meet with him. They had rejected his plan, calling it a step backward.

And the Mothers' League and the Citizens' Council rejected it because they didn't want to support the idea of integration even in the far distant future.

Nevertheless, there were signs all around us at school and in the newspapers that segregationists were making headway. The later it got in the month of May, the more the pace of harassment quickened. After Terry got hit on the head by a rowdy group of boys who cornered him, Mrs. Huckaby suggested we come to school only when we had to take final exams or attend classes critical to our completing the year. We would enter school, go directly to those classes, and leave immediately after them. She instructed us to let her know when we entered the building and where we were at all times.

We were told that the school board was hiring private guards to beef up hall security in response to threats of major violence. Word also came that the FBI would be present at graduation because of the threats of bombs and Ku Klux Klan activity planned to disrupt the ceremony. Little Rock police and armed federalized Arkansas Guardsmen would also be on hand to keep the peace.

"Stay home. Promise me you won't go to graduation," Link pleaded on the telephone.

"I'm not gonna let them scare me away," I protested.

"Listen, I've been in rooms where people are talking about harsh ways to stop that boy's graduation. They're saying if they let the first one of you graduate, there'll be no end to integration. Melba, listen up good. They're bragging about using high-powered rifles. They're taking bets about which way you'all are gonna fall when they shoot you."

The shooting idea is a really really drastic idea to get them out. You want them out not dead.

28

CENTRAL HIGH SCHOOL NEGROES PASS: ONE ON HONOR ROLL.
PRINCIPAL MATTHEWS SAYS HE WILL NOT REVEAL GRADES
BUT CONFIRMS GREEN WILL GRADUATE.
—*Arkansas Gazette*, Wednesday, May 23, 1958

"LET'S KEEP THE NIGGER FROM GRADUATING." THAT WAS THE RAL-lying cry in the halls of Central High that unleashed unimaginable terror upon us. Pressure was exerted on all eight of us; the goal was to get us out by any means possible. In case that plan failed, our antagonists worked at convincing us that even if Ernie had the grades to graduate, he should not march with the other seniors to receive his Central High diploma.

"We ain't gonna let no nigger wear our cap and gown," one boy shouted at me as I walked the hallway to English class. I pushed my way past him, flashed a smile and a pleasant "Thank you."

At first, some of my late-night telephone callers pleaded with me in a civil tone to ask Ernie to receive his diploma by mail. "We don't want his picture taken with us. My daddy says you'all ain't getting back in our school next year, no how. So this is

299

the only time we'll have that ink spot in the middle of all those pictures the news people take."

Another gruff-voiced man became angrier with each rude call. "We're gonna hang us a nigger at the same time your nigger takes our diploma," he said. On and on those calls came, keeping our phone ringing almost as much as it had at the beginning of the school year. At the same time, I received threatening notes sneaked into my books and in my locker.

I could see more evidence that the principal, vice-principals, and teachers had lost any hopes of corraling belligerent students. Even as school officials observed them, clusters of students threw rocks as we entered or exited the building. The hallways were like a three-ring circus, with hooligans completely ignoring commands to cease their outrageous behavior.

Because the situation was growing more explosive, Mrs. Huckaby called us into her office to double-check on our scheduled exams. While inside school, we were once again closely followed by bodyguards.

I was much more frightened than I had been in recent months because there were no longer islands of sanity within the insanity of that school. Just outside the principal's office, people threw rotten eggs and walked on my heels, whereas before that area had been a comparatively safe place to walk.

During those last days, time seemed to drag on and on as though some divine force were slowing the hands on the clock. I had no choice but to perform one of the most hazardous duties of the day—opening my locker. That meant standing still for several minutes, with my eyes and attention focused inside while my back was exposed to passersby.

I had developed a habit of reaching my hand into my locker to find hidden objects before I poked my face in. On Tuesday afternoon, I was searching my locker for my eyeglass case when I reached my hand down deep inside to see whether or not it had fallen. Suddenly there was the sound of popping guns and the smell of smoke just behind me. I quickly turned to see a flaming object flying toward my face. I put my hand up to deflect it. That's when I felt the pain on my first three fingers. I had shielded my eyes from several sparking hot firecrackers linked together by a wire. My hand hurt, but I could only be grateful it wasn't my eyes that had been burned.

As I was issued bandages from the office to dress the wound, I consoled myself by thinking of the calendar on the kitchen wall. I had marked off almost all the days of the month of May. Ernie would attend baccalaureate services the following Sunday evening, and graduation would be the following Tuesday, one week from this day. I would be an unwelcome Central High student in that building only a few more days.

"What are you staring at, nigger?" I was indeed staring, transfixed and elated at seeing what the boy was carrying. It was the sight I had been waiting for, praying for.

"The graduation gown Ernie's gonna wear," I said loud and clear. I couldn't help responding to his snide remark as I glared back at the boy wearing a flattop haircut and black shirt. In his right hand he was carrying his gown on a hanger, and his left hand was holding his cap. He was attempting to block my way, but he had no free hands. I simply made a wide circle around him. Nothing, not even his foul mouth spewing ugly words, could make me unhappy at that moment. The sight of that gown meant summer and freedom were right around the corner.

At home the phone calls were coming fast and vicious. "We got a way of gettin' you darkies now, for certain. We're offering ten thousand dollars for your head on a platter." I gulped as I replaced the receiver in its cradle. I couldn't help thinking about how that was an awful lot of money. Poor folks might take a notion to collect. They'd get ten thousand dollars for my head. Did that mean they'd have to cut it off to collect? I told Grandma India of my fears.

"Surely you've got something better to do besides speculating about white folks' silliness," she said.

"I can't help worrying about Ernie. One of those students could be an impostor—anybody could wear a robe."

"Impostor?" Grandma looked up from her needlework with a question.

"You know, someone from the KKK who wants to collect that reward money could pretend to be a graduate."

"I don't think Ernie is in any real danger during graduation because he'll be there among six hundred and one white graduates. Besides, God's watching after Ernie just like he's watching over you."

"But. . ." I tried to continue being in my pity pot. She motioned me to shush my mouth and hold my hands out so she could circle the embroidery thread around them to straighten it out. After a long moment she said, "You're fretting a mighty lot this evening. Hard work is always the cure for worry. So busy yourself doing those dishes and getting ready for your final exams."

I had always imagined that my last day of the term at Central High School would be marked by a grand ceremony, with a massive choir singing hallelujah, or perhaps some wonderful award from my community—a parade maybe. I imagined the roar of helicopters overhead towing flying banners of congratulations—something—anything. But it was just the same as any other day. Four of us, Thelma, Elizabeth, Jeff, and I, rode home together early that afternoon. We wouldn't be going back to Central High for at least three months. Long spaces of silence punctuated our talk about how we thought we did on our exams.

"It's over," Conrad said, greeting me as I climbed the steps to our front door. "You don't have to integrate anymore."

"Well, praise the Lord," Grandma India said, her arms wide open to receive me. "You see, you made it." She squeezed me and kissed my cheek.

"Well, well, young lady, welcome to summer." Mother Lois handed me a large box that I rushed to open. "You're very special to have come through all this. I thought you deserved a special summer outfit."

Early on Wednesday morning, I built a fire in the metal trash barrel in the backyard, fueled by my school papers. Grandma had said it would be healing to write and destroy all the names of people I disliked at Central High: teachers, students, anyone who I thought had wronged me. It was against the law to burn anything at that time of the year, but she said a ceremony was important in order to have the official opportunity to give that year to God. Grandma India stood silent by my side as I fed the flame and spoke their names and forgave them.

After a long moment she walked over to water her flowerbed. The four o'clocks were blooming purple and red. We stood together for what must have been half an hour, with only the sound of the crackling fire and the garden hose. Finally she said, "Later, you'll be grateful for the courage it built inside you and for the blessing it will bring."

Grateful, I thought. Never. How could I be grateful for being at Central High? But I knew she was always right. Still I wondered just how long I would have to wait for that feeling of gratitude to come to me.

———

COVERAGE CURBED TO ASSURE DIGNITY
OF CENTRAL HIGH SCHOOL GRADUATION:
Each Graduating Senior to Receive
8 Admission Tickets;
Press Admitted Only by Ticket.
—*Arkansas Gazette*, Tuesday, May 27, 1958

Even though I had made it through the school year, Ernie still had to survive that one final brave act. I counted on being with him, on applauding for him from our isolated though well-guarded section of the audience.

"None of you will be allowed to attend either the graduation commencement or the baccalaureate service," Mother Lois announced over dinner. "The authorities believe it would not only risk your lives, but also make it more difficult for them to protect Ernie and his family should they have to do so. They've also forbidden any non-white reporters or photographers to attend."

"But, Mom!"

"But nothing. This is no time to satisfy a whim and unravel

303

everything you've accomplished. There'll be enough of a circus, what with the soldiers, FBI, city police, and who knows all."

"The paper says every policeman not on vacation will be on duty from six o'clock on," Grandma said. "They wouldn't go to all that trouble and expense unless they expected something to happen."

"Besides," Mother Lois continued, "their best efforts should be directed to protecting Ernie."

She's right, I thought to myself. It was selfish of me to want to go, I suppose. But what I knew to be practical advice didn't lessen my disappointment at not being able to watch Ernie march triumphantly to the stage to receive that diploma. That night I wrote in my diary:

Dear God,
Please walk with Ernie in the graduation line at Central. Let him
be safe.

Quigley Stadium was where the 101st troops set up their headquarters. It was there, on Tuesday evening, May 27, with 4,500 people looking on, that Ernie received his diploma. I held my breath as I listened to the radio broadcast news of the graduation ceremonies. At 8:48 P.M., Ernie became the first of our people to graduate from Central High School in all its forty-nine years. Chills danced up my spine as I sat in the big green living room chair with Mama and Grandma nearby. "It really happened," I whispered. "We made it."

The audience had been applauding those who previously marched, but when Ernie appeared they fell silent.

"What the heck," Mother Lois said. "Lots of people in the rest of the world are applauding for Ernie and for all of you who made it through this year."

"Who cares if they applaud, they didn't shoot him. There was no violence. Everybody is alive and well." Grandma stood and applauded.

Ernie was escorted from the stadium by police to a waiting taxi in which he, his family, and their guest departed. The newspapers said Ernie's diploma cost taxpayers half a million dollars. Of course, we knew it cost all of us much, much more than that. It cost us our innocence and a precious year of our teenage lives.

The next morning, Link called, sounding as though he would fall apart. He was grieving because Mrs. Healey had died on the day of his graduation. He insisted I come to meet him. When I said I couldn't get away, he called me a thousand times that day insisting he had to see me or something awful would happen.

Late that afternoon, I had no choice but to meet him. He threatened to come right over to my house if I didn't agree. I figured I had to quiet him down or he would explode. He seemed inconsolable and really crazy. So I said we could walk around the block near the Baptist college. It was a safe place for me in my own neighborhood. Besides, when I asked Mother if I could go to the Baptist college library with a friend, I wouldn't be telling a lie—at least, not altogether.

When I arrived, he was red-faced and teary-eyed, insisting that I go with him to the Northern town near Harvard University where he would attend college.

"Things will be much better for you there. I'll take care of you until you get a job." He was so distraught that I felt sorry for him. He insisted that I leave Little Rock immediately.

"You're just saying this because you're sad about Nana Healey," I told him. "You'll feel differently tomorrow, next week."

"I've thought about this a lot. I'm tired of worrying about you. What will you do when I'm gone?"

"I can't leave. I have to stay here and go back to Central," I argued. "Everything depends on it."

"You keep acting this way, girl, you are gonna get yourself killed. I told you, there's a price on your head. They have posters all over offering that money. They'll never let you come back next year."

On and on he went, talking loud and frightening me. To calm him down, I told him I'd think about running away to the

North. But when I waved good-bye to him, I knew I would never, ever see him again, although I would remember him forever.

By May 29, the eight of us had flown off to Chicago to receive the Robert S. Abbot Award conferred by the Chicago *Defender* newspaper. I was so excited because Minnijean joined us there. It was the beginning of a whirlwind tour and another in the series of awards we received for "bravery and significant contributions to democracy."

In Little Rock we had been "niggers," but up North, we were heroes and heroines. We were paraded across stages before adoring audiences, chauffeured about in limousines, and treated like royalty at luxurious hotels.

In New York, we had suites at the Statler Hilton, took limos to Sardi's, and lunched with United Nations Secretary General Dag Hammarskjöld. We hobnobbed backstage with Lena Horne and Ricardo Montalban at their Broadway play *Jamaica*. In Washington, we had a private tour of the White House and posed on the steps of the Supreme Court with Mr. Thurgood Marshall.

In Cleveland, we received the NAACP's highest honor, the Spingarn Medal. We received so many other awards in so many cities that I lost count after a while. The first time I was asked for my autograph, I was astonished; afterward, I went to my room to practice a special signature.

But by late June, even as Minnijean and I were whirling about our hotel room, dressing to see a man we thought of as a deity, Johnny Mathis, Little Rock school integration was unraveling. On June 22, Federal Judge Lemley granted the school board's request for a stay in the integration order for Central High School, delaying it for three and a half years. The NAACP began a round of appeals up through the courts, trying to get us seven students back into Central High.

By September 1958, we had won our court battle. Armed with judgments in our favor, we prepared to reenter Central High. But Governor Faubus had the last word. He closed all of Little

Rock's high schools. So we began the school year waiting for the law of the land to blast Mr. Faubus out of his stubborn trench.

I couldn't know then that I would spend the entire school year of 1958–59 in lonely isolation and despair—waiting in vain. We had come back home, to Little Rock, back to being called "niggers" by the segregationists and those "meddling children" by our own people. Our friends and neighbors resented not only the school closure but most especially the negative economic impact our presence in that school had on our community.

By that time, segregationists were squeezing the life out of the NAACP and the Bates's newspaper, the *State Press*. Our people continued to lose their jobs, their businesses, and their homes as pressure was exerted to convince them to talk us into voluntarily withdrawing from Central High.

During those lonely days of what would have been my senior year, I waited for legislators and Faubus and the NAACP to resolve the entanglement that surrounded Central High's integration. As September days turned to late autumn, my world fell apart with the onset of Grandmother India's leukemia and her death on October 24. Ultimately, I was alone, at home, waiting to restart my life—waiting to live my teenage years.

By September 1959, we had waited as long as we could for Faubus to open the schools. The unrest in Little Rock and the bounty on our heads had by that time forced two of our seven families to move their homes away from that city forever. NAACP officials sent an announcement to chapters across the country, asking for families that would volunteer to give us safe harbor and support us in finishing our education.

I was fortunate enough to come to the Santa Rosa, California, home of Dr. George McCabe, a San Francisco State University professor, and his wife, Carol, and their four children. They were a family of politically conscious Quakers committed to racial equality. When I arrived I was frightened to see that they were white. But they became the loving, nurturing bridge over which I walked to adulthood.

More than their guidance, it was their unconditional love that

307

taught me the true meaning of equality. To this day I call them Mom and Pop and visit to bask in their love and enjoy the privilege of being treated as though I am their daughter.

The love of George and Carol McCabe helped to heal my wounds and inspired me to launch a new life for myself. It was also their voices echoing the same words of my mother that made me enter and complete college. In fact, George took me to college in January, 1960, to register for my first classes.

Not until September, 1960, did the NAACP, with its tenacious legal work, force Central High to open to integration once more—but only two black students were permitted entry. Carlotta Walls and Jefferson Thomas ultimately became graduates of Central along with Ernest Green.

Looking back, I suppose that had Faubus not called out the troops on that first day, had he remained silent, the integration at Central High would not have been as difficult. By dispatching the Arkansas National Guard to keep us out of school, he set the tone. His bold, defiant act gave renegades, who had until then been only a very minor thread in our city's fabric, the green light to play a major role. They took that opportunity and made the most of it, because or in spite of the fact that the world was watching.

As I watch videotapes now and think back to that first day at Central High on September 4, 1957, I wonder what possessed my parents and the adults of the NAACP to allow us to go to that school in the face of such violence. When I ask my mother about it, she says none of them honestly believed Governor Faubus had the unmitigated gall to use the troops to keep us out. Mother explains that they assumed he would order the military to quell the mob.

Since Little Rock's citizens had in most recent years behaved fairly rationally, Mother assumed the mob would be dispersed by the police and that would be the end of that. She recalls as well that even when a rational voice nudged her to keep me home, there seemed to be that tug to go forward from some divine source.

308

Many historians contend it was a brilliant stroke on the governor's part suddenly to remove the Arkansas National Guard from around Central High School in response to Judge Ronald Davies's ruling for integration on Friday, September 20, 1957. It allowed Faubus to set up an explosive situation, while maintaining a veneer of innocence. He could ignite and fuel segregationists' anger without being caught holding the matches.

When on that ominous day, Mob Monday, September 23, 1957, the NAACP officials and ministers dropped us off to go to Central for the second time under court order, I wonder how in their minds they justified such an act. As an adult, I believe had it been me driving, I would have kept going rather than allow my children to face that rampaging mob. And yet had we students not gone to school that day, perhaps the integration of Central, and of a whole string of other Southern schools that eventually followed, would never have taken place.

When I watch news footage of the day we entered school guarded by the 101st soldiers, I am moved by the enormity of that experience. I believe that was a moment when the whole nation took one giant step forward. Once President Eisenhower made that kind of commitment to uphold the law, there was no turning back. And even though later on he would waver and not wholeheartedly back up his powerful decision, he had stepped over a line that no other President had ever dared cross. Thereafter the threat of military intervention would always exist whenever a Southern governor thought of using his office to defy federal law.

I marvel at the fact that in the midst of this historic confrontation, we nine teenagers weren't maimed or killed. Believe me, it was only by the grace of God and the bravery of those few good men—some of them white men. I never allow myself to forget that although I was abused by many white people during that incident. Without the help of other law-abiding whites who risked their lives, I wouldn't be around to tell this story.

Yet even as I wince at the terrible risk we all took, I remember thinking at the time that it was the right decision—because it felt as though the hand of fate was ushering us forward. Naive and trusting, adults and children alike, we kept thinking each moment, each hour, each day, that things would get better, that these people would come to their senses and behave. This is a land governed by sane citizens who obey the law, at least that's what we're taught in history class.

So we headed down a path from which there was no turning back, because when we thought of alternatives, the only option was living our lives behind the fences of segregation and passing on that legacy to our children.

Today, when I see how far we have progressed in terms of school integration, in some instances I am pleased. In other areas I am very angry. Why have we not devised a workable plan for solving a problem that has so long plagued this nation? We put a man on the moon because we committed the resources to do so. Today, thirty-six years after the Central High crisis, school integration is still not a reality, and we use children as tender warriors on the battlefield to achieve racial equality.

It would take years of sorting out my Central High experience before the pieces of my life puzzle would come together and I could make sense of what happened to me.

In 1962, when I had attended the mostly white San Francisco State University for two years, I found myself living among an enclave of students where I was the only person of color. I was doing it again, integrating a previously all-white residence house, even though I had other options. I had been taken there as a guest, and someone said the only blacks allowed there were the cooks. So, of course, I made application and donned my warrior garb because it reminded me of the forbidden fences of segregation in Little Rock.

One night, a brown-haired soldier wearing olive-drab fatigues stepped across the threshold of my suite. His name was John, and he was a blind date for Mary, my roommate. Of course, for just an instant, he reminded me of my 101st guard—same stature, same uniform. When he tried to talk to me that evening, I ignored him. But the next morning, Saturday, he rang our

310

doorbell. When I told him that Mary had already left, John said never mind, he'd really come back to see me.

He brought me strawberries in dead of winter and flowers every weekend. Six months later I had married this bright, kind, green-eyed martial arts expert, who said he would protect me forever. Later I would come to understand that he represented Danny, my 101st guard; Link, my protector; the power of those who held sway over me at Central High; and the safety that my black uncles and father could not provide in the South.

"If you can't beat them, you're going to join them," my mother said when I nervously announced my wedding from a phone booth in Reno. "I hope you've thought this over, young lady. It's not the racial difference, it's the philosophical difference that is most important."

Seven years later John and I split up because he had been a farm boy who wanted a wife to putter about the house and have babies. I wanted to be a news reporter. But he had by then shared with me the most wonderful event in my life, the birth of our daughter, Kellie. As I held the cinnamon-colored bundle with auburn hair and doelike eyes in my arms, I swore she would never have to endure the racial prejudices I endured. I was wrong. But then that's a story for another book.

Until my marriage, I had been hearing from my old friend Link, living in faraway places as he piled up awards and degrees from this country's most prestigious educational institutions. He was livid about my marriage, saying I'd all along told him we couldn't date because he was white, and now look what I'd gone and done. I never heard from him again. Still, I think of him as a hero, yet another one of those special gifts from God sent to ferry me over a rough spot in my life's path.

Indeed, I followed my dream, inspired by those journalists I met during the integration. I attended Columbia University's School of Journalism and became a news reporter. I always remembered it was the truth told by those reporters who came to Little Rock that kept me alive. Later as an NBC television reporter, covering stories of riot and protest, I would take special care to look into those unexposed corners where otherwise invisible people are forced to hide as their truth is ignored.

I look back on my Little Rock integration experience as ultimately a positive force that shaped the course of my life. As Grandma India promised, it taught me to have courage and patience.

Some observers have said that its negative impact may have been that it forced me to live my life as a marginal woman, in two worlds—white and black—by virtue of my early experience with the McCabes and my marriage. But I see that as a distinct advantage, for it has allowed me to know for certain that we are all one.

If my Central High School experience taught me one lesson, it is that we are not separate. The effort to separate ourselves whether by race, creed, color, religion, or status is as costly to the separator as to those who would be separated.

When the milk in Oregon is tainted by the radiation eruption of a Soviet nuclear reactor, we are forced to see our interdependence. When forgotten people feel compelled to riot in Los Angeles, we share their pain through our TV screens, and their ravages impact our emotional and economic health.

The task that remains is to cope with our interdependence—to see ourselves reflected in every other human being and to respect and honor our differences.

Namasté
(the God in me sees and honors the God in you)

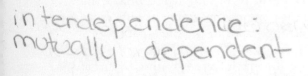